PRAISE F~~ ~
DEAR BI ~

"Raw and unflinching, *Dear Bi Men* is a must read for those navigating their identity.

J.R.Yussuf doesn't shy away from sharing his personal journey of coming to terms with his bisexuality. Through his own experiences navigating religion, race, and gender expectations,Yussuf deconstructs society and the harm it causes to bisexual men and other marginalized people.

More than this,Yussuf utilizes the wisdom he has learned through his journey, as well as his years of research and activism, to impart incredibly useful advice to those who are questioning or struggling with their bisexuality.

Dear Bi Men is a vital lifeline that every bi man needs on their bookshelf."

—VANEET MEHTA, author of *Bisexual Men Exist*

"Bi activist and writer J.R.Yussuf brings a thorough, thoughtful analysis to bear on his unique and enlightened perspective, combining epistolary and journal formats as entry points for his personal dialog with the reader.

The arena for bi men's voices to be raised and heard must be built on a solid platform of intense self-examination and honest acknowledgment of all aspects of one's male bisexuality. For far too long, immense societal forces have not allowed stories like J.R.'s (and mine) to be told. The way things were, however, is not how they exist now or how they should be. This book shines with an informed and articulate perspective that will speak to many men and others.

Perhaps the best endorsement I can offer is that listening to his authentic and loving voice restores my belief that bisexual men's stories must be told. His book informs and reaffirms my bisexual nature."

—RON SURESHA, editor of *Bi Men: Coming Out* and *Bisexual Perspectives on the Life and Work of Alfred C. Kinsey*

"This is a searing and soaring contribution to the development of men who have long existed in the shadows of our time. Understanding the mental health and socio-emotional impacts of being bi+ is an encouraging step forward to becoming a fully integrated and powerful society that will accept, encourage, and protect the most vulnerable men from harm, persecution and exclusion.

Navigating from margins to center, we can expect *Dear Bi Men* to be the book that pushes society toward greater understanding of human sexuality, while giving bi+ men the resources to advocate for themselves. A book worth buying if only for the personal learning journey you are bound to embark on."

—ALEX HOLMES, author of *Time to Talk: How Men Think About Love, Belonging and Connection*

"A must-read for anyone seeking to understand the rich diversity of the bisexual heart.

This is a how-to book for deconstructing internalized biphobia. Yussuf enriches personal stories with much-needed bi+ education.

This book is an antidote to society's biphobia. It seeks to build a more inclusive vision of manhood through practical coping skills and a future where hearts can love freely.

Importantly, Yussuf deconstructs colonial mindsets and shows how stereotypes about bi black men are deeply rooted in white supremacy. An important addition to the queer conversation."

—DR. JULIA SHAW, author of *Bi: The Hidden Culture, History, and Science of Bisexuality*

Dear Bi Men

Dear Bi Men

A Black Man's Perspective on Power, Consent, Breaking Down Binaries, and Combating Erasure

J.R. Yussuf

North Atlantic Books
Huichin, unceded Ohlone land
Berkeley, California

Published by
North Atlantic Books
Huichin, unceded Ohlone land
Berkeley, California

Cover design by Amanda Weiss
Book design by Happenstance Type-O-Rama

Printed in Canada

Dear Bi Men: A Black Man's Perspective on Power, Consent, Breaking Down Binaries, and Combating Erasure is sponsored and published by North Atlantic Books, an educational nonprofit based in the unceded Ohlone land Huichin (Berkeley, CA) that collaborates with partners to develop cross-cultural perspectives; nurture holistic views of art, science, the humanities, and healing; and seed personal and global transformation by publishing work on the relationship of body, spirit, and nature.

North Atlantic Books's publications are distributed to the US trade and internationally by Penguin Random House Publisher Services. For further information, visit our website at www .northatlanticbooks.com.

Library of Congress Cataloging-in-Publication Data

Names: Yussuf, J.R., 1989- author.
Title: Dear bi men / J.R. Yussuf.
Description: Berkeley, California : North Atlantic Books, [2024] | Includes bibliographical references and index. | Summary: "An unapologetic guide for readers who are Black, masc, and bi-unlearning biphobia, coming out, combatting erasure, and embodying your whole self"-- Provided by publisher.
Identifiers: LCCN 2023031760 (print) | LCCN 2023031761 (ebook) | ISBN 9781623179687 (paperback) | ISBN 9781623179694 (epub)
Subjects: LCSH: Bisexuals. | Men, Black. | Minorities.
Classification: LCC HQ74.8 Y87 2024 (print) | LCC HQ74.8 (ebook) | DDC 306.76/5--dc23/eng/20231030
LC record available at https://lccn.loc.gov/2023031760
LC ebook record available at https://lccn.loc.gov/2023031761

1 2 3 4 5 6 7 8 9 MARQUIS 28 27 26 25 24

This book includes recycled material and material from well-managed forests. North Atlantic Books is committed to the protection of our environment. We print on recycled paper whenever possible and partner with printers who strive to use environmentally responsible practices.

To Junebug,
I'm sorry I lost you.
Thank you for leading me back.
I vow to protect you from here on out.

CONTENTS

FOREWORD

The Black South is my dwelling place. I grew up here; I have planted and watered seeds here; it has become an embedded part of my being. The (Black) South, also known as the Bible Belt: where sex is too taboo a subject to explore; where queer sexuality can only be explored insofar as it must be condemned; where love and romance are defined by, as, and for God; where gender is static. While this is not unique to a Black experience, nor is it necessarily a uniquely Southern experience—as evidenced by the fact that the author of this text is not writing it from the South—I write about this here to share that this is the context under which I was and am being socialized.

While I knew from an early age that I was attracted to more than just one "type" of person, and thus attracted to more than just one gender, I didn't have language to describe that attraction, nor did I have a desire to traverse waters that I was taught would kill me. It wasn't until I was a first-year student at Morehouse College, where I was surrounded by a plethora of other queer and trans people, that I not only found the language I was looking for, but also a sense of self. It was there that I came into my transness and, for all intents and purposes, my bisexuality. As a gender abolitionist, I have long referred to myself as "queer" to specify my politic. Queerness is not just or only a mark of sexual (un)desire. As a politic, queerness has always referred to that which is non-normative; it has always suggested that those who exist outside of what is "default," or what is "inherent," are weird and peculiar people. It is supposed to be subversive and seditious, and it opposes cis/heteronormativity. Queerness is anti-assimilationist and it defies societal norms. Said differently, it's not an identity, it's an act. J.R.'s writing invites us to think about bisexuality in this way. Through *Dear Bi Men,* he invites the reader into thinking of bisexuality as a politic that requires one to reckon with power, sex, and consent, and how these things are distorted and shaped by our relationship to each other and to the world.

When I first discovered J.R.'s #BisexualMenSpeak initiative, while I didn't think it was necessarily for me as someone who is not a man, it spoke to so much of my experience as a person who was once being socialized as a boy in a cisheteronormative—by which I mean antiblack—world. With the friends I made in college, and the work that J.R. and others were doing online, I quickly understood that our struggles for any semblance of so-called liberation are relational and interconnected. This is essential to share as this book is being written and published in the midst of increasing bans against books by Black and/or LGBTQ+ writers; in the midst of legislators codifying or further systematizing violent sentiments about trans and other LGBTQ+ people; as cultural, societal, political, and legislative attacks against anomalous gender and sexual subject-positions become an even greater part of our everyday reality. It is perhaps more important now than ever that we understand not only how sexuality is constructed, but also how the binaries it erects and fortifies profoundly impact the ways so many of us experience and are actively erased from the world.

We are all inculcated into a social world order predicated on power and control, created and sustained by the western world—the imperial core, especially and particularly the united states. Knowing that this is the world in which we are indoctrinated should lead us to make a collective demand to destroy it; to run away from all attempts to salvage these structures that produce this fascistic social world order and instead become part of the reason that it burns. With *Dear Bi Men,* J.R. clarifies the ways that biphobia cannot be divorced from misogyny, cis/heterosexism, rape culture, antiblackness, and all other forms of violence through which one (or some) are afforded power over others. He problematizes our relationship and commitment to "health," our relationship to normative sex and dating practices, our relationship to representation, and ultimately, our relationship to ourselves in connection to one another. This text is a generous and generative offering. We should all hold it with care and use it to further develop our politic on and around (bi)sexuality and the world.

Da'Shaun Harrison

INTRODUCTION

I call myself bisexual because I acknowledge that I have in myself the potential to be attracted—romantically and/or sexually—to people of more than one sex and/or gender, not necessarily at the same time, not necessarily in the same way, and not necessarily to the same degree.

—ROBYN OCHS

The earliest I can remember having a crush was kindergarten. There was a little girl in my class who was nice to me and smelled good and a little boy who had shiny sneakers and shared his toys with me. Crushing on them came with a belly full of butterflies and uncontrollable giggling whenever they were in proximity. They always had brand-new name-brand clothes, faces shiny with Vaseline—other signs of being looked after—and were well-liked by the other kids. I, on the other hand, was not. On any given day during recess I'd find myself gravitating to both of them, wanting each of them to play with me, think I was funny, prefer me over the other kids. Not much has changed for me as far as valuing hygiene, grooming, and being attracted to more than one gender. My type is pretty boys and girls who are into serving looks, find creative ways to put together clothes, and are kind. In kindergarten I don't know that I considered what would happen if anyone learned of my crushes or that it was anything other than partly exhilarating and partly unremarkable in the way all crushes are. I'd learn soon enough that boys were not supposed to like other boys—and further—boys were not supposed to like *both* girls and boys.

As I got older, anti-LGBTQ+ messages on the radio, TV, and in movies became barriers, screen doors impeding me. People in my surroundings doubted and harried me, and I soon began to doubt myself. Though I was ten years old in 1999 when I first used the word *bisexual* to describe myself, it wasn't until 2014, when I was twenty-five years old, that I finally became comfortable with using it and what I knew it to mean. I had a friend who was nine months older than me who'd known he was gay early on and eventually taught me about sexuality, the word *bisexual,* and gender norms as best as an eleven-year-old could. Because of the lack of accessible, comprehensive bisexual-specific information in the world as it relates to men and people who identify with masculinity, I struggled to understand my thoughts, fantasies, dreams, butterflies in my stomach, and erections.

As a society, we've been conditioned to hear the word *bisexual* in men—in Black men especially—and think, not only are they lying because they're actually gay, but they're also going to cheat and spread HIV. I was born in 1989 at Long Island Jewish Hospital in Queens, New York, and grew up in the nineties, when so much of the stigma around the *down-low brother* was at its height and seemed to multiply at an exorbitant rate. A lot of time, money, and resources went into proctoring fear of the down-low brother: a handsome, smooth-talking Black man whose sole purpose seemed to be to deceive naive, unsuspecting straight Black women into having unprotected sex with them. Meanwhile he was having unprotected sex with HIV-positive men behind their back. The down-low brother put copious amounts of time into appearing as masculine and heterosexual as possible yet seemed to have no time to buy or use condoms. The down-low brother was a nightmare come to life and became synonymous with Black bisexual men. He was dangerous, irresponsible, malicious, and the perfect specter to pin the blame of the AIDS epidemic on.

Blaming things on the down-low brother (and other LGBTQ+ people) allowed the president of the United States, Ronald Reagan, along with the government, the pharmaceutical industry, the media, and the educational system to sidestep their negligence, social stigma, and absolute blame. Many people would not have died from AIDS-related complications, and the stigma around bisexual men, specifically Black men, would not be what it is today had the president not taken it as a joke and showed complete apathy when it was thought to be a gay disease that five thousand people had already died from. It would have been very different if the Centers for Disease Control and Prevention and the medical and pharmaceutical industry had sought out affordable antiretroviral medication sooner or made early versions of the postexposure prophylaxis (PEP) medication—a decades-long standing-emergency measure taken by health care professionals who may have been exposed to HIV at work—available back then. If the educational system had taught a wide variety of safe-sex methods as well as comprehensive education about sexuality and the risk involved with different kinds of sex so that more people were informed, instead of just teaching abstinence or never mentioning sex at all, I believe much of the negative impact could have been prevented.

As I navigated hostile attitudes about the down-low brother refracted back at me as a teenager in the 2000s, the early onsets of shame began to set in, as did the beginnings of internalizing biphobia. I felt immense shame surrounding my attraction to guys and girls because at every turn there were consequences for and messaging against feeling what I did. Shame gets magnified the more it goes unaddressed. It was clear I should not want to be close with other guys, and even more explicit that I should not desire to be close with guys *and* girls. Shame germinates like a fungus left in the wet and dark. Even when I eventually found a bit of succor pumping The Pier in the West Village or browsing on Black Gay Chat—BGC for short—I was told over and over again that I simply could not be bisexual. I was illegible. At the time, older gay men in particular had incredibly rigid views on sexuality and gender performance, and were critical, callous, and dismissive toward anyone or anything outside of what they understood to be true. They'd internalized the messages society meant as weapons for them and repeated them to anyone who would listen. Unlearning both homophobia and biphobia has not been fun or easy, and finding pride in something I once loathed about myself has not been a linear process.

In the essay *Never Too Much* by Marc Lamont Hill, he writes:

> *Black men model manhood after those who oppress us. We measure our humanity against the humanity of those who seek to kill us, our families, and maybe most of the planet. We imagine freedom to be the ability to accumulate the kind of unchecked power and privilege of cisgender*

heterosexual white men. We eagerly embrace the toxicities of this conception of manhood: hypermasculinity, hypersexuality, homophobia, misogyny, and violence. Anytime we deviate from this script, we feel less masculine. And when we feel less masculine, we feel less human.

What Marc describes is patriarchy and the way its power calls to and simultaneously subjects Black men. Feeling fear, deep sadness, and shame are seen as the absence of masculinity in wider society and male culture in particular. To admit to certain emotions is to admit defeat, to admit fault, to admit weakness, to admit to being inferior. There was a common sentiment growing up that emotional boys and gay boys didn't have fathers in the home, or they weren't raised right according to the guidelines of what boyhood and manhood should look and feel like. Women in my neighborhood would scold me for wanting to watch them in the kitchen instead of going outside to play with the boys. Men in my neighborhood would often try to toughen me up with cruelties in an attempt not only to shape me but also to *correct* my deviance. They drilled into me that exuding confidence at all times was imperative to being a man, especially with how I introduced myself and said my name. Boys and men were supposed to be strong and able to protect the women close to them. As a child I was timid, whimsical, and had a singsong way of speaking, where my vocal inflections were completely random and unrelated to the message I was trying to relay. My voice ought to be commanding, booming, steady. Some men likely meant this as a show of community, surrogate fatherhood, and helping, even though it was terrifying, domineering, and humiliating.

Patriarchal thinking, action, and inaction are dehumanizing for its victims and its willing participants. The way it demands we act as sentinels on behalf of upholding its ideals terrifies me, and as I get more context for how and why I've experienced what I have, I become certain that it must be obliterated. Being struck when teachers weren't looking, chased by a mob through the halls of my middle school, and followed home by straight boys who would throw rocks at me while calling me slurs was a lot of what I remember about the 1990s and early 2000s. My friends who were girls would sometimes tell popular straight boys I liked them or unnecessarily throw me into other petty drama. At the time I thought, *At least these girls were willing to be friends with me, unlike most boys.* Surviving middle school was harrowing, as it can be for many, but it was exacerbated by my Blackness, femininity, *and* bisexuality.

Learning that femininity is not only inherent in girls—and masculinity is not only inherent in boys—is something that's healed me, but had the communities I moved through, and the world, already embraced this, there wouldn't have been a wound to heal in the first place. If the kids and adults in my surroundings didn't see being gay or bisexual as a bad thing, I'd have had a tremendously different experience. There may be an instinct to judge or curse the people I've mentioned, and by all means have at it, but just know their beliefs about gender and sexuality did not develop out of thin air. These beliefs are the very fabric of the Western world.

I want to share a brief story about how being accustomed to being demeaned about my sexuality and gender expression conditioned me to be used to being put down in general. I grew up on Beach 9th Street on the peninsula of Far Rockaway. It's a very unique beach town that's part of Queens but bordered by Long Island on one end and connected to Brooklyn by a bridge on the other. Most of the people I went to elementary and middle school with were Black Americans. There were also many Afro Latinx kids, Caribbean American kids, and Nigerian American kids like me, though this didn't prevent me being taunted with "African booty-scratcher" on occasion. There were some non-Black Latinx kids, and almost no Asian or white kids, and yet anti-Blackness abounded. Though there were few white kids at my school, I lived across the street from a synagogue, and many white Jewish people lived in the houses surrounding my apartment building. During the summers my friends and I would befriend Jewish kids from around the way, and it was mostly fine, though there'd almost always be racist comments from their mothers about how surprisingly well-behaved we were. As a kid, I didn't really understand what they meant or that there was anything wrong with their responses. They'd say these things with a smile, and it felt like there was a level of approval that children can sometimes confuse with like or love.

There was a day I remember leaving my friend's house in the neighboring building and riding the elevator down alone. It eventually stopped on the fifth floor, and a Hasidic Jewish man in his fifties or so got on. After he got on, the elevator surprisingly stopped on each floor until we got to the ground floor. It was a prewar building, so the buttons didn't light up. I went to step off of the elevator first, and before I knew it, I felt a swift kick to my rear. I quickly looked back, and the man hadn't moved, and wasn't even looking at me. I obviously didn't imagine being kicked, but him seeming unchanged, casual even, and my own timidity, fear, and lack of confidence prevented me from saying anything. I hopped off the elevator and crossed the street to go to my building. I kept thinking about whether or not I'd made it all up, and determined that I couldn't have, and that he did kick me.

I told my oldest sister, who was the only one home and only four years older than I was, and she marched me back to the building. I remembered the floor he'd gotten on at, and we placed our ears to each door, hoping that he'd returned home and that we'd be able to find his door, until we did. My sister, who couldn't have been more than fourteen, had a firm talk with the man, who admitted he did kick me because he thought I'd pressed all of the buttons going down to the ground floor. My sister rightfully said that whether I'd done it or not, kicking me was completely inappropriate and wrong. The man eventually said he was sorry, and we went home. I couldn't understand why that'd happened, much like I couldn't understand what was wrong with the way I walked or comments about how surprisingly well-behaved my Black friends and I were. But to be honest, at that point I was used to being a target no matter who I was around for reasons I couldn't understand. All of it had a numbing effect. I learned this is not uncommon for Black kids, and more specifically Black LGBTQ+ kids. Hari Ziyad coined the term "misafropedia" in their book *Black Boy Out of Time* to connote the particular vitriol and marginalization Black children navigate:

> I offer "misafropedia" to mean the anti-Black disdain for children and childhood that Black youth experience. As a term, "misafropedia" helps me to describe the systematic oppression of and disdain for Black children— a disdain that culminates in discarding Black children's existence. Their

existence is discarded literally in the abuse and incarceration of Black chil-
dren within systems such as the school-to-prison pipeline—as when police
handcuffed six-year-old Kaia Rolle and held her in a detention center for
throwing a tantrum in class in 2019.

I was shown over and over again that bisexual Black men were deceptive and that they were also a myth. I had no tools to process the derisive representation of Black bisexual men in the media and no historical figures whose bisexuality was readily available or wasn't completely erased. I was ill-prepared for the questions I regularly got upon using the label *bisexual* or simply moving through daily life as a feminine Black boy. I was not aware so many people had such a problem with the word *bisexual* and had to learn, decades later, that *bisexual* is not a bad word. Knowing who to tell, why to tell them, and how to tell them I'm bisexual were hurdles I had to figure out as I went along. Having the cognition to know the pros versus cons of being out at work or on the internet was an exercise I had to go alone. Learning about the atrocious health stats of bisexual men and how to combat them was not something I can say was readily available to me growing up in the 1990s or even entering LGBTQ+ spaces as a young adult in the 2010s.

I wish I'd known about the peril I'd face going into LGBTQ+ spaces specific to being bisexual and how much bisexual history is consistently erased. I was never explicitly taught about consent, power dynamics, and the ways race, age, class, and gender can impact these things, though these topics are urgent. I couldn't articulate the ways Eurocentric ideas of what it means to be a man have made it contradictory to being a Black bisexual man, and how *maintaining* my manhood under patriarchy is wagered on who I want to share pleasure with as well as the ways I experience it. I think about how tumultuous my time being a devout Christian was because I was never able to reconcile being bisexual and being devoted to my faith. I felt like I had to choose one over the other, and my mental health and self-esteem suffered greatly because I didn't have access to affirming resources for LGBTQ+ people of faith. I didn't know of or understand the various kinds of partnerships a bisexual man could take part in or craft for himself, or that being bisexual and in a relationship often means you'll have to continuously come out or have your sexuality erased or that being bisexual is not synonymous with being polyamorous. I was unaware of the ways seeing through a bisexual lens could impact my political scope or the ways in which talk of a gay agenda would impact the way I saw myself and the potential attitudes I'd be met with socially, politically, religiously, and in the workplace because of it.

A lot has changed since the 1990s and 2000s, but not much in the realms of widely distributed depictions, public thought, and gossip about bisexual+ (pansexual, fluid, bi-curious, queer, etc.) men. This obscurity does an incredible amount of damage not only to our reputations but also to our psyches and the resources made available for us. There's a limited number of equally positive, equally complex LGBTQ+ characters in the media, even fewer bisexual+ ones, and almost none who are men or people who identify with masculinity to some extent. All of this led me to write *Dear Bi Men*. When bisexual+ men speak, we are doubted. When bisexual+ men speak, we are no longer seen as an individual but as a stand-in for every negative thing every bisexual+ man has ever said or done. When bisexual+ men speak, our issues are disregarded. When bisexual+ men speak, we're told other groups have it worse. When bisexual+ men speak, we face rejection. When bisexual+ men speak, our voices are drowned out. When bisexual+ men speak, we are disrespected. When bisexual+ men speak, we are accused of being liars. When bisexual+ men speak, we are mislabeled as gay or straight. When bisexual+ men speak, we face death. When bisexual+ men speak, we are villainized. When bisexual+ men speak, we hit a wall that is miles high. When bisexual+ men speak, we come up against a deep-rooted stigma that has entered chrysalis, gearing up to produce a very particular kind of swarm. This has the power to steal one's voice, to create an environment where we begin to doubt ourselves, to sabotage our imagination, and to take away the life we imagined in the first place. There are many adverse effects to not being heard, both individually and collectively, ranging from rage and exhaustion to self-doubt and despair. Being heard and understood is not something that's consistently offered to bisexual+ men in this society. That is withheld from us. My hope going forward is that when bisexual+ men speak, we will be listened to, understood, supported, respected, embraced, provided for, and acknowledged.

To be clear, I am not interested in further demonizing bisexual+ men who are unpalatable, chaotic, problematic, or *messy*, for lack of a better word.

Bisexual+ men who have unprotected sex without knowing their own status or the status of their partners, bisexual+ men who do not disclose, bisexual+ men who cheat, bisexual+ men who fuck for money, bisexual+ men who engage in other kinds of sex work, bisexual+ men who break up with their girlfriend and get into a relationship with a man, bisexual+ men who break up with their boyfriend and get into a relationship with a woman, bisexual+ men who use their sexual prowess to influence people to get what they want, bisexual+ men who lie about who they are attracted to, bisexual+ men who want to fuck (or be fucked by) multiple people at the same time, bisexual+ men who are polyamorous, bisexual+ men who only have sex with cisgender masculine men and cisgender feminine women, bisexual+ men who play games, bisexual+ men who struggle with boundaries, bisexual+ men who are inconsistent, or bisexual+ men who don't share who they're attracted to with the important people in their lives. Bisexual+ men exist and are not inherently worse than our straight or gay counterparts, and these bisexual+ men will likely continue to be demonized; but not here and not by me. Being complex and misunderstood is a part of being human—especially as a teenager and young adult—and I don't intend to further shame or contain anyone who lives their life marching to the beat of their own drum. I am not glorifying or validating abusive or manipulative behavior, but I refuse to spend time in this book shaming bisexual+ men when it is so ubiquitous regardless of our actions. Our bisexuality does not make us bad or automatically any of the aforementioned; but either way, bisexual+ men deserve a full picture.

As an educational memoir, this book unfolds in sections—first, the focus is on my experiences throughout childhood, navigating the understanding of being a Black bisexual+ boy. The focus changes to shine more light on you, the reader, and provides feedback that may help you navigate this experience.

I've included blank pages to use as a way to integrate what you are reading into your personal experience and make your engagement practical and intentional. I also recommend using a journal as your companion on this journey to write responses to the "Things to Consider" at the end of some chapters, and to ponder the "Questions for Reflection" that you can find at https://jryussuf.com/additionals.

─────────────── NOTES ───────────────

Richard Lawson, "The Reagan Administration's Unearthed Response to the AIDS Crisis Is Chilling," *Vanity Fair,* December 2015, www.vanityfair .com/news/2015/11/reagan-administration-response-to-aids-crisis.

Gus Cairns, "New PEP Studies Revive Interest in Post-Exposure Prevention," Aidsmap.com, March 11, 2020, www.aidsmap.com/news/mar -2020/new-pep-studies-revive-interest-post-exposure-prevention.

Roger Peabody, "How Effective Is Post-Exposure Prophylaxis (PEP)?" Aidsmap.com, April 2019, www.aidsmap.com/about-hiv/how-effective -post-exposure-prophylaxis-pep.

Marc Lamont Hill, "Never Too Much," in *You Are Your Best Thing: Vulnerability, Shame Resistance, and the Black Experience,* eds. Tarana Burke and Brené Brown (New York: Random House, 2021).

Hari Ziyad, *Black Boy Out of Time: A Memoir* (New York: Little A, 2021).

Understanding Yourself
and Labels

Males do not represent two discrete populations, heterosexual
and homosexual. The world is not divided into sheep and goats.
Not all things are black nor all things white. It is a fundamental
principle of human taxonomy that nature rarely deals with discrete categories. Only the human mind invents categories and
tries to force facts into separated pigeon-holes. The sooner
we learn this concerning human sexual behavior the sooner we
shall reach a sound understanding of the realities of sex.

—ALFRED S. KINSEY,
SEXUAL BEHAVIOR IN THE HUMAN MALE

The key to understanding yourself and what bisexuality is begins with
understanding the difference between sexual orientation, sexual history,
and identity.

Sexual orientation: I like to define sexual orientation as something
no one can see or really know other than you. It includes, but is not
limited to, who you've had sexual or romantic feelings toward, including
romantic or sexual fantasies, crushes, intense feelings of admiration or
attraction masked by jealousy, and romantic or sexual dreams. This can
develop over time and even be unknown to you. Studies have shown
attraction is based on three core things: someone displaying features of
your subconscious comfort zone, someone meeting deeply unmet needs,
and someone expressing traits that you're repressing.

Sexual history: Connotes who you've had physical or sexual contact or experiences with, including, but not limited to, kissing, caressing,
mouth to genital, mouth to body, hand to genital, hand to butt, frotting,
intercourse, circle jerking or baiting, etc.

Sexual identity: Your identity may be the most complicated of all
of these because it may line up with your orientation and history or it

may differ. Your identity is the label, or refusal of a label, that feels the most freeing for you; the most accurate, the most comfortable, the truest. It's where you don't feel confined and where you feel most at home, especially when it comes to presenting yourself to others, though this can be severely impacted by internalizing biphobia or homophobia that says only heterosexuality is legitimate and acceptable. Your identity can change throughout your life because even though many people have a bisexual orientation, they may feel most comfortable with a straight or gay label, or no label at all, and that is completely understandable and up to the person. Many men and masculine-identified people use the label *gay* because they often get less resistance than if they were to use *bisexual*. Many use the label *straight* because it puts their life in the least amount of danger and because they often get less resistance than if they were to use *bisexual*. Many also default to either gay or straight when they're in a relationship as a way to make their partner feel less insecure or threatened or embarrassed.

Regardless of whether you've only had experiences with one gender, or if you've never had any experience at all, if you feel that you're bisexual+ (a label and an umbrella term I will get to shortly), then you are. Being bisexual is about desire that you cannot see. There is no litmus test. You don't have to check a certain amount of boxes, and you don't have anything to prove to anyone.

The line between admiration and attraction is very thin for many bisexual+ people. For me, admiration is an opening, an invitation into attraction. Sometimes my attraction toward celebrities or public figures will begin with admiring their talent or their style, and then over time it will morph into something else. In the past I've had small crushes on friends that would wax and wane like the moon or fizzle out completely like a candle. Some bisexual+ people have trouble with boundaries when it comes to their feelings for friends, sometimes put a lot into friendships, and occasionally fall in like or love with friends. The way I define having a crush on someone is when I think about them, it makes me smile; when I think about being around them, I get excited, and I really want to be around them; when I think about their voice, I may get a chill up my spine as I imagine them saying complimentary things about me, and I often rehearse conversations or scenarios I want to engage in with them.

I want them to be impressed by me. I want them to think of me in a special kind of way, similar to that of a best friend but more intense and with more possibility. I've come to think of bisexuality+ as *the* source of how humans experience connection and romantic and sexual desire unadulterated, not a derivative like being "part straight–part gay" suggests. I've come to see "part straight–part gay" thinking as a distortion. This reframe has affirmed me tremendously and made me realize cisheteronormative society intentionally omitting that humans can be, and are, bisexual+ is astoundingly oppressive.

You don't have to be attracted to one gender as often as you are to other genders, and it doesn't have to be as intense or feel the same at all. That was one of the big reasons I'd go from using *bisexual* to using *straight* to using *kinda gay* to describe myself as a teenager and young adult. I thought in order to be *truly* bisexual, you had to be equally attracted to women as you were to men. I thought it was a numbers game—that if I was physically attracted to men more often than I was to women, that I was a gay man in denial. Many men are in denial about being gay, and feel immense shame around their sexuality, and attach the same deal of weight and importance to being straight that the society around them does. In the 1980 essay "Compulsory Heterosexuality and Lesbian Existence," Adrienne Rich writes, "I am suggesting that heterosexuality, like motherhood, needs to be recognized and studied as a political institution—even, or especially, by those individuals who feel they are, in their personal experience, the precursors of a new social relation between the sexes." Society helps support this without fail or nuance.

When it came to developing romantic or emotional feelings, I disregarded how easy it was for me to form meaningful bonds—and eventually crushes—with women because as a man we are often taught that sexuality is all about who you have sex with, that sex is penetrative and perfunctory, not intimate, and that intimacy has little consequence. Sexuality is vast and can be quite complex, though society generally says otherwise. I am not suggesting that because an ease may exist when relating with women that means you're bisexual+, or that this ease suggests automatic romantic or emotional attraction or potential. I am saying that as a teenager and young adult I met far more girls and then women who I was attracted to romantically and emotionally than I did boys and then men.

Many boys and young men are mean as fuck, yet I still yearned to reach out and touch them. These attractions to girls and then women would sometimes start out there and develop into a physical one, where I'd see them in a different light, where I'd want to learn everything there was to know about them, where I'd want to hear them talk about anything and everything.

Figuring out what it was about men and women that usually drew me to each, verbalizing these things, incorporating them into my relationships, and trying to find those qualities in one person across genders has been rewarding. Perhaps most important is acknowledging and nurturing those qualities I'm attracted to in others within myself. What I will say is that an important part of intimate relationships for some people relies on sex, whereas there are other important things people along the asexual spectrum value. If you're not sexually attracted to your partner, yet you're forcing yourself to be sexual with them or be with them because of societal pressure, that societal pressure is violent. Regardless of how charming or conventionally attractive someone is, you cannot will yourself to be attracted to them, especially if it's a person of a gender you're simply not attracted to. In other animal species that engage in sex for pleasure, fun, exercise, intimacy, or more than just for procreation, bisexuality (and homosexuality) exists and is a regular occurrence. I wish there wasn't such an extreme sociopolitical importance placed on sexuality and gender among humans. I hope everyone is able to make peace with their sexual orientation, learn to revel in it, have the best love (and sex) life possible, and do so without shame. Many of us are working on making that hope a reality of the world we live in.

According to the Williams Institute, more people identify as bisexual+ (1.8 percent) by a slight margin than gay or lesbian (1.7 percent), with these numbers rising in younger people. Adults are two to three times more likely to say that they have same-sex attraction or have engaged in same-sex behavior than they are to identify as LGBTQ+. An estimated 19 million Americans (8.2 percent) report that they have engaged in same-sex sexual behavior, and nearly 25.6 million Americans (11 percent) acknowledge at least some same-sex sexual attraction. I expect these numbers to continue to rise as comprehensive education, adequate support, acceptance, and protection continue to grow.

Returning to my earlier point of finding myself frequently developing romantic or emotional feelings with girls, especially as a teenager during the early 2000s, it's important to acknowledge what is demanded of girls and women in this realm: being unfairly conditioned to be nice, being unfairly conditioned to be conversationalists, being unfairly conditioned to be good listeners, and being unfairly conditioned to tend to the emotional needs of those around them. Obviously not every woman excels at these skills, and on an individual, anecdotal level, there are many men and nonbinary people who are great in these areas, but this society has a stringent set of punishments and rewards for women in these arenas that is not the same for men. Because of that, many people of different genders often have an easier time connecting with women and developing an emotional bond, usually predicated on women's emotional labor. This is not a concrete basis for being attracted to women. It is an example of sexism.

Another reason I bounced between the labels *bisexual, gay,* and *straight* was because I was raised Christian and became a devout born-again Christian in 2004, at the age of fourteen, until I was about twenty-two years old in 2011. During that time I thought that simply acknowledging my attraction to any other gender besides women was a sin. I will delve further into this in the "Bisexuality and Spirituality" chapter. Many of us have been conditioned to expect and accept the bare minimum from men in the realms of emotional intelligence, conversation, and connection outside the physical, and it's clear how blatantly dangerous and deeply depressing that is. Some bisexual+ men and masculine-identified people have a radically different point of view on the aforementioned, and I just want to start off by saying that's valid, and special, and important.

To recap: Sexual and romantic history is purely objective and based on the genders you've been in sexual or romantic situations with. For example, because of compulsory heterosexuality, many gay and lesbian people have been in sexual or romantic situations with a gender different from their own. This does not make them bisexual+. Many straight people have been in sexual or romantic situations with the same gender for a variety of reasons. Just because your history has people of different genders does not mean your identity or orientation is aligned with that. Just because your history does not have people of various genders does not mean your identity or orientation is aligned with that.

Orientation includes things like thoughts, desires, fantasies, crushes, romantic feelings, and sexual feelings, and it can include dreams. Your orientation can sometimes be hidden from you because of societal pressures, its intensity and frequency across genders may vary, and some may not know bisexuality is an option for men and masculine-identified people. Because of heteronormativity, we are conditioned to desire women and to pursue relationships with women only. Some people don't realize they have a bisexual orientation until later in life. Some people don't realize they have a bisexual orientation until they have their first experience with the same gender or until they have their first experience with a gender different from their own. Orientation is not something you can see.

Identity is perhaps the most complicated of the three. Someone might identify as straight or align with *straight culture,* only go to straight clubs or watch sports or whatever other things are deemed part of *straight culture,* but they may have a bisexual+ orientation (or a gay one). There are people who acknowledge their bisexual orientation but prefer to identify as gay or straight for a variety of reasons; perhaps the most important one to mention is that they feel most at home with gay or straight people. They feel community in these spaces, and though they may occasionally or even frequently be attracted to someone who does not fit the expectations of these communities, they're able to find their footing and voice identifying as such. Orientation is all about what you can't see, not necessarily what practices you take part in or what scenes you prefer. These are really important to talk about, as are the way they relate to one another and the ways society can shape or occlude our sexual orientation and identity.

BISEXUAL+ VIRGINS

It's important to note that the concept of virginity was created by patriarchal societies and is still used to police, violate, punish, limit the agency and social mobility of, and justify purity killings of women and people assumed to be women. I personally do not like the concept of virginity or the hyper-focus on it, though I recognize having a sexual experience for the first time is an event that can be significant for many people, and that the concept of virginity is still a cultural norm in many Western societies.

In order to be bisexual+, a person does not have to have romantic or sexual experience with people of more than one gender. Bisexual+ virgins exist just like gay and straight virgins exist. You can be bisexual+ and have only dated or had sexual contact with one gender, and you're still completely valid and bisexual+. There's something about the idea that, in order to be *legitimately* bisexual+ you've had to have sex with men and women, feels very binary and Christian to me. It's a sentiment that's often used to torment bisexual+ people and falls into problematic territory. The idea reminds me of the concept surrounding consummating a marriage; as though the legitimacy of a relationship is not sealed until sex has been had post-nuptials. Relationships don't *really* mean anything until you've had sex. This is not true and the idea teeters into the noxious waters of rape culture, pinning penetrative sex as the goal and characterizing factor. It's a warped way of looking at relationships and sexuality. I know many people who dismiss, disregard, and downplay relationships because they haven't yet had sex even though they've shared intimacy in other ways and created important memories. All that's been felt and experienced is not *really* important because sex hasn't happened? Then do friendships, which often supply us with a necessary feeling of understanding and community, not truly matter? I intensely dislike that idea. You're bisexual+ if you have a desire for more than one gender and you say you are—plain and simple.

LABELS

There are many labels under the bisexual umbrella (which I will use *bisexual+* to indicate going forward) and though there is a lot of overlap, there are differences that matter to some. Being someone who doesn't like labels—or hates them altogether—is completely valid as well and quite common among many individuals past and present. Labels make many people feel boxed in, like a product on a shelf, instead of a living, breathing human being. On the other hand, labels make some people feel seen and validated, less alone and able to find community. Whether you hate labels or don't mind them, it's important to acknowledge how you feel, how other people feel, and to understand what works for you in this department will not work for everyone else.

A Twitter user whose intention was to put an end to the bi versus pan discourse asked, "Do any of y'all use bisexual and pansexual interchangeably? Or do they mean different things to you and if so ... can you explain the difference?"

I absolutely love this question, especially coming from a person who is not interested in positioning non-monosexual individuals against one another. *Bisexual* is the first term I learned to describe a person who is attracted to more than one gender, and in my experience it is the most recognizable under the umbrella. With the term having origins in the world of medicine, it is the term that the most scholarship and activism has been done under, and using the term does not make me feel boxed in or like it's inaccurate, so I use *bisexual* to describe myself online and *bi* to describe myself when I'm disclosing to new people in real life. In my experience, when I've used *bisexual* in real life, I almost always get inappropriate comments or invasive questions about my sex life that adds another layer of dread onto disclosing. When I use *bi* without the *sexual,* people usually nod and the conversation moves right along. There is an aspect of identifying as pansexual as a display of full autonomy, getting to clearly name and define one's sexuality, and be in clear solidarity with nonbinary and transgender people that really resonates, but ultimately I've seen many examples of bisexual+ people who've reclaimed a word defined by the world of medicine and simply lived their truth as people who experience attraction across genders. Also, one of the large differences I've observed between bisexual+ and pansexual is that gender and gender expression are not deciding factors or influences on attraction for pansexual people, whereas they definitely are for me.

As I've done a lot of healing work and more living, I've realized that my sexuality is fluid, more specifically, and that fluidity really depends on my overall well-being, fears I've worked through, positive versus negative experiences across genders, and the traits within myself that I'm repressing versus embracing. My personal goal is to get to a place where I've addressed most of my big fears surrounding dating men, women, and nonbinary people so that when I find myself attracted to a man or a woman or a nonbinary person, there is not this overwhelming fear that prevents me from being present or trying to see where things go. Smaller fears may eventually arise, and I plan to remind myself that I'll be able to work through them as long as I'm patient and kind with myself. Making sure I'm reflecting on any stories I'm telling myself, such as *I will no longer be queer if I date women, I will be gay if I partner with a man, My attraction to women is me objectifying them, I'm not a real man if I'm with another man, I'm faking my attraction,* or, *A romantic relationship can't work between two men.* What works for me may not work for you, and that is okay.

This is a bit of a sticky one. As I said earlier, labels can make some people understand themselves in a very real way that they never have before. They can pinpoint and relay exactly what their experience is, which can be thrilling and validating. Many of these words under the bisexual+ umbrella were created on Tumblr, or elsewhere online, where many people offered very good insights on identity and understanding one's attraction and oneself. I think that work was really impactful for tons of teens and young adults and seems to have a hand in why Gen Z is not only the most pro-LGBTQ+ generation but why they are also the most self-identified LGBTQ+ generation to date.

I recognize that some of these more obscure labels—while they may be helpful for oneself when trying to gain clarity and specificity about exactly what you feel inside and how it works—may not be useful in everyday conversation. You will likely run into difficulty using some of these labels to communicate your sexuality to someone else who is not part of this niche. If you do not mind explaining, or if you're opening up to someone and it is important to you that they know your label and understand how it works, by all means.

I cannot ignore how the creation of some of these labels originated with, and still sits in, internalized biphobia. When someone says they're straight, it is not assumed that they are attracted to every single person of another gender. It is only when someone is not straight does it become a catchall. Gay men and lesbian women are often shunned and avoided because the assumption is that they're attracted to every man or woman, respectively. That is homophobia and lesbophobia. Bisexual+ people are often thought to be willing to fuck anyone, be attracted to everyone, and as hypersexual, which leads to an incredible amount of sexual violence against bisexual+ individuals, especially women and people assumed to be women. That is biphobia. Creating a label that is not *bisexual* simply to signal that you're not in fact attracted to every single person seems like a lot of work. Keeping oneself safe is paramount, and I know many people who use *queer,* though they mean *bisexual* or *pansexual,* as a way of keeping themselves safe. I do that in my own way by saying *bi* instead of *bisexual.* It makes complete sense. However, if the use of *queer* instead of *bisexual* is because the thought is that *bisexual* implies attraction to everyone, or that it means attraction to more than one gender equally, that sounds to me like a misunderstanding of what bisexuality is, or internalized biphobia. Bisexuality is about you simply acknowledging your attraction to two or more genders. It does not mean you're attracted to men and women to the same degree or as frequently, and it doesn't mean that you have slept with or even plan to sleep with more than one gender. There is no one way to be bisexual+.

EXPLORING WESTERN PSYCHOLOGY'S HAND IN BI ERASURE

In a seven minute YouTube video titled "How Men Confuse Sexual Attraction With Emotional Connection," Thais Gibson breaks down the three core tenets of attraction: (1) your subconscious comfort zone around what love is: the way you've historically received it, witnessed it, and what you've understood it to be; (2) a person meeting, or promising to meet, deeply unmet needs; and (3) having someone express traits you're repressing, or trait variety. She also acknowledges other biological factors being present with regard to attraction in other videos. Gibson is a licensed therapist, with over a decade of experience running a private practice, who avidly researches neuroscience and produces groundbreaking work involving understanding and reprogramming the subconscious mind. Gibson mentions how the topic was posed from prior clients and several men within her online school, The Personal Development School.

"How and why do some men get romantic-emotional connection and sexual connection intertwined and why?" She starts by asking the listener to imagine they were in the habit of chronically repressing their own emotions, then one day someone comes along and makes them feel really seen in their emotions. They hold space for their emotions and connect with them:

> *What's going to take place for you as a human being—as an attachment-seeking species—what's going to naturally happen is that you are likely going to associate this person with some kind of positive emotional associations, positive feelings, because somebody is seeing your inner self. When people—specifically men—are getting emotional connection and sexual attraction confused, the real core reason tends to be that exact reason. It tends to be that there's two things being hit at the same time. And so, if we are repressing a part of ourselves, we may not consciously recognize it, but we have a deep need for somebody to hold space for that part of ourselves, feel safe expressing that part of ourselves, and the moment that somebody comes along and gives space to that, it's such a fulfilling thing that it is not uncommon—even if somebody is in a relationship, somebody is experiencing something—it's not uncommon to feel such a strong pull toward that person because they seem to be holding space in a way that's allowing us to get a need met, to express our emotions, and maybe to be the container for that.*
>
> *This is not an uncommon space for different individuals, if they're experiencing this, actually sometimes to question their sexuality because that strong pull of attraction, though it may not be rooted in something sexual or romantic, can get confused there, and lines can get blurred. I have seen this many times before, and the person who actually asked this question cited an article that touched on males having this experience with a male therapist.*
>
> *What's essentially happening is because the subconscious mind wants trait variety and wholeness, if somebody's expressing something repressed in you, the subconscious mind is deeply drawn to that to create wholeness.*

What I got from this video is that the subconscious mind is bi or pansexual; it experiences various kinds of attraction across gender and gender expression. I want to make clear that because I view being bi or pansexual as distinct identities, and identifying as such a personally empowering and inherently political stance, especially in this society that is so virulently oppressive to polysexual identities, I do not find it helpful to label everyone as bi or pansexual, especially without robust plans to address and undo the myriad ways this specific oppression manifests. One thing about the subconscious mind is that it seeks to avoid pain a lot more than it seeks pleasure, and pain is often associated with being gay or bi or pan, whether that be eternal damnation or intense societal adversity. For some queer and trans people, the pain of denying their truth outweighs the pain of societal rejection and violence. For others, the opposite is true.

This idea of entryways into attraction is particularly fascinating to me as a bisexual+ person. Love languages—though rife with white Christian fundamentalist patriarchal white-supremacist thought—are another concept that's entered the mainstream lexicon, making legible the varying ways people give and receive affection and love. It was helpful to understand that as a bisexual+ person, I might have one point of entry for one gender and a completely different one for another gender, which may make attraction easy to misread or miss entirely. It was going to be up to me to value this, nurture it, and respect it. Learning about the concept of the mother-father wound and then addressing each of them helped contextualize so much for me regarding my beliefs, thoughts, emotions, and history surrounding engaging men, engaging women, and myself. It's been helpful asking myself, What would my particular entry point of attraction or met needs have to be in order to consider engaging with a particular man or woman? What fears would I need to work through? What skills would I need to learn? What beliefs about myself and others would I have to let go? What environments would I need to be in?

Terms like *sapiosexual* and *demisexual* are perhaps the better-known versions of this idea that in order for sexual, emotional, or romantic bonding to occur, it usually begins in a particular place. *Aromantic* and *gray-ace* are related terms.

Asexual writer AVENite Rabger, also known as Forbidden Fury, poses a hypothetical model of human attraction:

- **primary sexual attraction:** A sexual attraction to people based on instantly available information, such as appearance or smell, which may or may not lead to arousal or sexual desire.

- **secondary sexual attraction:** A sexual attraction to people based on information that's not instantly available, such as personality, life experiences, talents, and so on. How much a person needs to know about the other, and for how long they need to know about them, for secondary sexual attraction to develop varies from person to person.

- **primary sexual desire:** The desire to engage in sexual activity for the purposes of personal pleasure, whether physical, emotional, or both.

- **secondary sexual desire:** The desire to engage in sexual activity for purposes other than personal pleasure, such as the happiness of the other person involved or the conception of children.

BEATING BI BURNOUT

Oftentimes on Bi-Visibility Day (September 23) and during Pride month there is a joyous side that is shown on TV and online, but there's also the other side of being confronted with some of the reasons these events are still necessary. Becoming aware of the reality of your orientation, some of the really frightening stats and oftentimes lived experiences of bisexual+ people can be really troubling and stressful. My friend Patricia Silva, creator of *Larker Anthology*, documenting and celebrating bisexual+ culture, calls this "bi burnout." Because of this, I often find myself unplugging and finding comfort in affirming bisexual+ media.

Here are some commonly used ways to beat bi burnout when it happens:

1. I remind myself that dark thoughts and feelings are temporary and will not last.

2. Taking a nap is something I do when I'm in a dark place. I can do it immediately and it involves very little energy.

3. I try to quiet my mind by getting into my body. Doing something physical like taking a walk around the block, doing yoga in my living room using YouTube or an app, going to the gym, or taking a kickboxing class is a start.

4. Visiting a pet shop or animal shelter and playing with puppies is one of my favorite things to do when I'm feeling down.

5. I read affirming bisexual+ literature such as *Best Bi Short Stories: Bisexual Fiction* (my short story "Face to Face" is in it!); *Rec-Og-Nize: The Voices of Bisexual Men;* and *Barriers to Love: Embracing a Bisexual Identity*, which is a great way to distract yourself.

6. I distract myself with some bisexual+ media like *How to Get Away with Murder, Lost Girl, The Bisexual, Faking It, Shadowhunters, Queen Sugar, The DL Chronicles, Orange Is the New Black,* and *Boomerang.*

7. Listening to the podcast *Two Bi Guys* (I'm a guest on the episode "Femininity and Forgiveness"!), *Bisexual Real Talk, Bad in Bed, Bisexual Brunch,* or *The Homecoming Podcast.*

8. Cooking, baking, or cleaning is another great distraction.

9. Contacting family members or friends who are affirming.

10. Planning a visit to a bisexual+ support group meeting is another alternative.

NOTES

Alfred C. Kinsey, Wardell R. Pomeroy, and Clyde E. Martin, "Sexual Behavior in the Human Male, 1948," *American Journal of Public Health* 93:6 (June 2003), 894–99, https://doi.org/10.2105/ajph.93.6.894.

Adrienne Rich, "Compulsory Heterosexuality and Lesbian Existence," *Signs* 5:4 (1980), 631–60, https://doi.org/10.1086/493756.

I Love Veterinary, "What Animals Have Sex for Pleasure?" July 16, 2021, https://iloveveterinary.com/blog/what-animals-have-sex-for-pleasure.

Gary J. Gates, "How Many People Are Lesbian, Gay, Bisexual, and Transgender?" Williams Institute, UCLA School of Law, April 2011, https://williamsinstitute.law.ucla.edu/publications/how-many-people-lgbt.

Samantha Schmidt, "1 in 6 Gen Z Adults Are LGBT. And This Number Could Continue to Grow," *Washington Post,* February 24, 2021, www.washingtonpost.com/dc-md-va/2021/02/24/gen-z-lgbt.

Simonefiii (@simonefiii), "Do any of y'all use bisexual and pansexual interchangeably? Or do they mean different things to you and if so ... can you explain the difference?" Twitter, March 5, 2021, 2:22 p.m., https://twitter.com/simonefiii/status/1367918370671063041.

Thais Gibson, "How Men Confuse Sexual Attraction with Emotional Connection," YouTube video, July 24, 2020, https://youtu.be/3i2rYgn5H5Q.

Therapist Lauren L., "The Bigot Who Wrote 'The 5 Love Languages' Might Hate You," Medium Blunt Therapy, November 13, 2021, https://medium.com/blunt-therapy/the-bigot-who-wrote-the-5-love-languages-hates-you-e2f65771a1c0.

AVENite Rabger, "Primary vs. Secondary Sexual Attraction Model," Asexuality.org, July 19, 2022, https://wiki.asexuality.org/Primary_vs._secondary_sexual_attraction_model.

Unlearning Biphobia and Homophobia

> Being heterosexual is not "normal," it is merely one other expression of sexuality.
>
> —GAIL HALL

"What's the difference between biphobia versus homophobia?" A gay male friend of mine asked a while back, and I let him know that although they are related and often overlap, there's a distinction that is important to note in highlighting some of the challenges bisexual+ individuals face.

Homophobia is dismissal, prejudice, negative feelings, aversion or a fear of same-sex attraction and unfavorable sentiments toward gay people. Biphobia is dismissal, prejudice, negative feelings, aversion, or a fear of someone's attraction to more than one gender and unfavorable sentiments toward bisexual+ people. For example, a heterosexual woman saying they would not date a man who they knew to be bisexual+ *because* he is bisexual+ is an example of biphobia. When your personhood, character, and individuality is overshadowed or affected by the fact that you're bisexual+, that is a clear sign of biphobia. She may go on to explain the reason is because she thinks bisexual+ men are liars and cheaters (biphobia) and that they have HIV (the HIV part is both biphobic and homophobic) but also that a man being with another man makes him less manly or is disgusting (homophobia) because he's "double-dipping" (biphobia).

Another example is a gay man saying they would not date a bisexual+ man *because* he is bisexual+ (biphobia). He may go on to explain the reason is because he thinks bisexual+ men can't be trusted (biphobia) and will eventually go back to a woman in favor of a societally approved pairing of a nuclear family, because they can't commit (biphobia), that they will want a woman again and because bisexual+ men are not pro-LGBTQ+

rights (biphobia). Biphobia is when *all* bisexual+ men are assumed to possess these traits. When your personhood, character, and individuality are overshadowed or affected by the fact that you're bisexual+, that is a sign of biphobia. When negative character traits you have are attributed to you being bisexual+, that is a sign of biphobia.

An everyday example of homophobia is coming out as bisexual+ and people having a negative reaction to you presenting a partner who is a man but not with a partner who is a woman. An everyday example of biphobia is mentioning an ex (or a crush) of a particular gender, while currently being with someone of a different gender, and people dismissing your attraction to either, calling the validity of your feelings into question, finding it worrying, finding it perverted, or paternalistically labeling you straight or gay depending on their preconceived notions. Bisexual+ individuals face biphobia *and* homophobia, as seen in the case of Channing Smith, a sixteen-year-old Tennessee student who died by suicide after being outed by his former girlfriend via social media, then being cyberbullied. If homophobia somehow collectively ended tomorrow, biphobia would still remain.

Lawyers in a Texas case filed a brief recently arguing the U.S. Supreme Court's ruling in *Bostock* v. *Clayton County,* in June 2020, does not apply to bisexual+ men. In that ruling the High Court held that Title VII of the Civil Rights Act of 1964 protects employees against discrimination because they are gay or transgender. Lawyers for Braidwood Management, a business owned by hardline anti-LGBTQ+ activist Steven Hotze, and Bear Creek Bible Church in Keller, Texas, argued in their brief that "an employer who discriminates on account of an employee or job applicant's bisexual orientation (or conduct) cannot engage in 'sex' discrimination as defined, because that employer would have taken the exact same action against an identically situated individual of the opposite biological sex." In other words, employment discrimination based on sexual orientation or gender identity does not apply to bisexual+ individuals—as long as bi men are being discriminated against "on equal terms" as bi women.

This continues down a dangerous path that's already been tilled, and I expect to see things like this happen more frequently in years to come, alongside the intensifying marginalization of transgender people. I foresee many gay and lesbian people being apathetic or even incited by these rulings and thinking, *Finally, bisexual+ people will have some skin in the game,* ignoring the fact that much of bisexual+ people's fate has been closely tied to that of gay, lesbian, and transgender people as we are subjected to the social, internal, and legislative impacts of heteronormativity, regardless of the optics of our relationships.

As we witness society begrudgingly move toward tolerance of gay people, we see an increase in biphobia on platforms like X (formerly Twitter), YouTube, Instagram, and TikTok, which frustrates the sentiment that Gen Z will instinctively lead us to a completely LGBTQ+ friendly future. Many people's argument for supporting gay people is that "They don't affect your life" and "What they do in their bedroom doesn't affect you since you're straight," but with bisexual+ people, that argument no longer holds. These people want to know that they're comingling with others who are cisgender and straight, who are *normal* like they are, who won't mar their world. People who are not bisexual+ are willing to dismiss biphobia as not that big a deal far too often, even though bisexual+ health and livelihood stats tell a grimmer tale, which I go into in the "Health and Wellness" chapter.

I had the opportunity to speak with Robyn Ochs, one of the best-known bisexual+ activists in the United States, recently over Zoom, and found out that we both grew up in Far Rockaway, Queens, only a few blocks from one another, thirty years apart. On the Zoom call, she gave me advice for this book and also taught me about a frame she created to help bisexual+ folks understand and navigate a world so intent on erasing, disparaging, and misunderstanding us. She calls it the Biphobia Shield. Ochs shares her Biphobia Shield at colleges and workshops across the globe to explain the root of biphobic stereotypes and provide bisexual+ people with a practical tool to protect ourselves from the everyday comments that can lead to internalized biphobia. Utilizing these tools helps to weed through the bullshit and to understand that these things are not caused by us; rather they are caused by limitations in other people's thinking. Biphobia and bi erasure are not our fault. These five insights, by helping me understand why these stereotypes exist, help soften the blow of, and prepare me for, most biphobic comments.

THE BI SHIELD

- The tip of the iceberg: Most bisexual+ people are assumed to be either straight or gay, depending on who they are publicly known to be partnered with. People only recognize bisexuality when they know that someone has both a same- and different-gender partner or partners. Thus, people draw the false conclusion that because the bisexual+ people that they recognize—the tip of the iceberg—are all or mostly polyamorous or promiscuous, bisexuality equals having multiple partners.

- Binary thinking: We are conditioned to frame things in binaries. Identities that challenge this false simplicity often face dismissal and intense pushback.

- Society has a perverse relationship with sex and sexuality: Though U.S. media may suggest otherwise, we are quite a socially conservative country when it comes to many laws, opinions, and cultural attitudes. This society exploits sex because *sex sells*, while also demonizing and shunning talk of safe-sex practices, conversations around consent, and so on.

- Ignorance: People are uncomfortable with things they do not understand, and most people have not been given access to a good education on LGBTQ+ issues.

- Hurt people hurt people: This speaks to experiencing biphobia within LGBTQ+ communities or media and references a sociological concept called *horizontal hostility*. All too often, members of marginalized communities take out their pain and frustration on other members of their own community who they perceive as even more marginalized than they are. Bisexual+ and transgender people can be targeted by some lesbians and gay men.

Ochs also makes the point that it's a function of oppression that the behavior of any individual member of a minority group is seen to reflect on their entire group. Certainly, there are many bisexual+ people who behave in ways that conform to bisexual+ stereotypes. But there are also many nonbisexual+ people who engage in those same behaviors. Ochs emphasizes that the prevalent stereotypes are just that: stereotypes, and not defining characteristics of bisexuality.

There's a common idea that bisexual+ people deal with less external and systemic, yet more internal, homophobia because in the minds of many people, bisexuality is not its own distinct sexuality but merely part gay and part straight. Let's unpack that a bit. The Kinsey Scale was developed in 1948 and is still one of the most widely disseminated bisexual+ pieces of copy, pointing to human sexuality existing on a continuum rather than being a binary, as was previously understood. The language used in the study and the scale, however, describes homosexual attraction (same gender) and heterosexual attraction (other genders), and instead of this leading to evolving public thought surrounding binaries, it was easier to simply apply this unexamined binary thinking toward a bisexual+ person's sexuality, splitting it down the middle into half straight, half gay.

The first known use of the word *bisexual,* according to Merriam-Webster, was in 1793, but the word only came to be more widely used outside bisexual+ communities in the 1980s. If bisexuality is believed to be a real sexuality, it is still understood using binary thought. The idea of bisexuality and sexuality in general as a fluid, evolving thing disrupts the way so many of us have been taught the world is and the way we've learned to view ourselves, interact with others, and navigate life. Bisexuality can make some acutely aware that binary opposition is not in fact the end-all, be-all, and although it has its uses, it also has its limits and contradictions. It can disrupt the certainty people grasp for in philosophy, culture, and language because we are taught to comprehend in a binary fashion. And since bisexuality disrupts, it must be ironed out.

Still, for others, it can rock their world, acting as the final straw to seeing the world in all its endless wonder and possibility and terror. It can cause some to deeply consider the question, What else might exist outside binaries? And that question is sometimes too much for people whose reality is more comfortable in black-and-white. It's too much to wrestle with, too much to process. It's easier to interpret bisexuality as part this, part that. By this logic, if bisexuals are only part gay, they only face partial homophobia. This is not true.

"Why does anyone else's sexuality matter? It's nobody's business what goes on in someone else's bedroom." That is a very privileged, ahistorical, detached stance to take. The truth of the matter is that it does matter, and

anyone asking this should aim that ire toward lawmakers, other government officials, and society at large. Sexuality has been politicized. People
base their life's vision, personal style, and aspects of their livelihood on
who they date and plan to end up with. It impacts micro choices as well
as macro ones; it influences the way boys and girls are raised and socialized, which I explore in detail throughout this book.

Of course who you're attracted to is important, and of course it
matters. Of course it dictates a lot about someone when so much of
our culture revolves around a person's wholeness and identity being
tied up in being partnered, especially as you age, especially if you're a
woman. Comments like "I can't believe you're single" are meant as a
high compliment of someone's appearance or personality. Saying that
someone has a beautiful heart and mind, or that someone seems to really
like themselves, is not as common a compliment, which I think reflects
our values and beliefs as a society. It's about desirability and it revolves
around how an attractive person has earned being spoken for or claimed,
romantically and sexually. Our conditioned imagination around identity is so narrow. I wonder how many people view singlehood as an
unbearable punishment meant for those with *bad* hearts and minds, an
uncomfortable thing meant for those who are undesirable. As I navigate
my mid-thirties, the lengths people will go to in order to be desired
and *taken* frightens me more and more. I see people turn their backs on
other forms of love, go against their morals, lose sight of their ambitions,
and forget their own boundaries. The way we act as sentries influenc-
ing others through our interactions on behalf of upholding these ideals
scares me infinitely more.

It's such a complicated thing, having grown up as a feminine bisexual+
boy, never having been allowed to forget it, and now being a dark-
skinned Black man on whom hypermasculinity and heterosexuality
are projected. I've noticed that beginning in 2015, when I entered my
mid- to late twenties, I've been increasingly perceived as masculine and
straight for the first time in my life. I will admit, I remember spending
hours in the mirror as a teen and in my twenties, observing and *correcting* everything from my hand gestures to the way I walked, the way I
laughed, the way I spoke, the patterns my voice fell into while speaking,
and so on. Add to this, I studied acting in undergrad, which included

learning how to pitch my voice down, adjust my energy level, the story gestures can tell about a person in a scene and in real life, and how to maintain authenticity even while presenting my voice and energy and body language differently.

But when I really needed to blend in, none of my efforts succeeded. I learned very early into auditioning, after graduating college in 2012, that if a director and casting people in the room during an audition sensed I was feminine or not straight but was auditioning for a straight character, it'd be very unlikely that I'd be cast, regardless of my ability—even though many straight men are feminine. If I wanted to have an acting career with longevity and a wide variety of characters to play, I'd have to tone my femininity down, even when I wasn't performing. I'd have to play their game. I think once I realized this, I started to unconsciously morph, little by little, even when I wasn't in the audition room. Since leaving undergrad, I also gained muscle mass and tools to manage my anxiety, which I suppose make me appear more mellow or masculine. More indifferent. Less queer. Essentially, I was spending more time in parasympathetic nervous system mode, which is when your mind and body feel safe and able to smoothly enter rest-and-digest mode, and less time in sympathetic nervous system mode, when your mind and body sense danger and are in fight, flight, fawn, or freeze mode.

Over the last few years, I've found that straight men and women are a lot nicer to me in casual situations now that the way I'm read matches their expectations and desires. I've also noticed many LGBTQ+ people are on their guard or hostile toward me. It's bizarre and disorienting. Part of it is the disconnect between how I still see myself—a young feminine bisexual+ boy who people see as gay—versus how people sometimes see me—a straight Black masculine athletic man. When I was young and desperately wanted to just blend in with straight people, I couldn't. Not without incident or interrogation. But now that I care less about blending in, and see the value in connecting and organizing with other LGBTQ+ people, I'm not read as a part of the community. Another part of the pie is knowing that the pleasant treatment from the former is incredibly conditional. Once enough time passes, or I start talking about Beyoncé's vocal mastery and my voice jumps an octave, once my aunty laugh is heard, there's no going back, and things become different. It's always jarring when you realize people only treat you with decency when they think you're one of them. It's isolating. My experience is very different now as a 5-foot-11 man in his thirties than it was when I was a child, teen, and young adult, but what I've been through to get here and how I currently navigate doesn't exactly feel like *privilege*.

As Jules Ryan argues in their essay on Medium, "Why I Don't Use the Term 'Straight Passing Privilege'":

If you have to earn privilege through self-repression, being in the closet, or having your gender and/or sexuality erased, then it's not privilege. My issue with the term "straight passing privilege" isn't so much that there aren't inherent benefits to appearing straight to the outside world, because of course there are. You're safer walking down the street, you can travel to any country, and you can freely hold your partner's hand at the grocery store. However, where there are benefits to not "looking gay," there are also drawbacks to living in that limbo, since you still aren't straight. To call the experience of being perceived as straight a blanket privilege disregards the lived experience of lots of multi-sexual* people. It also insinuates that all LGBTQIA2S+ people who aren't in a same-gender relationship are automatically read as straight by the world as individuals or within their couple. It feels like there's a gap in our language to discuss what it means to be visibly LGBTQIA2S+ and how that affects us as individuals or couples. All I know is, the terminology we have seems to alienate certain people solely based on who they're dating or what they look like, which feels reductive.

In addition to having to overcome internalized homophobia, feeling that your attraction to the same gender is wrong, bisexuals also have to reckon with internalized biphobia that says that being attracted to more than one gender makes us greedy or filthy or untrustworthy or liars or all the other horrible things society parrots. Putting so much pressure on your sexuality is really unhealthy, and so is celebrating your attraction to a particular gender yet attaching shame and loathing to another. A common perception is that our sexuality is split in half, with our attraction to the same gender over here on the left and our attraction to another gender over here on the right. But it's not like that for me. My sexuality is not made up of these two separate things that exist in isolation of each other; it's one beautiful sexuality. Since that's the case, when I'm receiving messages from larger society that say my attraction to men is the problem, my attraction to all genders will bear the brunt of that bashing. If I'm internalizing messages that there's something wrong with my attraction to men, then there is something wrong with my entire sexuality because it's a whole thing. Feelings of guilt and shame and disgust that I may feel about my same-sex desires will weigh on my attraction and interaction with other genders. It will affect my entire sexuality and my entire self-esteem. Another part of why people think bisexual+ men deal with less homophobia is because people deeply believe that all bisexual+ men are masculine. That is not true.

It is important to break this assumption down a bit. A feminine man's experience with homophobia will likely be very different, as he will be met with constant criticism and violence on many levels. As I've shared, before I began engaging sexually with anyone or even having fantasies that I can remember, the way I expressed my gender was a big problem. A masculine man's experience with homophobia may not be about how he speaks or dresses, and it will be different, but he still faces homophobia, externally, internally, and systemically. It's not the same experience, and the urgency should be placed on feminine men, and yet they both face homophobia. I grew up as a feminine bisexual+ boy and it was hell. You do not have to be masculine in order to be bisexual+. You do not have to be feminine in order to be gay.

Our needs get neglected by LGBTQ+ programming, media, and outreach because of biphobia. According to a report from Funders for LGBTQ Issues, the total amount given from foundations for bisexual+-specific grants in 2009 and 2010 was zero. In 2017 and 2018, grants that specifically targeted bisexual+ people amounted to less than 1 percent of the funded amount. *And* many of the gay people in leadership positions think that since there are resources available for gay men and because larger society supports heterosexuality to a fault, bisexual+ people are getting their share of what they need from each space. That idea goes back to not seeing bisexuality as a whole sexuality with its own distinct needs and challenges and not seeing biphobia as a legitimate societal ill rampant in LGBTQ+ culture.

SEVEN WAYS TO ADDRESS
INTERNALIZED BIPHOBIA

1. **Stop gaslighting yourself.** Doubting your own bisexuality is destructive. Whatever you feel is what you feel, and whatever you have felt in the past *is* what you have felt. It is valid. If you've had crushes on guys or girls or nonbinary people, if you've wanted to get to know people on a romantic level or sexually, stop gaslighting yourself. Stop doubting the legitimacy of your own feelings or saying iterations of "This doesn't really count, and it doesn't matter." Pause. Take a breath, and accept what is. Accept the feelings that come up and don't judge them.

2. **Read bisexual+ literature.** I cannot stress this one enough because there is something so incredibly powerful about seeing experiences similar to yours in written form. It can make you feel a rush of excitement or just feel normal. Try any genre from fiction to nonfiction to memoir to speech transcriptions. A book that I return to is *Barriers to Love: Embracing a Bisexual Identity* by Marina Peralta with Penelope James. It's a memoir that chronicles the life of a Mexican woman who is a psychotherapist and takes you on a journey from some of her earliest memories all the way to her vibrant life in her sixties as a psychotherapist and moonlighting dancer. It really resonated with me because she talks explicitly about some of the differences in her experience dating men versus dating women, compulsory heterosexuality, and an attractive balance between being reflective and living out loud. It holds lots of insight that promoted a lot of healing and self-acceptance.

3. **Bisexual+ support groups.** Depending on where you are in the world, this unfortunately may not be an option available to you, but YouTube and other forms of social media, where you can remain anonymous if you need to for safety reasons or because you want to, exist. Certain places might not have bisexual+ support groups or an LGBTQ+ support group at that, but I definitely recommend traveling to larger cities once in a while

when it is within your means. Or go while you're on vacation in a metropolitan city. Even if you can only find a gay men's support group, I'd recommend going, though I'd be cautious about revealing your bisexual+ identity in groups that are not explicitly bisexual+. You can simply connect to being able to talk about being attracted to other men without fear of your safety being compromised or being scorned. The pros of going to one of these meetings is off the charts in the realms of feeling less alone, feeling affirmed, meeting people at different parts of their journey than you are who could potentially help you, or who you can help. Even if you just have to drive out or get on a train on a weekend for a few hours, it is worth it. It reminds you on a really substantive level that you're not alone, because you're not alone. There are so many bisexual+ people in this world.

4. **Stop putting pressure on liking a particular gender.** Before I'd done the work to be more comfortable in my own skin, I placed so much importance on my attraction to women. In retrospect, a lot of this was because of the faulty ideas I had about manhood, which was heavily intertwined with my attraction to women and the access I had to them. This is not surprising when you consider the way this society conditions boys to be, and when you look at the expectations around manhood in this society. A lot of it is centered on how much power we have over women, how we feel about women, and how women feel about us. This is one of the many pitfalls of Eurocentric ideas around gender; it says that men are nothing without the *other* gender: women. It says that we are only half of a whole. As I said, I was putting so much weight on my attraction to women, and when I began to ease up on that, my sexuality was really able to bloom, and I began to be attracted to men, women, and nonbinary people who didn't fit inside the neat little boxes I'd prescribed. I could feel a lot better about myself and my sexuality. Though we live in a heteronormative society that praises our attraction to another gender only, it's just not healthy to

put so much attention and focus on your attraction to a particular gender. It's not healthy to wrap your self-esteem and self-worth around how attracted you are to women. Accept what is.

5. **Stop assigning negative meaning when comparing your sexuality and desire to other men's.** I've berated myself so many times for not wanting to immediately fuck women or men I was attracted to. It has led me to be physically ill on more than one occasion. In these moments I'd tell myself there was something wrong with me or my sex drive because what I felt wasn't overtly sexual; *real* men not only had the ability to be sexual at will but also had to desire people they were attracted to, sexually, at all times. I'd tell myself these stories that said what I was feeling was illegitimate and didn't measure up in comparison to what other men felt. This is incredibly unfair, unkind, and steeped in rape culture and gender expectation. It's important to accept yourself and your sexuality as it is instead of trying to force it to be something else.

6. **Allow yourself to feel the excitement and the rush of being attracted to somebody.** Whether it's a celebrity crush or somebody you see on the street or a friend, allow yourself to simply appreciate how good that feels and how exciting it is to be attracted to somebody without all the judgments, without all the labels, and without the questions of "What does this mean?" and "Are we going to wind up together?" Allow yourself to just feel it, and hopefully one day you'll get to a place where, experiencing attraction, the only feeling you have is excitement and joy and not shame.

7. **Foster a kinder, more accepting internal dialogue.** I notice my bisexuality and subconscious speak to me more often and are easier to hear the kinder I am to myself internally. If my internal dialogue is kind, forgiving, and accepting, all sorts of bisexual+ desires reveal themselves to me. Whenever I am critical, think in binaries, and am judgmental of myself or others, it is inaudible.

ACCEPTING YOUR SEXUALITY
AND BEING ACCOUNTABLE

Trigger warning: misogyny, mention of violence against boys and men.

Being uncomfortable with one's sexuality may explain a person's behavior, but it does not necessarily excuse their actions. Prior to becoming fully comfortable in your bisexual+ identity, you may have harmed people, aimed disparaging comments at gay men and other LGBTQ+ people, joined in on criticizing feminine men, and reinforced the fallacy that men who are not cisgender and straight are inferior. That is reprehensible and incredibly damaging. This is obviously a symptom of internalizing biphobic and homophobic ideas from larger society and then lashing out. Hurt people hurt people. It makes complete sense that people from marginalized groups who are constantly mistreated and disregarded would internalize some of that. However, I notice that there are bisexual+ and gay men who expect that letting people in about their sexuality, or coming out, absolves them of the harm they may have inflicted. Hell, no. Coming out does not absolve you of misogynistic, biphobic, homophobic, or transphobic violence you participated in. Only accountability can. It may give context for why you lashed out and did what you did, but it does not repair the damage you wrought.

The ways I interacted with women and gay men prior to beginning the work of introspection was often born from a place of misogyny and homophobia. Prior to 2012, I was a devout Christian and had the foundational belief that men and women *belonged* together, that the union between a man and a woman with the man as the head of the house was holy, natural, and for our own good. This belief came with arrogance and entitlement when it came to women I was attracted to who found me even somewhat attractive or simply engaged with me in conversation. Everyday consent was not a precept encouraged in the Christian spaces or communities I passed through. Everyday consent means we communicate our boundaries *and* ask others for their perspective before taking both sexual and nonsexual actions that impact them.

At church and in Christian communities, I regularly witnessed coercion and people's everyday consent violated. This was in the form of people not asking prior to laying hands, telling someone else's story or intimate secrets during a sermon because god told them to, or because these things were believed to be something that would bring them closer to god, something done for their own good. People wouldn't blink an eye when these things happened, so I grew up thinking this was unremarkable and made sense, especially if it was done by an older person or a person farther into their walk with god. One of the ways this showed up in my everyday interactions with women is if I thought a woman could find me attractive, or if I thought we were a good fit, I'd often insist that we exchange numbers, get to know each other, be together. I regularly violated younger people's everyday consent, and gave them advice when they protested, and dressed it as spiritual discernment. I was doing it for their own good. There are plenty of men who are Christian or have had similar upbringings who haven't interacted with women or younger people in this way, and yet I recognize how naive and willfully ignorant it is to pretend like these widespread attitudes and customs don't contribute to a culture that does not center consent.

If you thought my treatment of women was bad, my treatment of gay men was abysmal. Though I was feminine and have been assumed to be gay from before I can remember all the way up until a few short years ago, I was prejudiced against men I perceived to be gay. I largely avoided them as friends because I didn't want to be associated with them—and I'm sure they felt the same way about my ignorant, self-hating, judgmental ass. I was unkind, quick to be irritated by, and quick to dismiss men I thought were gay. I had double standards; one for men I perceived to be straight and another for men I perceived to be gay. I did not think a romantic relationship between two men would last because I believed it was unnatural and that humans needed to be with the opposite sex. Same gender marriage was not a reality when I was growing up during the nineties—though civil unions were—cementing a ubiquitous sentiment that two men did not belong together and couldn't ever form a legitimate family. (It's important to mention that marriage equality is still not a reality for disabled people, according to the World Institute on Disability; there's more about the marriage penalty tax on the institute's website, https://wid.org.)

I relegated men to late-night rendezvous, experiences that helped me purge the gay out of my system after years of trying to pray the gay away.

I did not always practice everyday consent with the men I was sexual with, and though my behavior was sometimes met with resistance, it was often met with an equal level of transgression, mistreatment, and roughness. I thought all of this was because they were men—as if these traits were exclusive to men or innate rather than encouraged and reinforced by society. It fortified my belief that a long-term relationship could never work between two men.

Upon leaving Christianity and trying to become more comfortable with my sexuality, beginning in late 2012, which I will go into further in the "Bisexuality and Spirituality" chapter, I quickly realized just how much I'd participated in misogyny and homophobia. I realized that on some level I participated in misogyny as a feel-good, knee-jerk reaction to my manhood being challenged, to display my desire for women, and out of a deep-seated belief that I was also somehow entitled to women. I realized that on some level I participated in homophobia to distance myself from what religion, society, and the community I belonged to believed should not exist, was wrong, and was inferior. A common thread here was how I would objectify both men *and* women. I obscured their humanity in the process, which made it easier to treat them poorly and without a deep regard for their autonomy. As I began to process many of my experiences in therapy, I began to realize that not only had I been hurt, disbelieved, manipulated, objectified, violated, and made uncomfortable, but I had done the same thing to others. I relived the ways I'd wielded patriarchy and heteronormativity where I could, both knowingly and unknowingly.

I reached out to some of these women and men in an attempt to apologize. This did not always go well or even get a response. Even when they accepted my apology and went on their way, it still ate me up that I'd done these things, that I'd tried to out men who did not disclose their gay or bisexual+ identity, that when jealous or upset I'd insinuate a straight man was gay to *bring him down a peg,* that I'd said such casually violent things, that I'd succumb to patriarchy, that I'd hurt people, that I'd been the bad guy in somebody's story. Not everyone cares to stick around for your redemption arc, and it is incredibly self-centered and troubling to insist on that.

Kevin Spacey is a two-time Oscar award winner who currently has over thirty sexual harassment, assault, and battery allegations from men and women spanning decades, with many of them alleging the incident happened when they were minors. He's also alleged to have had sex with young interns on set and abused his power. When the news broke, he came out as gay and made a three-minute YouTube video invoking counterarguments to "cancel culture" and "impeachment without a trial," as though that would excuse the violence he enacted and the unethical power dynamics he orchestrated. Let me just say, I hated every minute of it. Conflating being gay with pedophilia is incredibly damaging and such a gross misrepresentation of gay men.

Accountability is community-focused and meant to repair harm that was caused and stop future harm from happening. The thing about accountability, though, is that the person who caused harm has to agree to an accountability process, and often has to initiate it. Our society responds to harm with punishment. Accountability, consequences, and punishment are often used interchangeably. They should not be because they are not the same. Punishment is an imposed penalty as retribution for behavior, whereas accountability is about a person taking responsibility for their actions and trying to rectify things.

Accountability can look like acknowledging one's actions and their impact on others, expressing remorse, taking action to repair the harm, and no longer committing similar harm. Accountability can look like Kevin Spacey being removed from positions of power and access so that he cannot further harm anyone else while he commits to working with a mental health professional to address the root of his behavior and fund whatever courses of healing his victims decide they'd like to take. Accountability can look like funding local and national educational programs around consent, rape culture, and enthusiastic consent. Accountability can look like a celebrity who was formally antagonistic toward LGBTQ+ people and has just come out as bisexual+ apologizing, funding LGBTQ+ education initiatives, and agreeing to fund local and national LGBTQ+ therapy or other health care needs. Accountability can look like a donation to an organization that helps survivors through their healing journey. Accountability can look like offering someone who you previously overlooked because of their sexuality a decision-making position with a competitive livable wage. Accountability can look like suggesting LGBTQ+ sensitivity trainings happen quarterly at work. Accountability is a process of admitting wrongdoing to the victim, taking ownership of one's actions, and agreeing to a solution.

If you've done harm, some people will only see you as those harmful things you've said or done, and that's understandable. I recommend trying to make amends, but you've also got to accept *and* respect that some people will not be willing to move on or see past the harm you've caused, and that's their prerogative. Making amends does not always have to mean asking to see the person or trying to get in direct contact with them because this may be triggering for them. There are other ways. Doing this shouldn't be about you or making yourself feel better. Accountability is about centering the person who's been harmed and trying to repair that harm. Sometimes being accountable means doing the really tough healing work to understand how it happened so that you never repeat it.

BLACK FEMINIST PRINCIPLES AT THE CRUX

For me, Black feminist principles are a cornerstone of my bisexuality, not an addition to it. These principles help me deeply understand what patriarchy demands, the violence it doles out at women, and how it impacts people of various genders. Bisexuality—and all the things related to and important to bisexual+ people—offers an opportunity to examine the white-supremacist ideals we've been taught to build our sense of selves on. I no longer wish to be helpless, cut off from, and underdeveloped in the areas patriarchy demands I be because of manhood. Black feminism offers space and a restoration of the self that has been mutilated due to patriarchy.

There are different kinds of Black feminists who practice feminism in their own way, but Black feminist principles examine patriarchy, sexism, race, social status, and economics in systemic ways that are far more conscionable and sounder. Patriarchy was created by white cisgender heterosexual abled moneyed Christian men, and today men are the largest benefactors of it, whether they mean to be or not—though I'd be careful when grouping all men in with patriarchy's inventors. Imperialist white-supremacist capitalist patriarchy disproportionately enables and encourages a level of entitlement, abuse, and labor theft to classed white men's benefit that is ongoing. Black feminism takes this and more into consideration.

Around these topics it can be easy to label women as solely good and men as solely bad, but that's a cop-out and is not in alignment with reality or Black feminist principles, which highlight systems of oppression. This thinking ignores interpersonal violence between Sapphics and when women cause harm, as well as men who do good and their many contributions. "Women are good and men are bad" is also an example of the golden prison patriarchy designs for women. As an act of compromise, it says women are the more mature, moral, superior gender if you really look at it. It may be alluring to parrot these talking points, especially because of all the adversity women face and have faced historically, but this is gender essentialism and in many ways a not-so-subtle threat to women. It does not end at a compliment like this. When you praise all women for being more sensible, nurturing, superior, and so on, assigning highly skilled labor—for free or for pennies—to the gender that's just naturally more competent is logical. *Women are better* and they must be selfless, rear children, cook and clean, perform emotional labor for the men and boys in their lives and more, *or else.*

THINGS TO CONSIDER

- If you believe women are inherently more emotionally intelligent and thus should be gentler with and teach the men in their lives emotional intelligence, can you consider how incredibly violent and unfair that is?

- Can you consider how this forces girls and women into these roles not only for their husband—if they marry or even partner with a man in the first place—and children but men at every step of their lives, who are bound to be there at every step because of the way authority roles usually change hands between men?

- Can you see how making someone else responsible for your emotional maturity is violent and damaging to them as well as to yourself?

- Can you see how this will create resentment from both parties?

- Can you see how unbalanced and outrageous this is?

- Can you see how men get credit by way of having a career and platform and power and respect and money because of their wives teaching them these skills?

- Can you see how words of praise about women's inherent emotional intelligence are both an obstacle and a threat?

- Can you see how this dynamic makes it harrowing for most women married to men to live full lives with themselves at the center?

- How much more patience, emotional intelligence, healthy communication, and healthy boundaries would be required of you to show up fully?

PORN

Trigger warning: if you have a problematic relationship with or are working on an attachment to porn or sex, you can choose to skip over this section if you need to. Trigger warning: mention of being rough with men.

Let me just start by saying there is no way I can really do justice to this topic in a few short paragraphs, as this topic is incredibly loaded. However, I will try to do my best to address a few major key points most relevant to the bisexual+ men and masculine-identified people I imagine are reading this. Take what I have to say with a grain of salt and make sure to center the varied perspectives of adult performers and sex workers in this arena.

To be honest, I'm not really able to enjoy porn between men and women that's produced by big porn companies. I find it overtly misogynistic, too out of character for how I'd personally want to engage with women, and the women usually seem like they're faking their enjoyment, which I find to be deflating. Literally. In my experience, lesbian porn has the same sort of awareness-of-the-male-gaze lacquer, where it's more of a show than passion on display. I love man–woman porn that couples post and that openly bisexual+ OnlyFans creators post, and porn where men please and interact with trans women who have a dick.

As a teenager in the early 2000s, I had a complicated relationship with porn that featured two men because a lot of it that caught my attention was really rough or hardcore (see: Tiger Tyson, Castro, Phoenix, and Dream). Even though the rational part of my brain knew I didn't necessarily want to interact with another person in that way, I was also incredibly aroused by it and had met many queer guys who either were really rough or expected me to be. I'm still unpacking this, but I think the draw to it was because a lot of it was simply hot, and also that it had something to do with thinking that men are naturally rougher, and perhaps physically stronger, so they can *take it*. Problematic, I know. I said I wasn't perfect. It was difficult to feel ashamed of my attraction to men, wonder if a relationship between two men could even work *and* be really stimulated by rough hardcore porn between two men. Shame is powerful and kept me in limbo until I put in the work to unlearn it. Nowadays, I love man-man porn that features passionate vers men, doggy-style clips where the POV is an overhead from the person topping, and porn where cisgender men please and interact with trans men who have a dick or pussy, though I wish there was more porn that featured trans men topping.

Supporting sex workers by paying for porn feels really good to me on an ethical level. I do have to be careful about making sure I do not watch porn every single day, or even more specifically, every single time I masturbate. Doing this means you will eventually run into erectile dysfunction trouble when you're engaging with another person in real life because your brain and body get used to a particular level of stimulation and intensity. Similarly, if you're using anal toys each time you're masturbating, or anal stimulation each time you're having sex, you will eventually run into erectile dysfunction trouble when you're trying to use your dick. Don't fret! If you go one week without doing either, your body sort of resets, and you will likely be able to use your dick for sex again or ejaculate without porn as long as you start using your imagination and physical sensations again. Also, switching up the hand you use to masturbate, where you masturbate, and whether or not you use a lubricant each time you masturbate helps too. I recommend daily Kegels, pelvic exercises you can easily find online or on an app. They can give you better erections with a bit more girth and length, delay how long it takes you to ejaculate (you can use sleeves if you have the opposite problem), and help intensify orgasms.

There is so much sexual shame at the center of our society. This country was established by white Puritanical Christian colonizers, so it tracks. Shame is a huge factor behind what makes people have such a negative relationship with porn and unsafe behaviors around sex. In some circles, it can be treated like a dirty little secret or not mentioned at all. Also there's often shame attached to watching porn in general, especially when it's not between a cisgender man and cisgender woman or that veers into BDSM or disrupting gender or sexuality expectations. Adult performers are often discussed in dehumanizing ways, mocked, are social pariahs, and their livelihoods are sometimes put in jeopardy if they have another job or have moved on from the adult entertainment industry, especially if they're women or assumed to be women. Although people casually joke about starting an OnlyFans, the reality is that being an adult performer is the ultimate societal taboo. People often learn about sex from watching porn, though adult performers say it is not meant to be educational— unless that's explicitly intended—and is best digested as entertainment or fantasy by adults. The truth is that mainstream porn companies are incredibly racist, colorist, misogynistic, biphobic, predatory in multiple ways, and intent on centering heterosexual male viewers. Gay porn can be just as racist, colorist, unrealistic, biphobic, predatory, and based on problematic portrayals of dominance and submission rooted in femme-phobia—which I will address shortly.

Comprehensive sex-ed is rarely taught in schools, or homes for that matter, so a lot of people do not wind up learning it. When people are taught about sex, the focus is often penetration, contraception, waiting until marriage, or the correct use of barriers to protect from sexually transmitted infections (STIs) and HIV. Things that are often left out are the emotional aspects of sex, the psychological aspects around sex, enthusiastic consent, how awkward and funny it can be, the etiquette of securely sending or receiving nudes, getting tested regularly, the social pressures and consequences, ensuring pleasure for everyone involved, the importance of peeing after sex, once you start having sex you will likely want to have sex regularly, sex toys, body positivity, sex positivity, BDSM, and so on.

In a #BisexualMenSpeak WhatsApp group that started shortly after my hashtag took off in 2018, one of the older married bi guys who mentors boys and young men made an analogy between porn and pizza that I found very helpful. He said that having pizza every once in a while is great and not bad for you; the problem becomes when you have pizza so much that it's the only kind of food you eat, truly enjoy, or can make you feel full. Substitute pizza here for porn. Obviously if you're lactose-intolerant or maintain a gluten-free diet or experience heartburn, this analogy doesn't exactly work for you, but you get the idea. I will take that metaphor with me for a long time because it makes sense, is simple, and attempts to discuss porn in a balanced way in a society that has a contentious relationship with it. Unless pizza (solo sex) is your preferred food. (I wonder what he'd say about porn where the adult performers *eat* pizza on camera.)

The thing about watching porn for bisexual+ men and masculine-identified people is that it can be affirming or help ease longing if you're in a monogamous relationship. Sometimes the fantasy the adult performers create can be really hot and can satisfy the desire or curiosity that you might have. I think more people would benefit from recognizing that their partner has a sex drive and sexual desires that existed long before they met that do not necessarily revolve around the other person. This does not mean they don't love you or aren't turned on by you. It means they have desires and a sex drive and they still chose you, and it's how human sexuality works. Masturbation and watching porn can be a time where your partner gets to fantasize and have things exactly how they want without having to be considerate or connected or experience anything more than a straightforward orgasm. That is okay and to be expected. If you're in a relationship with a man, occasionally watching porn featuring a man and a woman or two women might be something you're interested in. If you're in a relationship with a woman, occasionally watching porn featuring two men or a man and a woman might be something you're interested in. Sometimes, though, it won't be enough. Sometimes a conversation will need to be had, a relationship will need to be remodeled, a relationship will need to end.

Often when people watch porn it is because they have a desire, born from an unexpressed need—often a nonsexual one—to connect with someone, feel seen and heard, feel physically alive, and live out a fantasy. Occasionally people in monogamous relationships find themselves deeply attracted to another person, and it isn't because they're bad people. It's human nature. Your capacity to find other people attractive or be drawn to people doesn't short-circuit when you decide to be monogamous. However, those *deep* attractions are usually trying to get your attention because there may be an area of your life or relationship that you're neglecting. For example, being deeply attracted to someone who is thriving in their career may be a sign you need to reexamine or establish a structured plan in order to make headway in your own career while getting in touch with what you really desire in that area of your life so that you feel on track, less stuck, or more significant. Being deeply attracted to a creative type may be a sign you need to nurture your own creativity and figure out ways to bring creativity back into your relationship or sex life. Being deeply attracted to someone who remembers little things about you or gives you undivided attention may mean you need to effectively ask for that in your relationship or stop putting your needs last.

Porn can be really healthy for bisexual+ men and masculine-identified people to use on occasion when they are curious about or miss being sexual with another gender. A few years ago I started having casual sex again with this guy after years of celibacy, and though it was some of the hottest, most connected sex I've had, having sex with him made me realize how much I missed having sex with women. It had nothing to do with not being satisfied by the sex, and a lot more to do with the ways being sexual again was bringing to the surface other things I'd been repressing sexually. Considering nonmonogamy is also an option, I'd seriously advise you to ponder, whether you're single or partnered, if only to unlearn potential bias you may have absorbed. You may not have a conclusive answer anytime soon, and that's okay too. I will go farther into nonmonogamy in the "Sex and Dating (and Marriage)" chapter. Adult performers fulfill a need, create a fantasy, provide a service. Sex work is work. If you value or enjoy that work, pay for it. You can also advocate for the decriminalization of sex work. It is preferable to directly support adult content creators over subscriptions to large adult entertainment companies; however, paying for your porn is better than not paying for it. Paying for porn is a step toward ethical consumption and won't be a huge financial burden if you put the pizza-porn analogy into practice, though you may need to discuss this with your partner if you have one.

Bisexual+ adult performers like Wolf Hudson, Dante Colley, and Michael DelRay have talked about the discrimination they've faced in the porn industry on the *Two Bi Guys* podcast at length. Hehe. Even Dwayne Mckell, a straight adult content creator, spoke up about the double standard in the industry he noticed between male adult performers and female adult performers who did things on camera with men and women. Bisexual+ male performers, or "crossover performers" as they're often referred to, have largely been shut out of the porn industry, which has made many resort to do either gay or straight porn, or more recently, turn to creating their own content. Biphobia aimed at men is commonplace in porn. Biphobia aimed at women in porn often takes the form of sexual harassment, assault, and manipulation. Even further, femmephobia also plays a part. A study from 2012 showed that a majority of gay men prefer masculine men and abhor femininity in other men. This attitude, obviously internalized from larger society, has a negative impact on their own self-esteem, mental health, and social life. This spills over onto attitudes about bisexual+ men who are feminine.

Although things seem to be slowly changing, much of the representation of bisexual+ men (and straight men who do sexual things with other men on camera) plays into ideas of the only legitimate kind of bisexual+ man being a masculine one. Even then, his true identity is often posited as a gay man so deep in the closet, so bound to performing masculinity and heterosexuality, that his status as a bisexual+ man is vapid, fleeting, and conditional.

The premise in bisexual+ porn is often about whether being with a man feels better than being with a woman, the secrecy of the same-sex encounter, and the seductive allure of the taboo being irresistible. That sucks. Male bisexuality in the media—especially porn—is very rarely displayed as a man who is simply open to, interested in or enjoys being romantic and sexual with more than one gender, ethically, and on his own terms. Masculinity, regardless of how subjective it is, is essential and assumed. This informs cultural attitudes around bisexuality and acts as a model many people follow for bisexual+ representation in the few instances it does appear.

HOW INTERNALIZED HOMOPHOBIA AND BIPHOBIA CAN AFFECT RELATIONSHIPS

Many gay and bisexual+ men who have ingested damaging messages about their sexuality take their frustration over not being straight out on their male partners. LGBTQ+ people experience domestic violence at roughly the same or higher rates than our heterosexual counterparts; it's worse still for bisexual+ people. This includes incidents of physical violence like shoving, spitting, hitting, throwing objects, as well as threats, intimidation, verbal harassment, sexual violence, and incidents involving a weapon. Very few initiate an order of protection, call the police for assistance, or see it as abuse since domestic violence is usually framed around cisgender heterosexual couples. It's an ugly skeleton that needs to see the light of day, and I go into more detail, including statistics, in the "Health and Wellness" chapter.

It's clear that nearly all the gay and bisexual+ men I've talked to know that hitting women is wrong, but when it comes to hitting other men, the verdict is still out, even for ones they're dating. Masculinity asks us to settle things with our hands or psychologically hurt others who we feel have wronged us. A gay man I went to high school with told me he beat up his boyfriend after finding out he'd cheated, and said his boyfriend deserved it. He told me his boyfriend even admitted to having "fucked up." Finding out a partner has cheated can make you fear for your life and sexual health, and it's a form of emotional abuse. Becoming physical with a partner does not remedy this and is reprehensible regardless of gender. There was something in how casual my high school friend told me about his course of action that was alarming. It was just what happened when his boyfriend *went too far.* That is telling and shows me that more of us need to learn more constructive, less violent coping strategies and relationship boundaries. Feeling like it is your place to hurt or *discipline* a sexual or romantic partner is a sign you may benefit from working with someone to learn healthy conflict resolution.

Instead of unlearning internalized homophobia and redirecting the frustration many of us feel—because we're not afforded the same access and safety as our cisgender heterosexual counterparts—at the system that marginalizes some and favors others, we find ways to abuse and devalue our partners because it is easier. Many of us go from being the traumatized to traumatizing others through physical as well as psychological means like mental torture, infidelity, manipulation, and cruelty. Even more specific to bisexual+ men, many of us do not take relationships with other men as seriously as we do with women because of internalized homophobia and compulsory heterosexuality.

Many bisexual+ men engage with other men as if they're doing them a favor, as though the end of said relationship is inevitable, as though men are incapable of being gentle, as if they already know the other man to be only as interesting as what he can provide sexually. This shows up in a trite cynicism and quiet disdain. It shows its face in the unwillingness to treat the other as an equal deserving of care, respect, intentionality, and grace as well as a refusal to be emotionally available, which might be fine sans the condescension rooted in the idea that queer men *cannot* maintain a healthy, functional relationship. I know this because I've lived it, seen it, *and* have been on the receiving end of it.

Many of these men in particular call themselves bi-curious, heteroflexible, heteroromantic, straight, mostly straight, and sometimes, bisexual+. I have connected with many bisexual+ men like this—who have not told anyone they're bisexual+ or who have just begun to tell people. They show very little care to the forming bond, and they condescendingly engage as though their preference for and access to women validates them as men in a way it could never do for me, someone they assume to be gay because I'm feminine and because of my sexual history. If there exists an element of mystery and deliberate pacing when it comes to dating women that does not exist with most men, it is okay to acknowledge that without belittling same-gender relationship dynamics. It is okay that dating a woman feels very different from dating a man. It is even okay to prefer one over the other, especially since you'll likely feel more confident doing the one you've done more. You can grow your confidence with either if you're willing to put in the work and experience some discomfort at first as you learn. It is not okay to look down on or bad-mouth same-gender dating.

A hetero-flexible colleague shared that with women there exists "the thrill of the chase" and that most women wouldn't "give up the cookie" without some work put in, which makes him respect women more. Conversely, he sees men as easy and only considers sexual relations with them. Basing a woman's—or anyone's, for that matter—value on their sexual modesty falls into murky waters deeply rooted in violent thinking that's been used as a means of controlling and demonizing women's sexuality for centuries. It's based in toxic purity culture and rape culture. It's naive not to consider the innumerable ways this system has shaped our desires and why we prefer what we do. The idea that gay and bisexual+ men are to only be engaged with sexually because all gay and bisexual+ men have less inhibitions and are more sexual is rooted in homophobia and biphobia, respectively. Though men and women are rewarded and punished in different ways regarding how to express themselves sexually, attributing a lack of value and promiscuity to all gay and bisexual+ men is homophobic and biphobic.

Prior to learning about the subconscious mind and attachment theory, which I discuss later, I would revel in saying to friends, *"men,"* in a flippant, glum, irritated tone, even if my frustration was a product of me not feeling empowered enough to speak my mind yet expecting that man to read it. I'd say it even if I was expecting a man I was still getting to know to be on the same page as me or behave exactly as I thought he should. After deeply understanding the ways attachment styles and the subconscious affect the pace at which people unconsciously expect relationships to move, what they make sex mean, how they maneuver in the workplace, how they interact with authority figures, the way they give and receive love, and so on, all I could see when it came to men was variety. Maybe there were similar initial shades of color but various undertones that were distinct from one to another, even if they were only one color over.

I do not think queer men are automatically more superficial or sexual than our straight counterparts, or even women, to be quite honest. Unlike many scientific studies insufficiently linking testosterone to a higher sex

drive, I recognize various hormonal, social, and psychological factors that
may influence men and the ways patriarchy assigns meaning and instruc-
tion surrounding our erections, libido, and behavior. I've learned enough
to know that many, many gay and bi men have fewer tools for connection
at our disposal, combined with popular beliefs about how to attract or
keep a man. I've heard enough to know that many queer men engage in
sex with one another because they want to be liked, think it's expected of
them, because it is a cultural norm, want to hold someone's attention, to
please someone, because they're afraid of losing the other person, because
they want to feel desired, because they want to feel significant, because
they want to feel like they're good at something, because they're bored,
because it feels good, because it makes them feel powerful, because they
want to express themselves, because they want to convey something they
can't say verbally, and so on. What I've noticed about many queer men is
that they yearn to connect with other men, but because of certain fears or
limited social skills, they default to sex as the main way they connect. I'm
not passing judgment here, as aspects of the sexual freedom many queer
men possess is truly admirable, healing, and trailblazing.

Sexual shame is so pervasive in our society as a result of Christian
dogma, misinformation, and societal control. Sex is good for your body, is
fun, and feels good. I'm simply making an observation and am interested in
alternatives for queer men who want to connect with other men in various
ways. Firstly, maintaining a strong daily connection to your subconscious
often helps this need for connection with others be more balanced and
authentic. Eating meals without being on your phone, or having another
distraction while noticing textures and flavors, daily meditation where you
observe your thought patterns and feelings in interactions with certain personalities then advocate for necessary changes, daily journaling via paper
or voice note, processing your emotions somatically and by questioning
the stories your mind comes up with about people and situations you're in
and whether those stories are completely true or subconscious associations,
asking for your needs to be met and your boundaries to be respected from
those you interact with, nurturing a more understanding internal dialogue,
less thinking in extremes of all or nothing and perfectionism, working on
various things you want to create in the world consistently whether that's
weekly or daily for as little as fifteen minutes.

What the world of neuroscience is uncovering more and more is just how malleable parts of our brains and the self are, for better or for worse. Epigenetics is the study of how your behaviors and environment can cause changes that affect the way your genes work. Unlike genetic changes, epigenetic changes are reversible and do not change your DNA sequence, but they can change how your body reads a DNA sequence. You are in conversation with your environment, and the environment not only says bisexual+ men don't or cannot exist, it's also calling us names, it's also creating systems that ensure our destruction, it's also stoking fear and hatred of us so that in the event we show our faces, they will be caved in. The way you're treated throughout childhood— as well as later in life—is how you learn to treat yourself. If bisexuality is repetitively dismissed, shamed, feared, rejected, minimized, and ignored in our world, it then teaches us to do the same to ourselves whether sexual or romantic feelings are just beginning to bud or have already bloomed. Epigenetic researcher and author Dr. Joe Dispenza states, "Epigenetics teaches us that we are not doomed by our genes and that a change in human consciousness can produce physical changes, both in structure and function, in the human body." He goes on to say that epigenetics "turn on and off like Christmas tree lights," highlighting that there's an immediate response to stressors in our environment. Change is possible.

BEING PRESSURED TO "PICK" WOMEN (AND HAVE CHILDREN)

There's this common idea with bisexual+ individuals that when we come out to our parents or other loved ones and people in our lives, we have it easier because to these people we are only *partly* gay. Recently while we were watching TV, my mom was suggesting that I don't tell women I'm bisexual+ right away, or at all really, as a way to protect myself, yes, but also as a way to make myself more eligible to a wider net of women and to increase my chances of being with a woman. She essentially said this so that I can get her a grandchild sooner than later. This may sound harmless to some, but it's coercive and underhanded and is merely one example of the challenges that many bisexual+ people face when we tell our families or friends we're bisexual+. They say they accept that we're bisexual+ but find ways to either subtly or overtly tell us to be with a particular gender—not necessarily the person who we happen to wind up with who makes us happy—which doesn't feel like acceptance at all. This can be crushing. This is a symptom of a heteronormative society.

Our loved ones do this without taking into account our personal preferences and whether or not we can, want to, or plan to date a gender different from our own. Many bisexual+ people acknowledge that they are in fact attracted to a particular gender but do not want to engage, and that is completely valid and understandable. For the majority of my twenties I'd sworn off women because I didn't feel desirable to them. I'd been rejected because of my femininity or because many thought I was actually gay. Playing into gender roles makes my stomach turn, and I didn't want dating to be such a charged site anymore. If so many of the women I was interested in thought I was gay, there was no point in trying to prove them wrong, as it'd be to no avail. I had more experience with men anyway, so I decided to date and fuck men for most of my twenties, and had a great time doing that. Loved ones often forget or ignore the fact that you may not always have access to a particular gender. For example, in response to my mom's sentiment, I let her know that a lot of women think I'm gay when we talk or they see my social media. I simply do not have access to a wide array of women, and I've made peace with that. I'm a feminine man, I love that about myself, and it's not something I want to change, even if it has over the years, so it is what it is. I do not have access to every woman I'm attracted to, and every woman I'm attracted to is not attracted to me, and the women I'm attracted to who are attracted to me and celebrate my femininity may not be a match for me, and so on. Being bisexual+ is not this inherent free-for-all that many people seem to think it is, especially when you're forthcoming about being bisexual+. Many think it means you have twice the amount of options as gay or straight people. For many bisexual+ people that is simply not the case, especially considering the biphobia in society at large and within many LGBTQ+ communities. Some would argue we have less chance of finding healthy relationships that are free from fetishization, intense suspicion, or outright disgust.

THINGS TO REMEMBER

- Being bisexual+ does not suddenly grant you access to everyone.
- Being bisexual+ doesn't necessarily mean you have more options.
- You're not compatible with everyone you have access to.
- Bisexual+ women don't owe bisexual+ men access or allegiance.

Next, I asked my mother if she wanted me to end up with a woman, and to that she quickly said no, that she'd be happy no matter who I brought home—but I suspect she wants it to be a woman. She answered too quickly for me to believe her, and in that moment, I couldn't help but remember her asking me if I was gay, when I was a lot younger, and her responding, "Thank god," after I said, "No . . . I'm not *gay.*" While staring at the TV, my mom made sure to say that she did in fact want grandchildren, and from the way she phrased it, it was as if that could only happen if I was with a woman. I turned back to the TV and didn't give voice to the fact that I do not want children or that her vision for me with a happy family and what it means to be a man is not one I'll likely ever take part in. I don't know why this sentiment is so common because people in same-gender relationships can still have children. There are many options and ways around this. The conversation ended there, with her smiling at the TV, having expressed her well wishes for my familial life and me watching along, slightly irritated but resolute and comfy.

The incident reminded me of how heteronormative this society is and how, even if your family and friends say they accept you being bisexual+, they can still encourage you to be with someone of a particular gender, which can influence your decisions. It's backhanded, and it really sucks. It can put pressure on who you allow yourself to date and which of those people you tell them about. It puts an unfair burden and importance on your attractions. Regardless of who you may have a preference for, it may sway your decision to either get into a relationship with someone or not, and it can make you internalize biphobic as well as homophobic ideas even more when people around you want you to be with someone of a different gender rather than someone of the same gender, or when these people only celebrate relationships you're in with women and are not excited when you're with someone of the same gender. The opposite is also true. It's very common and it's horrible. So many people downplay their attractions to the same gender because of this, or they internalize the idea that a relationship with the same gender is not legitimate, or it's only good for sex. Some people only want to have sex with the same gender, and that is completely valid as well. I just wanted to point out that I notice, because of society's heteronormative assertions, many bisexual+ people internalize these ideas. Some of us place a lot more value and importance on relationships with people of a different gender than we do with people of the same gender.

NOTES

Tim Fitzsimons, Alexander Kacala, and Minyvonne Burke, "Tennessee Teen Dies by Suicide after Being Outed Online," NBC News, September 30, 2019, www.nbcnews.com/feature/nbc-out/tennessee-teen-dies -suicide-after-being-outed-online-n1060436.

Brody Levesque, "Bisexuality Not Covered by Federal Employment Law Lawsuit Claims," *Los Angeles Blade,* September 27, 2022, www .losangelesblade.com/2022/09/27/bisexuality-not-covered-by-federal -employment-law-lawsuit-claims.

Andrew Schneider, "How Conservative Activist Steven Hotze Became a Harris County Power Broker," Houston Public Media, January 28, 2021, www.houstonpublicmedia.org/articles/news/politics/2021/01/28 /390247/steve-hotze-gop-republican-activist-houston-harris-county -politics.

Veronica Zambon, "What Is 'Biphobia'?" Medical News Today, January 12, 2022, www.medicalnewstoday.com/articles/biphobia.

Jules Ryan, "Why I Don't Use the Term 'Straight Passing Privilege,'" Medium, October 16, 2020, https://radiantbutch.medium.com/why-i -dont-use-the-term-straight-passing-privilege-f7f0b06a2c49.

Amy Andre, "Show Us the Money: Funding for Bisexual Community Lacking," HuffPost, January 4, 2012, www.huffpost.com/entry/bisexual -funding_b_1178932.

Funders for LGBTQ Issues, "2021 Resource Tracking Report: Lesbian, Gay, Bisexual, Transgender, and Queer Grantmaking by U.S.

Foundations," 2023, https://lgbtfunders.org/research-types/tracking -report.

Aja Romano, "Kevin Spacey Sexual Assault Allegations: Everything We Know So Far," *Vox,* December 24, 2018, www.vox.com/culture/2017 /11/3/16602628/kevin-spacey-sexual-assault-allegations-house -of-cards.

Alissa Wilkinson, "Kevin Spacey Released a Bizarre Video Evoking Frank Underwood, Apparently to Defend Himself," *Vox,* December 24, 2018, www.vox.com/culture/2018/12/24/18155150/kevin-spacey -sexual-assault-arraignment-frank-underwood-youtube.

Kevin Spacey, "Let Me Be Frank," YouTube video, December 24, 2018, www.youtube.com/watch?v=JZveA-NAIDI.

Ramani Durvasula and MedCircle, "The Magic of Therapy: Indulge in Your Fantasies. Here's Why," YouTube video, May 24, 2021, www.youtube .com/watch?v=909dpQTCwB0.

Francisco Sánchez and Eric Vilain, "'Straight-Acting Gays':The Relationship between Masculine Consciousness, Anti-Effeminacy, and Negative Gay Identity," *Archives of Sexual Behavior* 41:1 (2012), 111–19, https:// doi.org/10.1007/s10508-012-9912-z.

Joe Dispenza, *You Are the Placebo: Making Your Mind Matter* (Carlsbad, CA: Hay House, 2014).

Man Enough: Masculinity and Femininity

Systems and structures dominate. But as human beings
we have choices. As individuals those choices are limited.
But collectively our choices add up to a force.

—FAHD AHMED

There's a great YouTube series called *Man Enough,* which is where I got
the name for this chapter. The series is hosted by actor Justin Baldoni, and
in it he gathers men from different walks of life to talk about masculinity,
femininity, sexuality, shame, body dysmorphia, the Me Too movement,
and what it means to be a man in the twenty-first century. The conversations are raw and vulnerable and funny and smart, and I could not
recommend the series enough, even though it's not without fault. While
watching, it becomes apparent that so much of what it means to be a
man, and to be masculine, is based on arbitrary identifiers like prefer-
ring blue over pink (though originally it was the other way around), not
wearing high heels (originally only worn by white men of a certain social
status), stoicism, athleticism, the access we have to women, the dominance we can assert over them, and how attracted they are to us. In this
society, what we call feminine is devalued, often represented as fallible
and corruptible. What we understand masculinity and manhood to be has
been forged by patriarchy.

I honestly can't remember a time when my gender was not being
policed and I wasn't told I was doing it wrong. My father was constantly
frustrated that I showed no interest in soccer and had a very hard time
viewing me as a separate person from him, with my own needs, quirks,
and desires. My male friends around the neighborhood I grew up in
would never pass up an opportunity to comment on how funny I walked:
"You be switching." As I entered adolescence, grown men—who I was

often nervous around to begin with—never failed to tell me to "put some bass in your voice." On occasion I still get called "ma'am" on the phone, and little kids sometimes ask, "Why you talk like a girl?" Whether their parents respond with horror or not, kids often help to hold up a mirror about what we put stock in as a society, and more specifically what is being taught and omitted in their household and community. Little boys and girls are really good at policing people's gender performance because most of us are. They learn it from the overt messages around them and the unspoken rules adults live by.

When I first got on YouTube as a teenager in 2007, I uploaded covers of Top 40 hits. I was trying to get discovered. Though I never did any speaking, I'd constantly get pejoratives, questions about whether or not I was gay, if I *believed in* same-sex marriage, and paternalistic comments of random people letting me know they accept me *no matter what*. I'd only get a few comments on the quality of my equipment and vocal ability, as though my femininity occluded the very subject of my videos. Everyday othering, combined with my profession as an artist, created an enormous incentive to sound and read as masculine and heterosexual as possible. I learned that if I wanted people to listen to what I had to say, if I wanted people to like me, if I wanted to gain more YouTube subscribers and book more roles, I'd play the game and tone down the feminine aspects of myself. Although a lot of this is birthed from a place of survival, in doing this I've felt like I lost touch with parts of myself, and that has been a very bitter pill to swallow.

I find a lot of joy and healing in that SpongeBob meme where his and Patrick's wrists are bent and they're giving one another a knowing look. It's a meme many queer Gen Z'ers have used to signify their own queerness. Having a limp wrist or a switch in your walk or a soft voice was evidence of weakness and queerness when I was younger, and it feels good to be able to laugh some of it off now. It helps to lighten a lot of that heaviness. Shout out to SpongeBob, who's asexual.

On the flip side, I remember one time, as a preteen, walking home from school, I was asked by a stranger, neutrally, whether I was a boy or a girl. It happened in the winter when I had on a hat on and a big puffer jacket. I had a soft baby face and high-pitched voice, so kids my age as well as adults, sometimes, simply weren't sure. I had a friend in middle school who'd grown to six feet tall by the time we were in eighth grade. He had a full beard, tons of hair on his arms and legs, and a really deep voice. I remained virtually hairless until I was about sixteen years old, and even now my Adam's apple is not very prominent, and I don't have any hair on my chest. I hated PE in high school because my thin, hairless legs would be on display, and I'd constantly get questions from girls about whether or not I shaved, and questions from boys about whether or not I was gay—even when I had a girlfriend. Having a girlfriend didn't suddenly mean I was no longer feminine or no longer assumed to be gay by my peers and elders, even though so much discourse about bisexual+ men insists it would.

Feminine bisexual+ boys and men are disbelieved in a way that is different than masculine bisexual+ boys and men. Femininity is proof of a man not being a legitimate man, in many people's minds; masculinity, which is understood as belonging to and innate in only boys or men, is necessary to like women, and to be desirable to them. Although self-acceptance, confidence, and healing cannot offset societal stigma or marginalization, Charles M. Blow offers an important quandary to us in *Shut Up Fire in My Bones.* He writes, "I had to stop romanticizing the man I might have been and be the man that I was, not neatly fitting other people's definitions of masculinity or constructs of sexuality, but by being uniquely me—made in the image of God, nurtured by the bosom of nature, and forged in the fire of life."

Growing up, I felt an immense disconnect from being a boy—and then from being a man—because so much of my experience as a feminine bisexual+ boy had been about how I wasn't manly at all, how I talked, walked, looked, and acted like a girl, how *different* I was. It's as if I didn't qualify for the moniker of man, as if I didn't register. The ways we measure up to cultural definitions of masculinity becomes the ink for the story of who we are, however faint. The widely used hashtag I created #BisexualMenSpeak—which I delve into later on in the "#Bisexual-MenSpeak" chapter—almost did not happen because I've regularly felt like I didn't have the authority to speak about masculinity or manhood. This book almost didn't happen for the same reason. Most of the time when I'd express an interest in or knowledge of certain *masculine* topics like sports, video games, or women, it'd be met with scoffs, antagonistic quizzing, doubtful looks, interruption, and outright dismissal from the straight men in my vicinity.

Throughout the 1990s and 2000s, we saw a plethora of men assembled on national TV talk shows, panels, news programming, and ESPN to talk about manhood or to represent the male perspective, but there were seldom openly bisexual+, gay, or trans men procured. It's as if manhood was synonymous with masculine cisgender heterosexual men, and everyone else didn't exist or qualify or matter. Thus, I grew used to feeling like I didn't have anything worthwhile to offer in the realms of manhood. I was too used to being disregarded, too used to being tolerated by cisgender heterosexual men and women while quietly disdained, too used to not seeing feminine or openly queer men invited to speak on forums about Blackness or manhood or social justice or fatherhood or video games or sports. We unconsciously believe straight boys and men to have a monopoly on all things deemed masculine and for boys and men to disregard, silence, and erase all other people's masculinity and relationship to boyhood and manhood. When they speak about manhood, it is from the place of authority and ownership and homogeneity. I've learned this belief is necessary in order to maintain social order.

Patriarchy tells boys they're not supposed to cry or feel emotion outside of anger, and tells girls they're supposed to always be nice, be good at cooking, and play with dolls. Those are small examples of a much larger issue, and these gendered lessons exist at every turn, are all-consuming, and ripple across our lives. We are deemed men because of our appearance, even when some of us say we are not. Many are deemed women because of their appearance, even when some of them say they are not. They're met with tribal gaslighting, a form of gaslighting involving many people who deny your reality over and over again. (I will circle back to tribal gaslighting and bisexual+ individuals shortly.) They're told who they know themselves to be is unnatural or irrelevant because that does not fit the tidy, cisgender-heteronormative white-supremacist patriarchal capitalist mold of things. They're told over and over again they must follow certain rules, their lives must be a certain way, their dreams must be a certain thing. In many precolonial non-Western traditions, gender was expansive, variation, a spectrum, "a horizon of identities," as filmmaker and writer Vernon Jordan III describes it, similarly to sexuality—whereas the Western gender binary is an unbending project. Of course all of this impacts bisexual+ men and masculine-identified people: who we find attractive, who we gravitate to, and what we expect from them upon meeting.

Equating femininity with weakness and women has all kinds of far-reaching effects, from self-esteem and relationship-building to ideas about god, divinity, who can be a religious leader, who we think has the ability or right to lead in government, and the entitlement we feel toward women's bodies, time, and emotional labor. These antiquated ideas about gender are largely subjective matters predicated on fabrication, exaggeration, violence, and role-playing. Nobody is one way all the time as far as expression is concerned, and simply allowing yourself to exist without inhibition, and encouraging others to do the same, is freeing.

SEXISM

- Consider for a moment that you are misogynistic. Consider that you are the bad guy in someone else's story, that misogyny is not simply one moment of calling a woman the b-word or thinking women are possessions or thinking a woman is unqualified even though her credentials or talent says otherwise.

- Consider that patriarchy and misogyny are ongoing and relentless systems.

- Consider that they warp reality and cast doubt, dislike, and resentment onto women automatically, that it is in the fabric of how one attains credentials in the first place, that it is in the fabric of what pursuits people are encouraged to dream about depending on their gender, that it's at the heart of major religions, that it's at the heart of people's ideas of divinity, that it's in everything we see and read and breathe.

- Consider that girls are taught to be nice to men—both strangers and associates—so these men's feelings won't be hurt and so these girls and then women won't be on the receiving end of violence.

- Consider the ways you've engaged in misogyny when your feelings were hurt, to make you feel or appear cool, the ways you're able to steal ideas from women in order to get ahead, the ways you engage in it to get what you want, the ways sexism says you automatically deserve certain things, the ways it protects you as well as the ways it hurts you.

- ◆ Consider that bisexual+ men are not exempt from playing into these systems.

- ◆ Consider that expecting bisexual+ women to be open to having a threesome, especially with another woman, comes from a place of entitlement backed by misogyny and fetishization.

In *For the Love of Men: From Toxic to More Mindful Masculinity,* Liz Plank details Nico's story:

> *"Masculinity can become a site of oppression if you are Native, but it also becomes an incentive. That you, as a Native man, want to access the things that masculinity tells you are yours, you might perform misogynistic violence because it's the thing that gets you the privileges of masculinity. But it doesn't seem to do that very well. So masculinity becomes this lure, without the social reward."* The way Nico described it, performing idealized masculinity seemed like a trap that marginalized men would fall into because of its promise to offer them the mobility they were so desperate to find. At the end of our conversation, Nico echoed one of the most important points I hope I've been successful in making in this book: that the doctrine of gender dictated by patriarchy doesn't just hurt women; it hurts men too.

So many of us internalize on a deep level these messages that expose men to constant emotional isolation, neglect, and violence whether or not they tiptoe outside of these preset parameters. There exists an idea among most men who engage with women that they are incomplete until they've found their soulmate in a woman. Femininity and women are seen as the polar opposite of masculinity and men, and in order for men or women to be complete, they need to find their other half to balance them out. This is anti-LGBTQ+ in nature and downright harmful. There exists a norm among men who participate in catcalling, who use the women in their lives as therapists, who're domineering, who view women as objects that exist for the betterment of and servitude of men; women are a means to an end. Nico goes on:

> *To express this, Nico quoted Fred Moten in* The Undercommons: Fugitive Planning and Black Study, *where he wrote in the context of racial justice that white people needed to see how racism hurts them too.* "I don't need your help," *he writes.* "I just need you to recognize that this shit is killing you too, however much more softly." *Nico explained how this applied to gender just as much as it did to race.* "To say we'll fix the problem together is not the same as saying you're wounded and I'm not, because the reality is that there needs to be a recognition that it's killing you too. Patriarchy is killing men too."

Moreover, this is about identity. It's about the avatar you're nudging through this world. It's about what gets you to fashion the idea you have of yourself that you share with others and why. It's about the forces that've pressed upon you as a child, as putty. The desire behind the hands that mashed you, that ground you down from the infinite radiating entirety you were born as, into this. In many households, boys aren't taught to cook, clean, caretake, or do other things seen as being domestic, which robs them of those necessary survival and bonding skills. I know this from lived experience. It's alarming how many people feel uncomfortable seeing men cry and reprimand boys who show any emotion outside happiness or anger. Still the responsibility of raising children and boys in particular is usually left up to women and people assumed to be women, thus making women shoulder the blame for boys and men being emotionally neglected when it is patriarchy that ensures this. It leads back to patriarchy regardless of who it's practiced by. This is key; identity does not determine sociopolitical practice. Women are ground down, forced, or expected to tend to children and perform emotional labor throughout their lives, even if they haven't been taught themselves, which includes teaching boys and men about suppressing their own emotions. Part of the emotional neglect boys receive is that they are conditioned to dump their emotions onto the girls and women in their lives, to only display a particular kind of emotionality around them. Children aren't usually taught self-regulation, emotional intelligence, de-escalation techniques, or breathing exercises to calm ourselves. Boys aren't usually taught how to perform emotional labor for others, and are usually taught they must be hard around other boys and men.

To recap: As a society we don't give boys the room to feel deeply without attaching weakness and shame to them.

As a society we do not provide boys with tools to do something constructive with their emotions or teach the importance of embracing discomfort.

Under the tenants of patriarchy, boys will continue to be emotionally neglected and women will be blamed.

Though there will be exceptions, culturally, this is a norm.

It's vital to be able to navigate certain physical challenges *and* to exercise emotional intelligence.

Collectively, we must stop insinuating that anything relating to emotion is synonymous with being weak or inferior, truly understanding that femininity is not only innate in women and masculinity is not only innate in men.

Further, neuroscience has proven that all human action stems from emotion. Acknowledging that you have emotions, creating solutions around them, and processing them in a healthy way is a sign of incredible strength. Emotions have been key to human survival, the ability to cohabitate, invent, have deep and complex relationships, and grow.

Each of us is made up of feminine and masculine qualities, and bringing the two into healthy harmony, without prizing one over the other, is a step in the right direction.

If you feel apathetic toward or accustomed to patriarchy, just know it harms you too.

Being apathetic about this injustice does not mean it has not or will not directly affect you and the people you care about.

DESIRABILITY AND WANTING WOMEN TO LIKE US

Many of us are unwilling to acknowledge our bisexuality because we fear rejection from women and losing access to women and whatever benefits being partnered with a woman may provide, even if that means attempting to suffocate another part of ourselves. Many of us attach our sense of worth to how attractive we are to women at large, which is dangerous and can lead to some dark places. Women do not exist in a vacuum and live under the same patriarchal society we do. Many women are biphobic and buy into patriarchal ideas that deem bisexual+ men as less masculine and therefore less desirable. It is not our job to prove our value, personhood, or bisexuality to anyone. Upholding patriarchy subliminally conditions us to feel inadequate and undesirable since we are bisexual+ men. Placing so much importance on being desirable to women is unhealthy and gets us to play into heteronormative ideas about gender expectation, all while our subconscious keeps a score that it will eventually need to cash out on. It keeps us afraid. It keeps us on the patriarchal hamster wheel that we must not only get off but also aim to destroy. Can we validate our own authenticity, expression, and self-actualization instead of depending on outward approval, or at least learn to seek it from better sources?

Many bisexual+ men who are assumed to be gay, or even thought they were gay themselves, are unwilling to acknowledge their bisexuality because they fear it will mean they are no longer aligned with LGBTQ+ communities, that they're betraying the cause, that considering sexual or romantic contact with women will deradicalize their sexuality and politics, that they're picking their *straight side* as a means of assimilating, even if it means attempting to suffocate another part of themselves. My hope is that every bisexual+ person makes the choice to look at their sexuality with eyes of acceptance and nurturing so that suffocating their sexuality is no longer an appealing option.

Imperialist white-supremacist capitalist patriarchy is obsessed with binary categorization and erasing bisexuals, whether we're in a relationship or whether we're single, whether we belong to an LGBTQ+ community or not. While bisexuals will be bisexual+ regardless of who we partner with, and while being with a woman may impact how others view us, the crux of LGBTQ+ oppression is not solely found in who we partner with. Though that is very important, that talking point only includes cisgender gay men and cisgender lesbian women. It is the hierarchy, it is that we are other, it is that we are made vulnerable, it is that we are kept from understanding ourselves, it is that cisgender heteronormativity is positioned as normal and natural, it is that we are posed as existing outside of what is natural and normal and holy and innocent. This is not magically reconciled if a bisexual+ man is with a woman. While their experience will be different from a bisexual+ man who partners with a man, especially if they are assumed to be gay and the bisexual+ man partnered to a woman is assumed to be straight, the oppression is not solely a topical one. I experienced rejection and violence and a sense of not belonging long before I became old enough to date. It exists when we're single and when we're partnered. It exists when we're children and when we're adults. It's about more than who we love.

Gabrielle Alexa Noel acknowledges the global sexual revolution we've been experiencing in *How to Live with the Internet (and Not Let It Ruin Your Life)*.

> *The rise of social media, video sharing, and free educational content [having] completely altered the politics and dominant ideologies of our sexual culture [while recognizing] some media forms continue to reinforce old-fashioned ideas about sexuality, the internet has allowed marginalized folks to take control of their own narratives and push forward a new culture of understanding and openness. Despite this, there are still inconsistencies in our sexual morality. There is a persistent view of sex as something sinful and corruptive, made apparent by our continued debates around abortion, birth control, abstinence-only sex education, and sexual violence. And so social media functions as both a battleground for our sexual politics and as an environment that brokers our individual sexualities.*

There's a lot farther to go. Patriarchy has a way of attacking the psyche and making some men who are not cisgender and heterosexual feel like they don't measure up. The stereotype of the bisexual+ man is that we do not exist, that we are secretly gay—which is another feature of this phallocentric white-supremacist patriarchal hellscape. This idea comes from prioritizing men and the penis, deeming sexual contact with men as a dominant, defining event that can characterize or even change someone's sexuality. Having contact with women is often seen as passive and fleeting, a nondetermining factor of someone's sexuality. As the days go on I find myself divesting from these sentiments more and more. I find myself divesting from the need to feel desirable to women *and* to men *and* to nonbinary people.

When your self-esteem largely comes from external forces, namely how attractive you are to women, it becomes very brittle, and you can lose yourself in that. There are real consequences to being other, to being a social pariah, to being largely undesirable on both your self-esteem as well as your livelihood that are not to be undermined, and no amount of self-help will prepare you for or alter that. This is the world imperialist white-supremacist capitalist patriarchy has created. Before understanding this deeply, the way I'd act would change depending on who I was around, and that was especially true with people I was attracted to. If I was attracted to someone, I'd find myself holding back, toning my innate femininity down, dampening my energy level, or putting on my idea of what it meant to be more masculine; adopting a persona. We're constantly bombarded with messages that masculinity is desirable and that femininity is not, especially in men. And some of us succumb. We play into it. With everything from the ways we obsess over our physiques, the normalizing of orthorexia under the guise of shredding-bulking culture, how we beat our bodies into submission at the gym, the clothes we wear, and the bass we put in our voices when we want someone to like or respect us. Consciously, I'm aware of how it sways what I wear and how I speak, but I sometimes wonder whether wanting to feel desired also sways subconscious actions I take, like where I live and whether it has ever been a spur for who I hang out with.

Becoming more desirable as I've gotten older and now perceived to be masculine means people are sometimes nice to me, more likely to listen to what I have to say, more likely to want to sleep with me, more likely to hire me. I am reminded of something Janet Mock wrote in an *Allure* article titled "Being Pretty Is a Privilege, But We Refuse to Acknowledge It": "Women have been trained to minimize their greatness in an effort to be more likeable." I think about all the ways patriarchy has made us morph in overt and subtle ways to be something *it* deems worthy, acceptable, attractive.

People can be really superficial, and our media certainly doesn't help. Our minds like to create stories, like how we can look up and see animals or faces in the clouds. We make split-second judgments and snap decisions about people's personality, ability, and morals based on how they look. Mock, and many other Black feminists, talk about how *attractiveness* often

reflects a woman's immediacy to thinness, lightness, Eurocentric facial features, European hair texture, being cisgender, and being able-bodied. This is
important to notice and understand. In a culture that objectifies us, getting
to know yourself deeply and connect with other people from the place of
intimate knowing can help.

It's been helpful for me to be critical about desirability and reflective
about how I perform my gender and how I acknowledge, explore, and
express my desires. It's been helpful for me to strive to be whole and
authentic regardless of what that may cost. It's been helpful for me to
question the voice in the back of my head that says, *Women or men or nonbinary people won't like you if you do this.* In this vast ever-changing world,
how can that possibly be true?

I've come to understand that I've expended way too much energy and
care over what people think about me because I want them to like me or
think I'm attractive. I've come to see that preoccupation as a cage. One of
the most impactful things for me about the 2016 film *Moonlight* was how it
made me reflect on the ways society and circumstances forced me to assim-
ilate, change, adapt, and develop a tough skin in the realms of performing
masculinity. I'd been conditioned over many years to drop my voice a few
octaves when speaking, or not to speak at all, and eventually I came to call
that and all the other ways I'd been instructed to perform masculinity, natural, my default, inextricable from who I am. I was shaken to my core after
seeing that film. In a now-deleted tweet, comedian Jaboukie Young White
said something very profound about coping with trauma and the ways we
adapt to it that helped me process this. Essentially he said that some of the
skills we developed and ways we adapted as a response to trauma are not
automatically bad. Sometimes they just are what they are. We find ways to
be ourselves, to let ourselves shine through trauma and conditioning, and
adapting in order to survive is not something we need to shame or fixate
on or judge. It may be something we want to grieve or acknowledge or
push back against, but it just is what it is.

PENETRATION AND SHAME

There's so much conflation around sexuality, masculinity, and what a man
should desire in terms of pleasure. So much of what it means to be a

man living under this society comes down to our ability to be dominant. Dominant in business, in conversation, mentally, emotionally, and especially sexually. What is dominance? Merriam-Webster defines it as being controlling, prevailing, or being in a powerful position, especially in a social hierarchy. Patriarchy says the only appropriate way for a man to receive pleasure is by being dominant when it comes to sex by using their penis for penetration, even if many men of various sexualities enjoy being penetrated, or some prefer nonpenetrative sex, even if they don't have a penis. These shared ideas around pleasure are antiquated and faulty when held up in the light, and yet they persist. If these ideas weren't so widely held, I don't think as many people would feel such intense shame around their sexual desires.

A straight adult content creator I follow strictly for scientific purposes began engaging in anal play when his girlfriend told him she was turned on by it. It started at rimming, then her inserting fingers, then dildos and strap-ons. Because he had a safe environment free from stigma and some openness on his part (he-he), he was able to explore and learned he liked something he previously hadn't given much thought.

In *Refusing Compulsory Sexuality*, Sherronda J. Brown asserts:

> *The gender binary has borders. It is a structure that requires the policing of those borders in order to remain intact. . . . And not only must these two binary extremes be explicitly different from one another, but one must be subjugated by the other. This Western gender binary has long been a racial project. In the nineteenth century and early twentieth century, policing gender became necessary for the "advancement" of the white race and the maintenance of white-supremacist cisheteropatriarchy. In order to further entrench myths about the natural superiority of white men, gender policing became a means to help establish whiteness as "civilized" and all other races as inferior savages.*
>
> *In Manliness and Civilization, Gail Bederman details how "'civilization,' as turn-of-the century Americans understood it, simultaneously denoted attributes of race and gender. By invoking the discourse of civilization in a variety of contradictory ways, many Americans found a powerfully effective way to link male dominance to white supremacy." In*

white civilized society, "women were womanly—delicate, spiritual, dedicated to the home [and] civilized white men were the most manly ever evolved," and these differences were an "intrinsic and necessary aspect of higher civilization." Men's institutional power within cisheteropatriarchy is dependent on strict gender differences, the gender binary, and specifically on defining "woman" as inferior to "man," identifying sexual roles as intrinsic to both gender categories. . . . Dutiful sex and sexual submission to men—meant to be reflective and reproductive of social submission to men—are integral to this script.

SEXUAL SHAME

Signs You Have Sexual Shame

Signs you have sexual shame and how to overcome them, by Morgan Mandriota via Well+Good:

- Sexual shame often manifests as an insecurity and disconnection with the self.

- Diminished voice or a certain kind of physical stature, like being unable or unwilling to make eye contact during sex. You can't vocalize what you want or need during sex, and you feel afraid to make sounds. You don't express your sexual desires or curiosities.

- Sexual dysfunction or dissatisfaction, since the presence of sexual shame interrupts the flow of feeling sexually expressive (I thought I'd add that there can be many other reasons for this besides sexual shame).

- Trouble with intimacy and relationships (again, I'd add there can be many other reasons for this besides sexual shame).

- Viewing sex as "bad" or something that you "shouldn't do." Feelings of shame or regret regarding having sex or masturbating.

- You're uncomfortable talking about sex.

- If you feel uncomfortable or guilty with the idea of using sex toys on others or yourself (I'd add that this may just be because of a lack of knowledge or experience with sex toys).

Ways to Overcome Shame

◆ Acknowledge that you have sexual shame. Shame only sustains itself by being hidden, something people don't talk about, something left in the dark.

◆ Pleasure is one of the first ways to get over shame, whether that is self-pleasure or pleasure with someone else. You have to be gentle with yourself throughout because for some people, things get worse before they get better. Think of it as a U-curve instead of a steady upward climb.

◆ You don't want to shame the shame that might come up.

◆ Be intentional about becoming less judgmental of others and, in turn, yourself.

◆ Be the observer, not the judge.

◆ Separate yourself from the source of the sexual shame. It may be a particular religion or denomination, ideologies, family, friends, particular kinds of media, and so on.

◆ Unfollow and block content creators who use terms like *alpha male, dominate, feminizing men,* and *Stacys or Chads.* Alpha-male thinking is steeped in eugenics, which is incredibly anti-Black, ableist, sexist, and anti-LGBTQ+.

◆ Explore your body's erogenous zones (neck, ears, inner wrists, nipples, perineum, and so on) so you know what you and your body like or don't like. It's a practical way of sharing intimacy and can help with self-confidence.

◆ Do some somatic work or chakra yoga, with a special focus on the sacral and solar plexus chakras.

◆ Stop giving negative meaning to the comparisons you make between your body or sexuality and anyone else's. It's really unfair to judge yourself or others while making observations or comparing. You deserve to feel good about who you are right now.

◆ Learn how to have a more compassionate self-talk where you talk to yourself compassionately and gently and do not shame parts of your body or put yourself down.

- Be a sponge and an observer instead of a judge or a critic.
- Educate yourself on every term and acronym under the LGBTQIA2+ label, especially demisexuality and asexuality.
- Watch shows like *Slutever* on Vice that help identify and tackle stigma around sex in society.
- Watch the videos within the #BisexualMenSpeak playlist on YouTube I created.
- Watch YouTube videos of LGBTQ+ people talking about their experience coming out and also talking about everyday things, sex and relationships, finding a therapist who is able to be supportive of bisexual+ individuals.
- Educate yourself on aspects of the BDSM world.
- Read bisexual+ fiction and nonfiction.
- Watch TV shows and films with positive bisexual+ representation.
- Frequent bisexual+ support groups.
- Make bisexual+ friends.

Back to orgasms we go! There are seven different kinds of orgasms people assigned male at birth can experience:

1. Standard orgasm: achieved through typical masturbation or penetrative sex.

2. Blended or whole body orgasm: occurs when stimulation to multiple erogenous zones results in an orgasm without being sure which stimulation zone caused it. Usually happens during fast sex or a slow build up.

3. Wet dream orgasm: often associated with being a teenager but happens to adults even during dreams that aren't sexual in nature. It's how some people realized they were bisexual+ in the first place.

4. Pelvic orgasm: occurs when practicing edging; getting to the point just before ejaculation and stopping then repeating this again and again until you're ready for your pelvic orgasm, which will be far more intense.

5. Prostate orgasm: the male G-spot, also known as the P-spot, is a walnut-size point on the prostate gland that's accessed through the anus. It's located at bottom of the bladder, is very sensitive, and an orgasm can be achieved through gently rubbing it.

6. Multiple orgasms: there two types of multiple orgasms. One is where you ejaculate, take a break, and then ejaculate again. The other happens with no intermission and can be more than two.

THINGS TO KEEP IN MIND

- The type of pleasure you want to experience in your body is not the same as who you want to experience that pleasure with.

- The submissive versus dominant roles within sexual dynamics or within the BDSM world does not necessarily have a bearing on the genders you find attractive, and actually speaks to *what* turns you on rather than *who* turns you on. The *Two Bi Guys* podcast has an awesome episode detailing this called "Queer Enough and Down to F*ck" with Karley Sciortino of *Slutever* on Vice. It's highly recommended.

- You can be a bottom, a man who is penetrated, and be dominant in bed.

- You can be a top, a man who penetrates, and be submissive in bed.

- You can be vers and either be a combination of dominant or submissive *or* prefer to be one over the other.

- You can be a side, which is someone who prefers nonpenetrative sex.

- Keep in mind that the prostate or male G-spot is located in the anus, and it's an enormous site of nerve endings, a.k.a. a pleasure center.

- Still, some men of various sexualities do not desire to be penetrated, find it easier to be the penetrator, or are simply not into it.

Lastly, in *Come as You Are* by Emily Nagoski, the subject of nonconcordance, incongruence between feeling sexually stimulated and genital arousal or vice versa, is thoroughly engaged as a way of combating shame as well as encouraging people to ask for enthusiastic verbal and energetic consent. Emily introduces the concept of humans having sexual accelerators and sexual brakes that are context-specific and have varying sensitivities from person to person that can fluctuate through a person's life as the context changes. Especially as men age, what they often need to sustain a satisfying and lively sex life is a continuously deepening sense of vulnerability and emotional safety rather than stoicism. Men must actively work to create this in their close relationships while choosing people who are willing to help cocreate this. Not everyone is currently able to do this, has learned to do this, or is willing to do this.

Power dynamics in the bedroom with men:

- If you are a feminine man, people will likely assume you're gay, and if you're masculine, people will likely assume you're straight. Going a bit farther, if you're a feminine bisexual+ or gay man, you're routinely expected to be a bottom. If you're feminine or a trans man, many men will not allow you to top them even if that's what they enjoy. Femmephobia and transphobia are rampant, but not every single person thinks this way, so just keep this in the back of your mind.

- Masculine bottoms, on the other hand, are either seen as hitting the jackpot by many femmephobic tops or a contradictory inconvenience by many bottoms. Gender roles and patriarchy strike again!

- Vers men are sometimes met with the "pick a side; which are you really?" sentiment that bisexual+ people face universally.

- Being masculine or feminine has no direct correlation with the type of pleasure or position you're into or should explore.

These ideas surrounding dominance and manhood, emasculation and pleasure are welded together and need to be replaced.

Something that's very common among bisexual+ men is the idea that we only maintain our bisexual+ status if we are never penetrated and never on the receiving end of anal stimulation. This idea is steeped in biphobia and homophobia. It's that same idea that says that being with men is wrong, dirty, shameful, or tainted. It's the same idea that says that being attracted to two or more genders is being greedy or indecisive or double-dipping or wishy-washy. It's the same idea that says you are defiled by being with another man. It's the same idea that says as a man you must be masculine and if you allow yourself to be penetrated, and like it, that's *too* gay. The fact is:

- Some bisexual+ men want to be penetrated when they're with men and to penetrate when they're with women.
- Some bisexual+ men only want to be penetrated by women.
- Some bisexual+ men enjoy penetrating *and* being penetrated.
- Some bisexual+ men only want to penetrate.
- Some bisexual+ men prefer nonpenetrative sex.
- All of them are still bisexual+.
- Being bisexual+ means you acknowledge your own capacity to be romantically or sexually attracted to two or more genders.

The idea that your attraction to women is delegitimized if you are penetrated, if you are with a man, if you are doing things considered *too* gay—like being penetrated—needs to die. The potential beauty, joy, fun, and pleasure of being partnered with a man ought to be acknowledged and uplifted. As a former devout Christian, I had to do a lot of work to undo the shame attached to being penetrated, being a sexual being, and having a fluid and free sexuality. I needed to understand that I deserve to feel pleasure in my body. I needed to learn that there is nothing wrong with feeling pleasure in my body, and being with another man does not diminish me. If, according to white supremacy, being with another man diminishes my manliness, whatever that means, so be it. It's taken all of ten years for this to sink in with me deeply and for me to realize that it was okay that I had sexual desires and needs that are valid that I have a responsibility of acknowledging and tending to.

To be clear, you can do whatever you want with your body. What you want and what you enjoy can and will change over time. I'm simply pointing out that shying away from being penetrated because you think it is less manly is a symptom of internalized homophobia that deserves your attention. At the end of the day, just trying to be present with another person without all this discourse floating around your mind is ideal. Go with what you feel, prioritize enthusiastic consent, try new things, figure out what you like, and have fun.

MASCULINITY AND FEMININITY

There was a time when I came to think of aggression, bluntness, and taking the lead as wholly bad, especially as a dark-skinned tall Black man, but that's simply not true. Sometimes being forward, taking the lead, and being aggressive can be a good thing. Each has some really great, necessary qualities to them, and each has a time and a place. I've seen them used in excess and with impunity for most of my life, plus I didn't want to live up to the racist stereotypes in the media of an aggressive, angry Black man. I didn't want to be dominant or play in those muddied waters, especially as it related to women, and I didn't want to be like so many of the toxic cisgender heterosexual men I've witnessed up close. I didn't want to associate with hegemonic masculinity because I'd seen it cause so much harm. This is another reason I didn't engage with women romantically or sexually throughout my twenties and instead engaged with men. My thinking was that with another man, gendered dynamics— and the patriarchy—would simply cease to exist, and I could escape the gender rigmarole. But it wasn't exactly so. Patriarchy seeps into every facet of our minds and lives and is central to our society, so it didn't stop spinning when I exclusively engaged with men. "Top" and "bottom" sometimes take on the functionality of man and woman, respectively, and if not, it's almost always who is more masculine and who is more feminine. Queer men definitely have their own brands of misogyny that largely goes unchecked in many circles, and being in a relationship with another man is not inherently antipatriarchal. But labeling, then writing off, taking the lead, directness, and aggression as completely bad is incorrect. Doing these things in doses at the right moments can be good and are requirements for a healthy, fulfilling, balanced life. I had to learn that taking the lead doesn't mean the other person no longer has ownership of themselves. Being direct doesn't mean they can't rebut or disagree with what's been proposed. Employing these doesn't mean the role is fixed, that it's my identity, or that the other party can't employ these too.

Your experiences and the way people respond to you as a bisexual+ man will vary dramatically depending on whether you're seen as more masculine than feminine and vice versa. There's something I've noticed

regarding bisexual+ men; we are thought to automatically be more feminine than our heterosexual counterparts, yet simultaneously, media mostly
focuses on bisexual+ men who are masculine and assumed to be straight.
The way the media sensationalizes and focuses on these men speaks to a
more disguised bias many of us have; prioritizing people we perceive to
be masculine cisgender heterosexual men above all, even when they're
not actually heterosexual. Society rarely pays attention to, offers empathy
for, or provides complicated representation about gay-assumed, feminine
bisexual+ men who primarily frequent LGBTQ+ spaces. It's another
form of bi erasure combined with femmephobia that plays out the way
it does, in part, because the assumption is that they're actually gay and
that these gay-assumed bisexual+ men are getting everything they need
from gay spaces. This couldn't be farther from the truth, but I suspect it's
something else. I think this particular societal response is a result of being
conditioned to center and coddle cisgender heterosexual men even if
they're only seemingly cisgender heterosexual men. Let me be clear that
I am not saying that straight-assumed bisexual+ men are less bisexual+,
or less legitimate, or are actually straight. I am pointing out a difference
in experiences and the ways society generally reacts in a less volatile way
toward you the closer you are to being perceived as a white cisgender
masculine abled heterosexual man.

Because society is heteronormative, it places a lot more priority and
importance on men assumed to be straight who are in fact bisexual+ than
it does on gay-assumed men who are actually bisexual+—though not by
much, and the psychological damage is still there. The assumption is that
straight-assumed bisexual+ men are closeted and lack the tools to express
themselves or to act on their desires for the same gender, are unequipped to
experiment, and are not given the space to be bisexual+ compared to their
gay-assumed bisexual+ counterparts; this is pathologizing and also incon-
gruous. This sentiment that only masculine bisexual+ men are legitimately
bisexual+, though inconsistent and fickle, is shown online when straight-
assumed bisexual+ men disclose, and is evident throughout culture.

This can be seen with the character Connor in the TV series *Dear White
People*. In season 1, episode 2, he is a partygoer at a theater congregation
who makes friends with Lionel and attempts to set up a threesome with

himself, Lionel, and his female roommate, Becca. The three of them are getting hot and heavy, but before they can, Lionel can't contain his laughter over the ridiculousness of the situation. Lionel says to Connor, "Look, you don't need the wing woman, okay? You're obviously just into guys." Connor and Becca get into an argument about whose idea setting up the threesome was, and the numerous MMF threesomes Connor has set up over the past two years, which seems to confirm Lionel's assertion that Connor was using Becca as a cover for his gay orientation. Underneath this stiff acknowledgment is the belief that being bisexual+ is fleeting; a blip along the way to Gaytown, and if Gaytown is the inevitable destination, there is no need to bolster gay-assumed bisexual+ men to embrace their full sexualities or to come out. The idea is they've already done so since they're assumed to be gay, one of the two recognized male sexualities.

The way desirability affects how society acknowledges and judges these men is worth noting here as well. Femininity in men is not seen as desirable, or innate, and when bisexuality occurs in feminine men, their bisexuality is mostly dismissed or scoffed at. This can be seen with audiences discussing the character David from the TV series *Schitt's Creek* as gay, especially because he winds up marrying a man named Patrick by the end of the series, even though his father uses "pansexual" to describe his sexuality. Requiring men to be masculine and punishing them if they step outside of the role of virility is a reality perpetuated by men and women because of patriarchy. Until femininity in and of itself is prized and priority is paid to gay-assumed bisexual+ men, the full gamut of bisexuality in men will never be seen as ordinary or common.

THINGS TO CONSIDER

- Are you still holding on to the idea that an array of bisexual+ men don't really exist?

- Do you believe that sexuality and gender exist on a spectrum?

- As men we help to cocreate what is included in what it means to be manly and masculine. I must caution against trying to absorb things currently deemed feminine into the fold of masculinity because it does not address the abhorrence and disenfranchisement of femininity and women.

- ◆ Men and people who identify with masculinity help to decide which expressions, desires, and behaviors are acceptable for men and masculine-identified people and which ones are not.

- ◆ What's at stake is personal identity, who has the right to exist, and how they get to exist.

I have a bisexual+ friend who is attracted to men and women just as frequently, but he has a lot more experience with women largely because of opportunity and access. He doesn't always disclose his bisexuality to women—and he doesn't have to—but in most of the instances where he has done so, most of the women pretend not to hear, brush it off, or worst of all, take it as a challenge to try to turn him straight. My friend is masculine, muscular, has a lustrous curly 'fro, and resembles actor Michael Ealy, except he has hazel eyes instead of Michael's blue ones. Because of white supremacy, colonialism, and chattel slavery, colorism has an enormous impact on racialized communities. In short, it deems lighter-skinned and lighter-eyed people as more desirable, innocent, and soft or human, often leading to better socioeconomic conditions for them, and the opposite the darker you are. Many women, and men, who engage with my friend view being with him sexually or romantically as a prize in and of itself, which is objectifying. Many of the women who brush his bisexuality off do so not necessarily because they are accepting, supportive, bi-friendly people but because being chosen by a light-skinned, muscular man with hazel eyes means something. He is not quite seen in all his beautiful, messy humanity in these instances but instead as a symbol with a shiny veneer, and though he is with them sexually, they are never fully with him. They're often caught up in their imagination of what being chosen by a light-skinned, masculine man who resembles Michael Ealy means about their value, and are willing to *overlook* his bisexuality. The ways race and colorism interact with gender expectation and bisexuality here points to the core of what I'm getting at: as long as bisexual+ men are still seen as living up to gender expectations surrounding masculinity, and are conventionally attractive, usually they're not rejected in the same way or to the same degree as feminine men, and the violence is not as apparent— though it is deeply problematic, looming, and there insidiously.

NOTES

Justin Baldoni, *Man Enough,* podcast series, 2021, www.youtube.com /channel/UC2MbPazrSLEbgiHT3yQ4DnQ.

Puja Bhattacharjee, "The Complicated Gender History of Pink," CNN Health, January 12, 2018, www.cnn.com/2018/01/12/health/colorscope -pink-boy-girl-gender/index.html.

Katie Scott, "Nickelodeon Announces SpongeBob Is Member of the LGBTQ2 Community," Global News, June 15, 2020, https://globalnews .ca/news/7066112/spongebob-lgbtq-community.

Charles M. Blow, *Shut Up Fire in My Bones* (Boston: Mariner, 2014).

Liz Plank, *For the Love of Men: From Toxic to a More Mindful Masculinity* (New York: St. Martin's Press, 2019).

Jason Pontin, "The Importance of Feelings," *MIT Technology Review,* June 17, 2014, www.technologyreview.com/2014/06/17/172310/the -importance-of-feelings.

Gabrielle Alexa Noel, *How to Live with the Internet (and Not Let It Ruin Your Life)* (Melbourne: Smith Street, 2021).

Janet Mock, "Being Pretty Is a Privilege, But We Refuse to Acknowledge It," *Allure,* June 28, 2017, www.allure.com/story/pretty-privilege.

Barry Jenkins, dir., *Moonlight* (Los Angeles: Plan B Entertainment, 2016).

Sherronda J. Brown, *Refusing Compulsory Sexuality: A Black Asexual Lens on Our Sex-Obsessed Culture* (Berkeley, CA: North Atlantic Books, 2022).

Morgan Mandriota, "6 Signs You Might Have Sexual Shame—and How to Overcome It," Well+Good, November 11, 2020, www.wellandgood .com/sexual-shame-signs.

Almara Abgarian, "It's National Orgasm Day, So Here Are Seven Different Types of Male Orgasms," *Metro,* July 31, 2019, https://metro.co.uk /2019/07/31/national-orgasm-day-seven-different-types-male -orgasms-10495431.

Emily Nagoski, *Come as You Are: The Surprising New Science That Will Transform Your Sex Life* (New York: Simon & Schuster, 2015), 46–49, 191.

Justin Simien, dir., *Dear White People,* Netflix TV series, 2017.

Fabrar, "Dan Levy as David Rose in Schitt's Creek Is One of the Best Comedy Performances in a Long Time," Reddit r/television, August 7, 2020, www.reddit.com/r/television/comments/i57cw8/dan_levy_as _david_rose_in_schitts_creek_is_one_of.

Processing Black Bisexual+ Male Representation

Eurocentric humanism needs blackness as a prop
in order to erect whiteness: to define its own limits and to
designate humanity as an achievement as well as to
give form to the category of "the animal."

—BECOMING HUMAN: MATTER AND MEANING IN
AN ANTIBLACK WORLD BY ZAKIYYAH IMAN JACKSON

Bisexual+ male representation in the media has gotten marginally better in recent years, though it is still scarce and oftentimes hit-or-miss. Though this is not great by any means, it seems to be on its way in the opposite direction, albeit at a snail's pace. Considering I grew up in the 1990s seeing depictions of bisexual+ men, in particular Black bisexual+ men, characterized in a harsh light, this sluggish turnaround once seemed to be a pipe dream. Dunking on the "down-low brotha," which has been made synonymous with Black bisexual+ men, was and still is an incredibly profitable and attention-grabbing business, regardless of someone's motives, lived experiences, scope, or concern over bisexual+ men's well-being. The "down-low brotha" tapped into many American fears all at once, namely the fear of Black male sexuality that's been cultivated since before white settlers touched down on this land with enslaved Africans in tow, then showed its face in the film *Birth of a Nation,* originally named *The Klansman* (1915), with white actors in blackface depicting Black male sexuality as threatening to whiteness, dangerous, aggressive, beastly, out of control, and violent. This evocative trope seemed to crystalize with the "down-low brotha," and a moot unanimity seemed to form between otherwise adverse groups; straight Black women, gay Black men, straight

Black men, straight white men, straight white women, and gay white men. Various sects of the media kept this phenomena alive, sensationalizing and pathologizing "down-low brothas" with little care for the impact it would cause, the ramifications of shame on human beings, the psychological damage to "down-low" men, an increase in comprehensive sex-education in schools and beyond, a clear picture of how government negligence led to this phenomena in the first place, an underscoring of how this targeted reprimand is a clear example of white supremacy demonizing Black sexuality yet again, underscoring how little tangible evidence that Black men are more likely to be "on the down-low" in comparison to men of other racial groups, educational programs or media to destigmatize "down-low brothas," educational programs or media to support "down-low brothas," public policy to address disparities, and so on.

In J. L. King's tell-all memoir, *On the Down Low*, he gave details about being gay and partnered with women, and aspects of the "down-low" subculture that landed him on the talk show *Oprah*. Those *Oprah* episodes of Johnathan Plummer and Terry McMillan, best-selling author of *How Stella Got Her Groove Back* talking about how their marriage ended with Johnathan admitting to living "on the down-low," being gay and having used her for American citizenship, are seared into my mind, and I'm not the only one. In 2010, during her final season of the talk show, host Oprah Winfrey invited a woman named Bridget Gordon on to discuss how she'd won her case against her former husband who was "on the down-low," gay, and how she'd contracted HIV. Bridget sued her ex-husband for fraud and won $12.5 million. Oprah spoke to Bridget again in 2014 during a *Where Are They Now* segment on the OWN Network. It is easy to see the pain these women endured and experienced at the hands of these men's actions. It's easy for some people to conflate "down-low" men with bisexual+ Black men with gay men thanks to these specials, the onslaught of media following *Oprah*'s lead, and cultural attitudes that existed prior. It is easy to see these men in particular as nothing short of villainous. What is harder is to see how "down-low" men more broadly have their own context, their own perspectives, and their own stories. The same is true for bisexual+ men who are not "on the down-low." Isn't it curious how Oprah and her producers never thought to bring on HIV researchers, medical experts with information on how HIV is transmitted, and groups of out gay and bisexual+ men who had nothing to do with these scandals to share their experiences with themselves at the center of their own narrative, rather than in relation to straight women? Oprah is well-known for her capabilities as a journalist who is well-researched and asks hard-hitting illuminating questions and yet in this area, even years after the end of the *Oprah* talk show, she dropped the ball and helped nurture biphobia. I have a hard time accepting that Oprah simply has not done the reading because questions would still arise from a brain with her capacity. Though I cannot know for sure, it is easier for me to accept that Oprah decided to see through this panic-inducing narrative as it's been lucrative and sensational, and provided an adversary to bond over.

DEMONIZING BLACK MALE SEXUALITY

Harry J. Anslinger (1892–1975) was a government official known for master-minding the war on drugs, which conflated drug use, race, and music in order to criminalize nonwhiteness and create a prison-industrial com-plex. He used yellow journalism and fearmongering to convince much of the country—mostly white Protestants—of just how corrupting weed and other drugs were to further reinforce the need for racial and social lines and to criminalize people of color. One of the methods he used was exploiting the fear of Black male sexuality in relation to white women. He's quoted as saying, "Reefer makes darkies think they're as good as white men. There are a hundred thousand total marijuana smokers in the U.S., and most are Negroes, Hispanics, Filipinos, and entertain-ers. Their satanic music, jazz and swing, result from marijuana use. This marijuana causes white women to seek sexual relations with Negroes, entertainers, and any others."

In interracial porn, we are almost exclusively presented with the trope of the small delicate white woman with the assuming dominant Black man with a large dick (I refuse to use the word c★ck). This racist fetishiza-tion spills over into everyday life with the use of "BBC?" aimed at Black men and Black trans-women as a pickup line on dating apps or listed as an interest in people's bio and beyond. Words like *buck* have an incredibly gruesome racist history and can be seen strewn about like parsley on porn sites describing Black men. Many cuckhold scenarios involve a white couple and a Black man with a large dick, and this of course spills into other areas of life. There are many white men, married or partnered with white women, obsessed with watching a Black man in particular have sex with her, and will go to many lengths or international destinations to achieve this. There's an assumption from many white people, especially white women, that they are desirable to Black men, and heaven help you if you don't feel that way or aren't willing to concede to their advances. As Sherronda J. Brown writes in *Refusing Compulsory Sexuality*, "Blackness negates the need for consent in the social imagination since we are constructed as always consenting—either passively or enthusiastically—to the sexualization imposed onto us."

These ideas don't appear out of thin air, and if you cannot tell by now, they derive from white supremacy. These ideas reinforce that Black men in particular are more masculine, more aggressive, more threatening, more sexual, more animalistic than white men—who are positioned as the balanced standard to aspire to. White supremacy pathologized and criminalized anything outside white cisgender heterosexuality for decades, and queer Black gender and sexuality meet a particular type of racialized classification that most of the population still regurgitates. The idea that Black people, especially Black LGBTQ+ people, are inherently more irresponsible and dangerous is a blatant symptom of this, and yet it is commonly seen in how Black STI and HIV statistics are disseminated and studied in the first place, who PrEP and PEP is marketed to, and in the case of the "down-low brotha" of the nineties. All humans can be sexually irresponsible, however overwhelming data points to class and comprehensive sexual education being consistent factors in what makes someone make sexually irresponsible choices and either have access to necessary resources or not. Because a priority of race, gender, and sexuality are about maintaining social order, this means large swaths of Black LGBTQ+ people will be born into this category and remain under-resourced for life.

In *Not Gay: Sex Between Straight White Men,* Dr. Jane Ward describes the ways whiteness protects straight-identified white men who engage sexually with men from societal stigma, harm, and the like, as well as the general phenomenon of white straight men seeking out sex with other straight men despite not identifying as gay, bisexual+, or bi-curious.

A related anecdote is the ways many white LGBTQ+ people refer to how lucky we are to live in such a great free country in comparison to countries in Africa, the Caribbean, or Asia. This completely ignores the perspectives of Black Americans, Native Americans and American Indians, and other people of color living in the United States, and the ways the United States, England, France, Portugal, and so on have had a direct hand in global imperialism, destabilizing governments, and enforcing the white-supremacist ideals of religion, gender, and sexuality that led to anti-LGBTQ+ legislation and attitudes in those places they vilify in the first place. The violence, ignorance, lack of self-awareness, and racism in statements like that is always mind-blowing yet remarkably common.

BIPHOBIA IN MEDIA

The aforementioned *Oprah* episodes sounded a biphobic dog whistle heard around the world, but there have been tremendous efforts from bisexual+ activists that just haven't been as widely consumed or disseminated. TV, film, and general media consumption has shifted dramatically in the last fifteen years, and with so many channels and various forms of social media, media today is siloed in an unprecedented way. It is incredible to have all the positive bisexual+ male representation that we have, but between television and streaming platforms, the public's attention is scattered. Things that are cultural resets or impactful moments for certain communities go completely unheard or unacknowledged in other circles, making media incredibly fractured. Obviously, this has meant that way more projects and characters that may have at one time been seen as too political, or a threat to family values, have been greenlit, made, and distributed. It also means it's easier for people who have been misinformed, whose fear has been incensed by the characterization, fearmongering, ignorance, and irresponsibility of the last half century are comfortably situated in their biphobic echo chambers, keeping those ideas alive and well. So what is the solution, and what is the problem? Where do we go from here when most people over the age of thirty largely think of the world in binaries, have grown up with deeply biphobic programming, governmental neglect, and bi erasure both broadly and within LGBTQ+ communities? (I'm not saying everyone above the age of thirty is biphobic, however maintaining that we have not been socialized to be is naive at best and gaslighting at worst.)

Many people recognize the limitations of binaries, and though they may reach for them out of habit, they recognize there exists a whole world between the north and south pole. Television was not the only source of learning, and even though biphobia is not exclusive to TV and film, independent thought remains. Many people of all sexualities saw those depictions and were mostly unaffected, outgrew that kind of thinking, or did not take them to represent all bisexual+ men. But bisexual+ men have been left to collect bits of seeing ourselves vaguely reflected from here or gather bits of hearing neutral opinions of us from there. Representation seems to be the vehicle through which many argue our liberation lies, but I like to push back on that. Representation is important, *and* buying into a system that is built atop and maintained by white supremacy can never lead to liberation. Positive representation can be a useful modern tool, but it is not a magic wand, and there are key things that're often sacrificed in order to participate in being represented.

Society has largely told a homogenous story about bisexual+ men up to this point, and that particular story was never led by or focused on bisexual+ men's wellness, various perspectives, and full context. I want to propose a critical exercise where we take past bisexual+ male representation in film and television, find places to relate to, and frame these bisexual+ men differently, their fucked-up actions and corrupted words momentarily suspended. In this section, I will briefly discuss well-known instances depicting bisexual+ male representation and reframe them using context and humanity in an attempt to offer perspective. It is crystal clear that these characters' behavior was vile, and I am not trying to excuse or justify their behavior because that would be wrong and encourage trauma bonding.

According to Medical News Today, a trauma bond is a connection between an abusive person and the individual they abuse. It typically occurs when the abused person begins to develop sympathy or affection for the abuser. Stockholm syndrome is a specific type of trauma bond. While this term typically refers to someone who is captive developing positive feelings for their captors, this dynamic can occur in other situations and relationships. Research in 2018 investigating abuse in athletics suggests that Stockholm syndrome may begin when a person experiencing abuse begins to rationalize the actions of the perpetrator.

Many of these men are obvious villains, and many of their actions were unacceptable, violent, and manipulative. I am saying, with the narrow representation that we have largely had that does paint many bisexual+ men as abusers, I'm choosing to turn toward it and see what else can be extracted.

Finding ways you're innocent is a technique I recently learned in therapy, and it's a powerful tool meant to foster self-compassion, recognize sponsoring intentions, and view my own feelings as equal to another's. It is not meant to justify harmful behavior, be weaponized, reinforce negative action or inaction, or evade accountability. This is a crucial step of an accountability process, emphasis on *process*. The exercise is useful in early stages of forgiving oneself and is only complete when your behaviors are appropriate and align with the innocence of your feelings and sponsoring intentions. You begin by validating the feelings and needs, then figure out the most effective, nondestructive strategies to getting those feelings heard and the needs met. It's extremely important that this exercise is not used inappropriately or taken out of the context of accountability and its roots in restorative justice. I had reservations about including this because it can be misappropriated to validate, normalize, and rationalize abusive behavior and trauma bonds, and even enable narcissists to continue to be abusive and self-serving. The unfortunate reality is that most characterizations of bisexual+ men, especially Black bisexual+ men, are as abusive, manipulative, or narcissistic because these representations are a result of people wanting to make money and how society perceives bisexuality in men. I think there is value in using it carefully here.

Finding Ways They Were Innocent

In the TV series *Queer as Folk* (2000–2005), the character Hunter Novotny-Bruckner, age seventeen, was formerly a hustler when he lived on the streets, but he was taken in by couple Michael and Ben. He starts attending school and eventually develops feelings toward a girl name Callie. Hunter has two adoptive gay men for caretakers, and they both express disappointment when he gets a girlfriend and act as though he is now a heterosexual outsider, even though they previously bonded over his shared HIV status and him expressing interest in boys. This underscores how isolating queer friends and communities can be for bisexual+ boys and men when they have a partner of a different gender and how the support of the aforementioned can disappear if you date a girl or woman. That sounds really tough.

In the series *Six Feet Under* (2001–2005), the character Keith is David's main love interest throughout the series, and they eventually wind up getting married and having two boys. During one of the times they were getting back together after a break, Keith has a one-night encounter with a woman named Celeste he's working as a bodyguard for. Keith identifies as gay but is shown having sex with a woman and mentions having been with women in the past. Keith's attraction to women is seen as a betrayal by David, not that he slept with someone else, as they were just getting back together, and is instantly politicized. Even while in partnership, many gay men see bisexual+ men's attraction to women or engagement with women as a threat to *the cause* and conflate attraction to women with a change of political allegiance or conforming to heteronormativity. David puts a pronounced distance between them once Keith tells him and appears to take Keith's attraction to women as an offense. To have a partner you love who feels this way about your desires or sexual history and express shock, disgust, and discomfort around having been with women sounds really tough. To be so incredibly proud of being a queer person, yet still encountering a lack of support within an intimate partnership, sounds really tough.

In the series *Prison Break* (2005–2017), the character T-Bag has power in prison and uses that power to try to make men do his bidding. He is a very sexual character. T-Bag had a wife on the outside and had a boyfriend while in prison during the first season. His boyfriend eventually dies. T-Bag has to process his boyfriend's death and what it means largely on his own. That sounds really tough.

In *Noah's Arc* (2005–2006), Wade is title character Noah's main love interest throughout the series, and they wind up getting married and living happily ever after with one another. Prior to meeting Noah, Wade identifies as straight and wasn't attracted to guys. Because of this, he crosses a lot of Noah's boundaries, figures things out surrounding his sexuality rather clumsily, and has a hard time not pursuing women or living the way he is used to. He has no guidance throughout any of this, as all of the people around him are either gay or straight. That sounds really tough.

When the main characters in the film *Brokeback Mountain* (2005) first began working together herding sheep on Brokeback Mountain, Eniss was an engaged recluse and Jack was talkative, hard-working, and single. Both were largely unable to reconcile or really make sense of their identity as masculine cisgender cowboys with their bisexual+ orientation. Both of them had a lack of validation, support, connection, and guidance from their fathers on what manhood is and can look like. Both came from Southern Christian households. Both had little to no sex education, especially not bi-specific sex ed. Eniss was a virgin until his encounter with Jack. Both had no one with their cultural lens who was affirming to talk to or process the complex emotions that may have arisen or persisted throughout their lives, or how to navigate the social stigma surrounding bisexuality, and the expectations of being a man. They had no tools or real examples to navigate these on their own. Eniss knew from a very early age that his father would not accept his sexuality, and his relationship with his father was already strained. Eniss's father shows him a queer man dead in a ditch as a child, which haunted and scarred him. Jack had a secretive father who didn't share his rodeo secrets with him and withheld as much as he could. There was inter-partner violence between them, and they were not given the tools to recognize it as that, or to navigate domestic violence in a same-sex relationship. The treatment from their boss worsens after he finds out they've been intimate and he fires them. They part ways thinking they'd never see each other again. Both of them experience poverty, though help from Jack's in-laws significantly bolsters his fate. Both their romantic relationships with women suffered because they felt shame over an aspect of their identity. Shame and not being able to disclose created the distance between them and their loved ones. All of this, and that his wife found out he cheated, lead to Ennis's divorce. Eniss's shame, secrecy, and fear of being found out and confronted by his ex-wife leads him to violence against his wife and to leave the home. Eniss's relationship with his children suffered. The murdered queer man he was shown by his father acted as a specter in the background of his life, guiding him and deterring him from looking at himself for fear of what he may find. He is unable to let anyone in because of the ways he'd been traumatized. Eniss is unable to love his wife or Jack or anyone else because of all this. Neither Jack nor Eniss were part of the others' family. Jack was murdered because of his attraction to men. Eniss loses the love of his life and a twenty-year relationship to a hate crime. It was not recognized as such, and Eniss was not able to attend the funeral or to grieve with Jack's family as a part of the family. That sounds really tough.

In *Trapped in the Closet* (2005-2012, episodes 2 and 3), after catching his wife cheating, we see the husband and pastor reveal that he's been having an affair as well and that his partner is a man. This makes the affair worse, as can be seen by his wife's reaction and the narrator's tone surrounding it. I can see how his life as a pastor and his duties as a husband may have felt restrictive, rigid, and suffocating. I can empathize with finding ways of rebelling when living under an immense amount of pressure. That sounds really tough.

Because the character Carl in the film *For Colored Girls* (2010) is not a heterosexual man, Carl's manhood comes under attack and is threatened, which causes him distress and to cling to performing hegemonic masculinity for dear life. This causes him to be disconnected from his wife, Jo. It also causes disconnection from himself, which led to sneaking, hiding, and lots of shame. It causes him to be mean and judge others, specifically his wife, much like he is mean to and judges himself. He has to engage his attraction to men in secrecy, which is putting his life, freedom, and dignity at risk, as he is arrested while receiving oral sex in a parked car. He had little to no resources available to understand himself and no examples or models of ways to have relationships with women openly as a bisexual+ man or as a nonmonogamous bisexual+ man. He likely suppressed or shrugged off his attractions until it got to a point where he couldn't ignore it. He may have started engaging with men "to get it out of his system" so that he could go back to only desiring women, specifically his wife. Carl cannot reconcile his desires for men and women with the political identity, ostracization, and stereotyping that comes with being public with another man or anything else other than heterosexual. Carl is not interested in the political, spiritual, moral, or societal backlash that often comes with being partnered with a person of the same gender. Carl's embrace of hegemonic masculinity leads him to betray his wife by taking her money without her permission (financial abuse) to use it to invest, though he wishes he hadn't. Carl is unable to reconcile his gender as a masculine cisgender Black man with his bisexual+ orientation. Carl is unable to allow himself to attach to men romantically. Carl's "truth" induces shame. When people feel shame about the core of who they are, it causes them to hide and to avoid those parts of themselves as much as they can. Carl had little to no sex education, especially not bi-specific sex ed. Carl finds out he is HIV positive and does not seem to have anyone he can turn to. Carl had no one with cultural competence who was affirming to talk to or to process the complex emotions that may have arisen or persisted throughout his life, or anyone to offer him ways to navigate the social stigma and expectations that are thrusted onto him. That sounds really tough.

In the MTV series *Faking It* (2014–2016), when asked, Wade is forthcoming about being bisexual+ and flirts with the guys and girls that he finds himself drawn to. He is later fought over by Shane and Karma, who view him and his sexuality as a challenge to be won. They both lie to him about being okay with the arrangement of them all going out to prom together, then having a threesome, and it ends disastrously. That sounds really tough.

The character Kevin in the film *Moonlight* (2016) grows up receiving messages about what it is to be an acceptable boy and then an acceptable man. These messages and pressure from a school bully lead him to physically hurt Chiron, someone he's known for a long time and cares about, shortly after they'd had sexual contact for the first time. Kevin talks about feeling like these messages and the pressure he was under caused him to do what people thought he should do rather than what he wanted to do. This led to estrangement between him and Chiron. That sounds really tough.

In the film *Call Me By Your Name* (2017), both Elio and Oliver had little opportunity to partner with other boys or men. This seemed to affect the plans Oliver made for his life and the dreams he allowed himself to dream. This limited the time they had with one another and meant Oliver was going to leave Italy at the end of the summer as planned and then go on to marry a woman, leaving Elio heartbroken. That sounds really tough.

How Black Mirror *Failed Bisexual+ Men and Genderqueer People*

"Striking Vipers," the first episode of season five of the television series *Black Mirror,* follows Danny, a married man bored by his mundane nuclear familial life, as he gets tangled in a virtual-reality affair involving his former roommate Karl. It has sparked a lot of conversation around virtual reality, infidelity, sexuality, gender, polyamorous relationships, and ways to spice up a romance when it falls into a rut.

Much of the reaction to the episode has been positive, although it is wrought with uncertainty. For *The Guardian,* Guy Lodge writes, "These are complex questions . . . yet there's a stale whiff of 'no-homo' coyness to the way 'Striking Vipers' dramatizes two ostensibly straight men's flirtations with homosexuality and genderqueer identity."

Many viewers were glad to see Black masculinity and queerness explored at all, yet the episode left something to be desired because it lacked a satisfactory resolve. "Striking Vipers" has just as many flaws as it does strengths. It's amazing to see an almost exclusively Black cast, aside from Asian avatars who were also crucial to the storytelling. It was great to witness spellbinding aspects of gamer culture, like escapism and getting to take on a different persona, on display, plus outstanding cinematography and the unforgettable visual assists of the blue versus yellow color palette, symbolizing the staleness of the real world versus the draw of the virtual world. Concepts around manhood—such as men not being in touch with themselves outside of performing masculinity, and being poor communicators—were explicitly engaged in satisfying ways.

But "Striking Vipers" also exploited the all too familiar trope of Black bi+ men as liars, cheaters, and sexually insatiable, all while further invisibilizing us by refusing to have characters who explore bisexuality to ever acknowledge it (in the minds of many, bisexual+ men don't actually exist).

Because of a lack of clarity around bisexualities that feels intentional as well as irresponsible, the recurring question many people had after watching "Striking Vipers" was, "Are Danny and Karl gay or straight?" After they have virtual-reality sex for the first time, while Karl's mind is in a female avatar's body, Karl tells Danny, "Guess that's us gay now." Danny replies, "Doesn't feel like a gay thing," in the only explicit acknowledgment of queer sexuality. But the problem goes beyond using the word *gay* instead of the seemingly more accurate *bisexual*. The characters' lack of self-reflection in general, and the show's inability to show them exploring and finding certainty in their own individual ambiguities, sexuality, and gender identity, makes the episode play more for shock value than the nuanced representation we deserve.

It's clear to me that Karl, the initiator of these virtual sexual escapades, has internalized heteronormative ideals that say a relationship between two men is illegitimate. What's less clear is whether he desires both sex and romance from Danny, which he seems to, because he is only allowed to vocalize wanting sex under the shroud of virtual reality.

Danny's predicament is even more complicated; he wasn't aware of wanting sex or romance from Karl until he was kissed in virtual reality by Karl's female avatar. He found himself enjoying the sensation *and* who it was coming from, but then he remembered his marriage, and he couldn't let himself go there, sexually or emotionally.

I empathized with Danny after the first kiss, which he did not see coming, because I know how overwhelming it must be to all of a sudden realize that you're capable of being sexual or romantic with a person of a gender you hadn't considered. However, Danny's atrocious communication became another flaw of the episode because it seemed designed not to let me feel bad for him for too long, even though empathy is too often withheld from Black bisexual+ men struggling with feelings such as this. Danny could have been shown speaking to his wife, Theo, afterward, or at least doing some soul-searching and research (although resources for bi+ men are scarce), but he was callously avoidant until there was no other option.

At the end of the episode, Danny and Karl simplified their relationship, agreeing to have virtual-reality sex once a year. This seems reflective of the experiences of many bi-curious and bisexual+ men who have a hard time reconciling their emotional, physical, and sexual attractions to other men because of internalized biphobia, homophobia, and heteronorma-tivity. Many never fully overcome this, nor come out as bisexual+ to their loved ones or to themselves, for a myriad of reasons. A generous read of the episode is that the relationship between Danny and Karl represents the very real and numerous struggles Black bisexual+ men face and ques-tions that remain for us. But in order to come to this nuance and the specificity of the characters, the viewer is required to know the difference between sexual orientation, sexual history, and identity, and that trans people are not *putting on* another gender in order to avoid being gay or make the person they're with avoid being gay, all context the show seems to go out of its way to sidestep.

Without making these truths plain, the episode is more easily read as painting Black bisexual+ men as cheaters who use the women in their lives to deflect the reality that they are actually gay, and trivializing trans experiences as something to take off, put on, and maneuver as a way of escaping being gay in the minds of others. That might make for a popular episode, but it does more damage to the psyche and reputation of Black bisexual+ men and gender-variant people.

What hope do Black bisexual+ men have if, even in our imaginings, in virtual reality, we can't escape the stereotypes that haunt us, that lead 35 percent of us to consider or attempt suicide (compared to 30 percent of gay men and a much lower number for straight men), as well as higher rates of anxiety, depression, mood disorders, intimate partner violence, discrimination within the LGBTQ+ community, heart disease, and tobacco use than our gay and straight counterparts?

Could this episode not imagine working toward a healthy nonmonogamous relationship, one achieved after Danny has difficult but necessary conversations with himself and Theo that we are able to see too? There have been many televised bisexual+ MFF threesomes, something often depicted for the straight male gaze, and it would have been refreshing to see an MMF scene for once, one that *included* Theo in the fun instead of keeping her in the dark until the very end, when they only negotiate their boundaries off-camera, and only because they reach an impasse.

Can Black bisexual+ men ever escape the specter of being the cheating down-low brother, responsible for spreading HIV in the Black community? The stigma remains at the core of our society that informs racist, biphobic attitudes that spill over into our media. If we hope to change any of that, to make room for Black bisexual+ men and begin to reverse some of the damage wrought on us, the work should resume in the imagining, in virtual reality, in fictitious depictions of Black bisexual+ men, because exploiting tropes about Black bisexual+ men, as "Striking Vipers" did, ain't it.

Vicarious Trauma

When people watch television and film, they can become emotionally invested in characters and their stories, and learn from their mistakes and other lessons. According to the Griefwork Center, "vicarious trauma is a psychological response that is associated with the disturbing experiences and traumatic events of another person, often victims of crime or abuse. The condition describes the indirect trauma or the result of identifying with a trauma survivor's suffering." When we are presented over and over again with bisexual+ men as perpetual cheaters and liars who are actually gay, that can create an emotional imprint or at least influence people to side with the *victims* of bisexual+ people and deeply believe that bisexual+ men are cheaters, liars, and secretly gay. Studies have found that when people watch television or film, alpha brain waves, which are associated with hypnosis and being highly suggestible, are produced. This can have a profound effect on the deeper, more subconscious parts of the mind, especially when bisexual+ men are characterized as unsafe threats. I do not doubt that there are real-life stories like these, or that there are plenty of bisexual+ men who have cheated, or men who've identified as bisexual+ or straight but are gay. The issue is that this is the dominant narrative—using an incredibly powerful tool—and it's what immediately comes to most people's minds when bisexuality in men is brought up. Most people think of these negative stereotypes when they hear of bi-sexual+ men, or assume they're secretly gay. Most people living in societies colonized by Europeans understand sexuality as a binary instead of as a continuum. White supremacy is responsible for that.

Good Representation

In season 2, episode 14 of the television series *Glee* (2010), Blaine accepts Rachel's offer to go out on a date after they'd had a great kiss. Kurt vehemently discourages him from doing that and says disparaging things about bisexuality in men. Kurt compares Blaine considering a date with Rachel to going back in the closet, not being proud, and being ashamed of his sexuality. This is a common experience that a bi+ man may have if they're surrounded by gay men, and seeing it displayed was validating, even though Blaine internalizes this and later goes back to saying he's gay. That is common without the right support as well.

In the BET television series *Boomerang* (2019), Ari is a complex, thoughtful, openly bisexual+ Black man who's working on getting more comfortable with his sexuality. He doesn't have all the answers and is not perfect, but that's part of what makes the character so compelling and relatable. Ari works a Pride parade, is confronted by a female ex-lover, experiences biphobia, and the legitimacy of his sexuality is called into question. It is a distinct bisexual+ experience that happens for many bisexual+ people, and having it displayed so accurately was refreshing.

In episodes 4 and 5 of season 1 of the sitcom *Grown-ish* (2018), Nomi dumps her bisexual+ boyfriend, Dave, because he's bisexual+, even though she's also bisexual+. Dave was really supportive, kind, and charming, but once he let Nomi know he was also bisexual+, all bets were off. Nomi goes on to verbalize societal attitudes surrounding female bisexuality, and it becomes clear that she is the asshole in the situation and he is better off without her. In season 4, episodes 8 and 9, Des corrects Skye's understanding of his sexuality to actually be a more fluid one, namely "queer," rather than what she'd assumed, which was gay. Skye seems fine with this and is intrigued. Because of everything they have in common and the flirtatious energy that's been building between them, they wind up hanging out later that night at a social gathering. Des shows up wearing a hoodie with a dress layered underneath, which takes Skye by surprise and completely turns her off. She has trouble being honest about this with Des for fear of being labeled problematic. She winds up seeing her ex kissing another girl at another social gathering they're all at just before she's about to break things off with Des and decides to kiss Des instead in an attempt to get over her ex.

In the animated sitcom *Big Mouth* (2019), Jay is a preteen who creates fantasy scenarios while masturbating with his pillows and projecting different genders onto them. Jay has a budding moral compass and openness despite his brothers being homophobic, other turbulence in his home life, and him being a preteen.

In the series *Schitt's Creek* (2015), David's definition of his sexuality is, "I do drink red wine, but I also drink white wine. And I've been known to sample the occasional rosé, and a couple summers back I tried a merlot that used to be a chardonnay, which got a bit complicated. I like the wine and not the label." This comedic definition of bisexuality and pan-sexuality was especially great and provided clarity into David's understanding of his sexuality. David is especially important for bisexual+ male representation because he's a man who's assumed to be gay, and we get to witness this underserved perspective and how he navigates that.

In the musical series *The Get Down* (2016), Dizzee is depicted as a sensitive artist, a free spirit, and a rebel. Throughout the progression of season 1, we see Dizzee develop a romance with Thor, and by the end of the season, they allude to the two kissing in an underground LGBTQ+ club, though this is not actually shown. Dizzee constantly refers to freedom and rebellion that can be linked to his Blackness and queerness.

In episode 3 of season 2 of the TV series *Good Trouble* (2019), we see Gael stand up to his father, who disowns and deadnames his trans sister Jazmin. Then Gael takes a stand and says if his sister is disowned for being transgender, he should be disowned as well because he's bisexual+. He navigates biphobia in the series really well, is charming, and is shown to have a clear moral compass.

In season 2 of the television series *Roswell, New Mexico* (2019), Michael Guerin is depicted as an evolving, passionate, spontaneous bisexual+ man who is not ashamed of his desires and is unafraid to act on them. He lives his life to the beat of his own drum while learning more about his past and juggling a full life.

The character Timmy begins the horror film *The Craft: Legacy* (2020) as an insensitive teen who has been harassing Lily since she got her period in class. Lily and her coven cast a spell to awaken him to his highest self, and Timmy starts treating people with respect, begins to be honest about his feelings, and chastises his friends for making light of consent in sex-ed class. During a game of Two Truths and a Lie with Lily and her coven, Timmy reveals that he hooked up with Isaiah for the first time ever and delivers a moving speech about some of the hardships of being a guy and liking guys and girls.

These examples show some variety, depth, and humor. There are more that I haven't mentioned, as this is not meant to be an exhaustive list, but the point is that instances of bisexual+ male representation are few and far between in the grand scheme of things, often involving the bury your gays trope, and is often a hit or a miss. We are rarely the main character. We need more. We need writers and directors of every genre to read *In Focus: Reporting on the Bisexual Community,* a resource guide to equip journalists and media experts to accurately and effectively report on the bisexual+ community, its experiences, and the important issues bisexual+ people face. This was created in 2016 by a partnership of GLAAD, BiNet USA, the Bisexual Organizing Project, and the Bisexual Resource Center.

Queerbaiting, Bi-Baiting, and Bi Device

Queerbaiting is a term originally coined in reference to politicians. Similar to "race baiting," the term meant implying the opponent was queer to diminish their image and campaign, but a new meaning and use for the word came about when users of the social media platform Tumblr began to use it. "Queerbaiting" is now used to describe a marketing technique for fiction and entertainment in which creators hint at, but then do not actually depict, same-sex romance or other LGBTQ+ representation in an attempt to garner support from liberal or LGBTQ+ communities. Think Dumbledore and Grindelwald in the Harry Potter series. Think Poe and Finn in the *Star Wars* series. Think Scott and Stiles in *Teen Wolf.*

On #BiTwitter, many bisexual+ users have used the phrase *bi-baiting* to describe a similar phenomenon in which a character is hinted at being bisexual+ and is actually gay or straight. I like the term *bi-baiting,* though I've come to create the term *bi device* to highlight how creators use a character's potential bisexuality as a plot device to spice up or create engagement around content without an actual bisexual+ character being present. The most egregious demonstration of this as of late can be seen with the character Victor in the television series *Love, Victor.* In the trailer and all the way up to episode 6 and 7 of season 1, Victor is positioned as a bisexual+ boy, and then at the midnight hour, the writers signal that he's actually been gay all along. There's a voiceover at the end of episode 6 from Simon, a digital mentor by this time, that's invalidating and out of step with the developments and portrayals made since episode 1. "Hey Victor, I know you really like Mia, and I know you've been trying to figure out if you're attracted to her. It sounds like tonight you realized that you're not, and that's okay. But maybe it's time for you to really figure out what you want. Before someone gets hurt." The voiceover is acemisic (discrimination against, invalidation or oppression of, or hatred of asexual people) and overlooks the ways attraction often feels and can manifest differently depending on the person or their gender, and it doesn't exactly match up with how the previous scenes landed.

Victor's inner monologue at the beginning of episode 7 is frustrating. The voiceover from Simon asks, "Victor, how'd it go with Mia? Did you guys . . . ?" Victor replies, "I choked. Big time. But honestly, Simon, is sex such a big deal? I mean, everything else about our relationship is picture-perfect. I know you probably think I'm grasping at straws, but if there's a chance for me to be happy and normal, why not try?" It lands like his characterization and the story has pivoted to represent a gay guy in the closet trying to force himself to like girls, which is a marked difference from his bisexual+ thoughts, like wanting to kiss Mia and enjoying it, his feelings for her, and behaviors in previous episodes. It did not feel like the natural progression of a gay guy discovering that deep down he was gay. A bisexual+ guy was marketed to us in the trailer, depicted for half the season, and then the rug was pulled from underfoot. The writers dabbled in harmful stereotypes about bisexual+ boys and men being cheaters, exploited the juiciness of a guy dating a girl but having secret feelings for boys, and ended the season showing a gay boy so deep in the closet that he dated a girl.

Many people do not agree with me on this and simply see this depiction as a gay guy needing to explore his sexuality by dating a girl to figure out that he's actually gay. I see it as exploiting the trope that exists surrounding bisexual+ men for a potentially juicy story, viewership, and a plot with twists and turns without any interest in or concern for the reputation, psyches, or representation of bisexual+ boys and men, one of the most underserved communities under the LGBTQ+ umbrella. Victor was positioned as a bisexual+ boy in the trailer for the series and is depicted as bisexual+ up until episode 6, when the writers shift gears and eventually end the season with Victor being caught by Mia kissing Benji while on a date with Mia. Why use the allure of a bisexual+ guy without the follow-through, care for bisexual+ communities, or understanding of what bisexuality can be or look like? Have we not

seen enough depictions that are similar? Does bisexual+ male representation not already feel degenerative? Is the reputation of gay men affected
by these depictions and realities, or is it a mark left on male bisexuality?
This bi device was what made the first season alluring, controversial, and
memorable.

I am reminded of another instance where this happened. Something
similar can be seen in series 2, episode 6 of the television series *Moesha*
(1996), though merely in one episode. The character Hakeem's cousin,
Omar, is a nice responsible young man who takes Moesha on a date. They
have a lot of chemistry, and Omar is caring, versatile, and open. Their
date is interrupted by Omar's friend, Tracy, who is obviously gay. The
date comes to an end with Tracy hijacking it, Moesha heading home, and
Omar going to a party with Tracy. Moesha later tells Kim and Niecy that
she suspects Omar is gay, and it doesn't take long until everyone in school
knows the latest gossip. Omar later comes out as gay, after being outed
by Moesha, Kim, and Niecy. Hakeem doesn't take it well. Though Omar
comes out as gay, he initially expressed interest in Moesha and took her
out on a date. The twist was Omar being associated with Tracy, and their
association being evidence that Omar was not straight. This bi device was
what made the episode exciting and controversial.

The writer of this episode, Demetrius Bady, talks about how hard
he fought for this episode to be aired, as the 1990s were a dead zone
for Black LGBTQ+ content on network television. What complicates
my assertion is that Demetrius Bady originally pitched the episode
during season 1 with Moesha attempting to kiss Omar, and when Omar
declines, she starts a rumor that he is gay, which would be a lot more
in line with the Moesha character as a bratty teenage busybody. Instead,
producers Ralph Farquhar and Ron Neal introduce Tracy, Omar's flam-
boyantly gay friend, to provide a reason for Moesha to think Omar
might be gay. This change in Bady's initial idea was meant to support
the pervasive idea that Black people are antigay, even more than other
racial groups. Let me be very clear in saying that white supremacy has
criminalized being gay and bisexual+, created the gender binary, and
through colonization, has enforced the same ideologies on communities
across the globe. Over the years, white people have largely been positioned as the most progressive in this arena, even though white people

colonized the world and are now appropriating and bastardizing aspects of pre-colonial African, Indigenous, and Asian norms around sexuality and gender. White LGBTQ+ people continue to keep this myth alive (Andy Cohen, I'm glaring at you), while skipping over the hundreds of anti-LGBTQ+—specifically anti-trans—laws passed within a predominantly white country and government.

What's missing in many white LGBTQ+ people's—and by result LGBTQ+ organizations—analysis or critique of anti-LGBTQ+ sentiment seen across Western society is its direct ties to white supremacy. If they know that, why don't they name it? If they don't know that, why don't they know it? After learning about it, why don't they explicitly name these ties? I don't want to repackage white supremacy as long as it is inclusive of bisexuality or men being able to express emotions or femininity without being met with violence or shunned or whatever the fuck. I want the whole pie. I want an end to the world as we know it. I am not invested in attaining more power in a system that's inherently oppressive. I want freedom for everyone. I must survive in this system for the time being, and I can do that without lifting radical thought from its context and purpose in order to attain power and false comfort in this white-supremacist society. I am asking white LGBTQ+ people to learn about freedom from white supremacy and what that will afford and what that will cost.

There is a more multifaceted use of bi device in recent television history that also comes to mind. In episode 6 of season 1 of the series *Insecure* (2016), we see the character Jared tell Molly, who he's dating, that he let a guy go down on him one drunken night, only after she shared having been intimate with a woman in college herself. After this revelation, Molly asks if he is bisexual. He says no, then she goes on to discuss his sexuality with her crew, and she eventually breaks it off with him because of his revelation. The motivation behind the writers including Jared's revelation definitely seemed to be about highlighting and challenging a double standard that exists surrounding Black male sexuality and the lack of room for exploration, fluidity, or being able to experiment without labels. It also underlined how the Molly character consistently self-sabotages and is biased and judgmental, and equates a past she finds less than respectable with minor flaws and deal-breakers. The very mention of the topic of bisexuality in Black men usually brings about a tremendous amount of engagement and controversy, though exploiting that may not have been the intention of the writers. There was more to their relationship and the story than Jared's presumed sexuality, but this can still be classified as a bi device—although not as obviously exploitative as the other two—as the question of Jared's sexuality is something that changes the trajectory of their relationship and is returned to over the course of the series. This bi device made the episode juicy and controversial, and fans of the show often refer to the character Jared as bisexual, even though he is not. The mere hint of a Black bisexual+ man is powerful enough to evoke panic, fear, suspicion, disgust, laughter, scandal, and more, all while no bisexual+ man is to be found.

Media that features or centers LGBTQ+ characters, and more specifically bisexual+ men, needs to move beyond our identity as a plot device or something to bring in ratings via tapping into harmful tropes. It is exploitative by nature, and a man possibly being bisexual+ is not a very creative or remarkable plot. It is not the most decorative display of creativity or skill, and I am asking creators to do and be those things if they hint at a man possibly being bisexual+ or if they include a bisexual+ male character. I don't think a lot of gay or straight people know just how many of us hold our breath when we see a bisexual+ character depicted in a TV show or movie, especially if it's an LGBTQ+-centered narrative. A lot of us are holding our breath hoping the characterization does not dip too far into common tropes because we know them all too well. Some of us hold our breath waiting for it to be over, having preferred no representation at all rather than representation that creates further harm.

NOTES

Jon Cohen, "A Silent Epidemic: Why Is There Such a High Percentage of HIV and AIDS among Black Women?" Slate, October 27, 2004, https://slate.com/technology/2004/10/black-women-and-aids.html.

Laura Smith, "How a Racist Hate-Monger Masterminded America's War on Drugs," Medium Timeline, February 28, 2018, https://timeline.com/harry-anslinger-racist-war-on-drugs-prison-industrial-complex-fb5cbc281189.

David Pilgrim, "The Brute Caricature," Jim Crow Museum, Ferris State University, 2023, www.ferris.edu/jimcrow/brute.

Sherronda J. Brown, *Refusing Compulsory Sexuality: A Black Asexual Lens on Our Sex-Obsessed Culture* (Berkeley, CA: North Atlantic Books, 2022), 11.

Teresa J. Guess, "The Social Construction of Whiteness: Racism by Intent, Racism by Consequence," *Critical Sociology* 32:4 (2006), 649–73, www.cwu .edu/diversity/sites/cts.cwu.edu.diversity/files/documents/constructing whiteness.pdf, https://doi.org/10.1163/156916306779155199.

Jane Ward, *Not Gay: Sex Between Straight White Men* (New York: New York University Press, 2015).

Lois Zoppi, "What Is Trauma Bonding?" Medical News Today, November 27, 2020, www.medicalnewstoday.com/articles/trauma-bonding.

Charles Bachand and Nikki Djak, "Stockholm Syndrome in Athletics: A Paradox," *Children Australia* 43:3 (June 20, 2018), 175–80, https://doi.org /10.1017/cha.2018.31.

Eliel Cruz, "MTV's 'Faking It' Big Bisexual Blunder," HuffPost, October 30, 2015, www.huffpost.com/entry/mtvs-faking-it-big-bisexu_b_8413276.

The essay "How *Black Mirror* Failed Bisexual Men and Genderqueer People" first appeared in Black Youth Project, June 21, 2019, under the title "How *Black Mirror*'s 'Striking Vipers' Episode Failed Bisexual Men & Trans Women," http://blackyouthproject.com/how-black-mirrors -striking-vipers-episode-failed-bisexual-men-trans-women-1.

Guy Lodge, "Queer Fears: The Problem with *Black Mirror*'s 'No Homo' Episode," *Guardian,* June 10, 2019, www.theguardian.com/tv-and-radio /2019/jun/10/black-mirror-charlie-brooker-striking-vipers.

Chris Longo, "*Black Mirror:* 'Striking Vipers' Star Breaks Down a Complex Relationship," Den of Geek, June 11, 2019, www.denofgeek.com/tv /black-mirror-striking-vipers-star-relationship.

Ta-Nehisi Coates, "A Low-Down Crying Shame: Why the Myth of the "On the Down Low" Brother Refuses to Die," Slate, March 9, 2007, https://slate.com/technology/2007/03/why-the-myth-of-on-the-down -low-refuses-to-die.html.

Paisley Gilmour, "Why Many Bisexual People Don't 'Just Come Out,'" *Cosmopolitan,* May 21, 2018, www.cosmopolitan.com/uk/love-sex/relation ships/a20769881/coming-out-bisexual.

Nissa Mitchell, "On Being 'Uber-Gay,' Trans Women and Sexual Orientation," Medium, March 13, 2018, https://transsubstantiation.com/on-being-uber-gay-ad360448e170.

Alia E. Dastagir, "LGBTQ Definitions Every Ally Should Know for Pride Month (and All Year Long)," USA Today, June 2, 2022, www.usatoday.com/story/news/nation/2022/06/02/lgbtq-glossary-ally-learn-language/7469059001.

Ellyn Ruthstrom, "Bisexual Health Awareness Month Draws Attention to Community's Urgent Health Needs," National LGBTQ Task Force, March 5, 2014, www.thetaskforce.org/news/bisexual-health-awareness-month-draws-attention-to-communitys-urgent-health-needs.

Black Youth Project, "How Biphobia Impacts Black Bisexual Men's Health," April 30, 2019, http://blackyouthproject.com/how-biphobia-impacts-black-bisexual-mens-health.

Barbara Rubel, "What Is Vicarious Trauma?" Grief Work Center, 2020, www.griefworkcenter.com/what-is-vicarious-trauma.

The Humble Bee, "The Effects of TV on Your Brain," Steemit, 2017, https://steemit.com/tv/@thehumblebee/the-effects-of-tv-on-your-brain.

TV Tropes, s.v. "Bury Your Gays," 2015, https://tvtropes.org/pmwiki/pmwiki.php/Main/BuryYourGays.

GLAAD, "In Focus: Reporting on the Bisexual Community," April 11, 2016, www.glaad.org/publications/focus-reporting-bisexual-community.

Mguzmanvogele, "Queer Baiting," 21st-Century Interdisciplinary Dictionary, blog post, March 29, 2016.

Chai Elemental, "Things You Didn't Know Were Acemisic," That Weird Ace Woman, blog post, June 24, 2022, https://thatweirdacewoman.wordpress.com/2022/06/24/things-you-didnt-know-were-acemisic.

Alfred L. Martin Jr., "Re-Watching Omar: Moesha, Black Gayness and Shifting Media Reception," Flow, February 1, 2021, www.flowjournal.org/2021/02/rewatching-omar.

American Civil Liberties Union, "Trans Rights under Attack in 2020," 2020, www.aclu.org/issues/lgbtq-rights/transgender-rights/trans-rights-under-attack-2020.

#BisexualMenSpeak

I tire of people telling me I don't exist and that I'm lying.

That was my very first #BisexualMenSpeak post, a direct result of a conversation between me and a Twitter (now named X) friend. We'd been gushing over celebrity couples that made our bi senses tingle, until one couple was mentioned and I was brought back to biphobic comments one of them made about bisexual+ men in particular. They said we didn't exist. They did wind up apologizing and making a commitment to educate themselves, and made it clear that it was a lack of knowledge and not malicious, and I believe them. The reminder of this whole ordeal reopened the wound for me, and I started tweeting. I invited other bisexual+ men and masculine-identified people to join in using the hashtag to talk about how being bisexual+ impacts the way they move through the world, and within minutes people from all over the world began responding. Bisexual+ men started using the hashtag to share their stories, voicing their frustration over being put in a box, voicing their fears, making light of their gripes, and speaking up about bisexuality not invalidating nonbinary or trans identities, to name a few. The contributions since have been varied and extremely vulnerable, which has been really lovely and an integral part of building a world many of us want to see. One of my most ambitious hopes for this hashtag, my work, and the work of my peers is that a man or masculine-identifying person being gay, bi, or pan will not negatively affect his social status, access to resources, reputation, experience, or desirability.

During the first year of the hashtag's inception I spent a lot of time and effort focused on visibility, declaring that bisexual+ men exist, have always existed regardless of people's ignorance, close-mindedness regarding sexuality, and the ways gender expectation affects people's ability to see bisexuality in men as valid. On July 15, 2019, the day the hashtag turned one year old, I began to move in a different direction with how I engaged, focusing my efforts instead on speaking to fellow bisexual+ men and masculine-identified people about any and everything. I've talked about the unspoken reality that some bisexual+ women find bisexual+ men disgusting, the misogyny so many bisexual+ men happily propagate, overcoming shame, going through spells of being primarily attracted to a particular gender, and how bisexual+ men are held to a more stringent standard of being safe than our straight and gay counterparts, to name a few. I also began making #BisexualMenSpeak videos on July 15, 2019, on topics ranging from how to make the world safer for bisexual+ men to how to know if you're bi, the pros versus cons of growing up bisexual+ and Christian, and how to be less afraid of dating men or women.

In 2018, when I first started this hashtag, you had to really dig to actually find a video on YouTube of a bisexual+ man speaking for himself about his experience. On the first few YouTube search pages, you'd find tons of videos of straight women sitting on panels talking about whether or not they'd date a bisexual+ man, or videos of gay men talking about how bisexual+ men are all down-low, are too scared to be seen as gay, that bisexual+ men *are* all gay and the only reason they're with women is because of the societal encouragements that come with it. There have also been videos that've cropped up of straight men going up to random women in malls and asking them if they would ever date a bisexual+ man. Although there are thousands of videos on YouTube of bisexual+ men around the world opening up about their experience, being visible and presenting across the vast spectrum of what people define as feminine expression to masculine expression, that is not what drives clicks, and it is not enough *proof* that we are not all ghouls set to trick or harm people. For some, there will never be enough.

Fear is a powerful emotion that drives us on a survival level. When bisexual+ men go from being nonexistent in people's minds to a singular sinister thing, it is easy to see why videos that do not feature us, but reinforce this ideal, dominate the subject. Most of the videos I've made or that other bisexual+ men and masculine-identified people have made don't get anywhere near the amount of views that these clickbait, simplified, fearmongering, shallow videos do. And I will be very surprised if they ever do. Videos that go beyond whether or not women would date us, onto the ways this white-supremacist society is set up to box us all into rigid categories, why bisexual+ people face the health and economic disparities we do, the bi erasure that has taken place and continues to, what it would require for us to be safe and supported in this society, get very few views in comparison. I think one of the worst things is for us to try to prove that we are not the stereotype of a bisexual+ man. Ironically, it's counterproductive. But people will ask you to do that over and over again. People will frame your existence through the lens of the "bad bisexual" and how close or far away you are from it. Call people out when they do this, but do not go out of your way to prove you are nothing like the "bad bisexual." The problem has never been the "bad bisexual"; the problem has always been our binary way of viewing things, which is what leads people to believe that bisexuality is not beautiful in and of itself. People draw conclusions about bisexual+ men based on fear, projection, insecurity, jealousy, ignorance, lack of context, and disdain.

The Ugly

Some of my frustrations with this hashtag and other bisexual+ men has been largely around femmephobia. When I first started making #BisexualMenSpeak videos, I'd get comments about how feminine I was and how they couldn't "get past that" to hear what I was saying. Many dismissed me and my bisexuality altogether because I'm feminine—or at least I *was* feminine. It's something I was used to, as I've described throughout this book, but these dismissals especially hurt because I was the one doing the labor to actually discuss these topics that affect us beyond the usual 101 coming-out stuff. I was having complicated conversations with as much grace, gentleness, and nuance as I had at the time, and I was supplying resources. My intention was to help try to put an end to our erasure by doing this work, but it felt like my contributions were being ignored, and none of that mattered to my fellow bisexual+ men—because they couldn't take my femininity.

I suppose this is a huge reason why I'm a writer in the first place. I seldom felt comfortable or supported speaking my mind as an adolescent because of people's reactions to my femininity. Whatever I had to say aloud was dismissed, but when I put my thoughts to the page, it felt as though people's bias was suspended for a minute, and I'd finally found the thing I needed to be understood. I didn't have to face the scoffs, smirks, or disgust that can come when you're a feminine Black bisexual+ boy. When I wrote, I was a *thinker*. I was intelligent. I was heard. It is why, for the first year of the hashtag's creation, it remained something I only wrote about on Twitter, even though inherent in the hashtag is the charge to *speak,* not write.

I'd already had a very small YouTube channel where I would talk about emotional intelligence and mental wellness because of my first book, *The Other F Word: Forgiveness.* But when I started talking about bisexuality in men, as a Black man, suddenly I had all of these eyes on me, perhaps determining whether or not I was actually bisexual+. I suddenly had men who were trying to become more comfortable with their bisexual+ identity projecting their disgust over their own smothered femininity, insecurities, and anxieties onto me. It was not fun, especially because I had no interest in talking to straight or gay people about who we are. I had no real interest in gaining tons of views educating the masses on bisexuality. I'd done my own research on human sexuality and figured they could too. I tried to center bisexual+ people in my content because I'm passionate about us feeling good about ourselves, having access to necessary resources, and combating our troubling health stats. There were also hordes of straight women telling me how disgusting I was, how they would never want to be with a bisexual+ man who fucked men in the ass, how I owed women disclosure of my bisexuality, and how I was infected with HIV. There were also hordes of gay men telling me how much privilege I have, how I value my relationships with women over relationships with men, and how *bisexual* was synonymous with lying and being masculine. I will continue blocking accounts like this. I do not enjoy these comments, and they oftentimes stay with me for a while. I'd like to pretend like I'm this unfazed person it doesn't get to, but that's not true. It hurts to feel attacked on all sides, and that is a very common experience for feminine Black bisexual+ men.

When I began sharing more of my personal experience being a bi-sexual+ man, it became clear that people could not really hear me as an individual. I'd share that my default was long periods of celibacy, a relic of my Christian upbringing that I hadn't quite figured out how to shake. This made me feel a bit insecure because I was now in my mid-twenties, and many of my peers had casual sex, knew what they preferred, and had multiple serious relationships under their belts, which I did not. It's like they didn't hear any of this and would go straight to advising me to use protection or ask about whether sex or dating was better with men or women. Many bisexual+ people experience being hypersexualized, but I felt that part of these microaggressions were also because I was a Black man. I'd watch as many of my Black female friends would announce they were practicing celibacy, usually after a breakup, and there would be interest and questions about how it affected their dating lives and what they did about urges. Yet with me, people pretended as if I hadn't said it, as though men were not capable of celibacy, especially not a Black man who was claiming to be bisexual+. Women and their sexual piety is praised even though it's rooted in religious dogma and patriarchal control. Women are shamed for being sexual or desiring sex while men are expected and encouraged to be hypersexual.

My experience as a feminine man is not the same as a woman's or a person who experiences misogyny, but I can't help but be reminded of a recurring theme that has happened in many social justice movements throughout history. Women and people who experience misogyny, who face the most marginalization, are expected to perform labor and are concurrently disrespected. The intense level of marginalization and antagonisms I've experienced since I was a child is what led me to learn so much about myself, to get involved doing this work and prioritizing unlearning misogyny and the disdain of femininity. I am not the first bisexual+ man to get involved in this work, but I am involved, and I have been trying to do something about what we face, whereas the masculine bisexual+ men who've criticized my femininity are not creating resources for all of us. I remember how hard it was for me to become comfortable in my own skin, not hate myself, and not lash out at fellow feminine boys and men. I also do not think it is acceptable or fair to be treated this way, especially as a person doing labor for an underserved community.

One of the large challenges of making and maintaining the #BisexualMenSpeak playlist on YouTube (with 1,000-plus videos of bisexual+ men and masculine-identified folk speaking about and centering their own experience) has been compiling this playlist while being who I am. I grew up feminine, I'm Black, I am committed to undoing patriarchy, I am committed to undoing transphobia, I am not affiliated with a religion and am not spiritual, I am against imperialism, and I think critically. Many LGBTQ+ news outlets and social media accounts take an apolitical approach and celebrate LGBTQ+ people from all ideologies and walks of life, recognizing that even those ugly parts are part of the LGBTQ+ community too. Touché. However, I didn't want to do that with the play-list. Unlike those LGBTQ+ platforms, I do not have the same power or privilege or access where I can afford to approach the playlist that way and still be mentally well. And it's my playlist. I can feature whichever videos I want.

From this dilemma, I was reminded of a few questions: What is the role of community—online or in real life—in meeting people where they are on their journey to unlearning, especially when people within that community also have their own wounds and things they're working to unlearn? Does sharing in oppression automatically mean someone else will be equipped to be supportive? What responsibilities do indi-viduals have when seeking out community? Has the idea of a singular, happy, healthy LGBTQ+ community even been realized? No; there is no such thing. What I mean by that is that I am not in community with every single LGBTQ+ person. I may try to stand in solidarity with global LGBTQ+ organizations and people, but I am not in community with them. There are LGBTQ+ communities across the globe that are thriving and work well and play well with one another, but I am not in community with them. I am in community with the people I have access to who have a vested interest in my growth, who share my political ide-ologies, and who I interact with regularly.

Yes, many LGBTQ+ individuals are invested in overlapping struggles. No, we are not all in community with one another, and we are not a singular community, although I can see how that idea offers some people comfort. We are a demographic, not a monolith. We do not all have the same attitudes, interests, or goals, even though we may share similar labels or experiences. Perhaps I'm simply making a distinction between com-munity and being *in* community with people. I think in order to be in community with people, you must be invited in and also have done some preliminary or ongoing work on yourself. I think when communities are welcoming and supportive, that can be an enormous incentive to unlearn and accept oneself and others. I also acknowledge that we are all responsible for our beliefs, words, and actions and need to be mindful of how they may impact people we are seeking to be in community with or gain support from. *Community* does not mean "punching bag" or "therapist." One of the great things about talk therapy is the confidentiality aspect and that you can get out all of your problematic thoughts and beliefs with the guidance and support of a trained mental health professional. Talk therapy can be a place where you won't be judged. Your words won't be held against you and likely won't cause harm to the other person in the room as they are trained to witness you on your journey. You can regurgitate the horrible things society has taught you about yourself and about other LGBTQ+ people, reflect, and choose to heal. In community, however, you need to be mindful of your words and respect that you're not the only person hurting or healing or growing or worthy of consideration. A community is made of members. Individuals. Human beings. Community also requires accountability. Being a person of your word and being mindful of differences and similarities. Community has its limits and benefits, as does talk therapy.

The Beauty

Many people from across the globe have reached out to me letting me know how much the #BisexualMenSpeak hashtag has helped them realize or admit to themselves that they're bisexual+, learn more about bisexuality, or give them a small corner of the internet that feels like a safe haven, and I couldn't be happier to hear that. I intend it to be a virtual community where we can be seen and accepted as ourselves, where we can heal, challenge each other, laugh, cry, vent, unlearn misogyny, and grow our confidence. Out of creating this hashtag and the supporting threads and videos came the idea for this book: to expand on some of what I've already discussed online and have it all in one comprehensive place. I wish I'd known as much about sexuality, gender expression, and gender expectation when I was a teenager as I do now, and though I can't go back in time, and wouldn't want to, even if I could, I can share things that may make someone's journey a bit easier or possibly nurture a growing desire to end white-supremacist patriarchy. I do not think I have a duty to do this. I do not *owe* it to the next generation or anyone to educate and share intimate details of my life. I do, however, see it as an

opportunity, and I sincerely hope this contributes to change in the world
and disruption in this white-supremacist nightmare.

The Unexpected

Though I spent the first twenty-five years of my life as a feminine guy
who was often mislabeled as gay, things began to shift as I entered my
late twenties. Many times I'd catch glimpses of myself in a shop window
as I was walking by and tone down the way my arms flapped around,
or other tells in my posture; that finally began to be my default. The
work I'd been doing to keep my head from dipping to one side or from
making random exaggerated faces in my acting for TV and film classes
had become something I didn't have to think about, even when I wasn't
on camera. Practicing using a deeper, more even tone when speaking
because of multiple studies that'd shown orators with lower pitches were
perceived to be more trustworthy and knowledgeable eventually over-
took my signature airy roller-coaster cadence. The shift in my awareness
of how people perceived me wasn't exactly immediate because I was still
surrounded by people who'd known me for a long time and envisioned
me the way I knew myself to be: dramatic, feminine, and goofy. But as I
inched closer and closer to thirty, and put on fifteen pounds of muscle,
I began to hear from new acquaintances that I was "straight-passing" and
couldn't understand what it was like to grow up visibly queer. Putting my
hands on my hips after a really tough set at the gym was all of a sudden
perceived as a Superman power pose instead of as a sign of me being
queer. The gentleness in my voice started to be read as a comforting display of my maturity and a sign of mental tranquility rather than a catalyst
for someone to tell me to put some bass in my voice. It was as if the possibility of femininity was now repelled from my tall, dark, muscular body
or being. Gone were the days when I was described as a bird after telling
an amusing story, and instead my masculine New York accent was seen as
passionate and was crooned over.

Comments poured in from bisexual+ guys on YouTube and Twitter
about how much they respected me and related to me rather than that I
was lying and too feminine to be bisexual+. Men and women would say
how brave I was for talking about being bisexual+ when I really didn't
have to reveal myself. My hashtag and movement had more credibility the

more masculine I was perceived to be in my videos. Speaking up meant something *because* I was masculine, and my work had legs because of it too. Having muscles while being visible meant if there'd ever been any curiosity or latent attraction from straight-identified men in my vicinity, it'd likely rise to the surface after some time or under the influence. I was more desirable to men and women because of my presumed masculinity. Having this range of experiences from childhood into adulthood while living in the same body is enough to split someone into two. In *Belly of the Beast,* Da'Shaun L. Harrison contextualizes this experience using the term *desire capital:*

> *When I capitalize the P in Pretty and the B in Beauty, or the U in Ugly, it is to name who does and does not have access to Desire Capital—that is to say, who owns or embodies more or less of the identities that grant one access, power, and resources. More to the point, "pretty," "beauty," and "ugly"—all with lowercase letters—are subjective. However, as with all capitals, one can embody identities that are valued in modern society and still also hold identities that are marginalized, which is why the term "privileged" is not quite specific enough and often does not go far enough. Desire is complex. Privilege insinuates that there is a possibility that you can opt out, and that if you don't* feel *pretty, then you can't possibly benefit from Prettiness or suffer the violences of Ugliness. Desire/ability politics and Desire Capital, however, suggest that one does not need to feel pretty to be Pretty; one does not need to feel beautiful to be Beautiful; one does not need to feel ugly to be Ugly. How one benefits or suffers from the subjugation of particular people is not determined by their feelings; it is determined by the identities they embody. Desire/ability politics is the methodology through which the sovereignty of those deemed (conventionally) Attractive/Beautiful is determined. Put another way, the politics of Desire labels that which determines who gains and holds both social and structural power through the affairs of sensuality, often predicated on anti-Blackness, anti-fatness, (trans) misognynoir, cis sexism, queer antagonism, and all other structural violence.*

The access bisexual+ men have to desire capital is stipulatory, yet being perceived as masculine felt like I was finally being let into the boys club that

I'd always been laughed out of. Being seen as a straight Black man came with its own challenges, however: I was now treated as a different kind of threat and something to be subjugated while simultaneously looked upon with a mix of revulsion and admiration, and emblematically placed on non-Black men's mood-board, even though they'd never acknowledge me and were now in quiet competition with me. Many see muscles and dark skin, and the possibility of that person being timid goes out the window. Many see dark Black skin as a personality trait, dark-skinned Black men as being automatically cool or aggressive, either sexy or irresponsible. People fail to be able to imagine Black people as anything more than objects to project what they will onto, diligently refuting our humanity.

Around 2019, when I was assumed to be straight more regularly and became open to dating women again, a few more things began to change. I became hyperaware of women who believed bisexual+ men to be beneath them. There seemed to be more YouTube videos of straight women talking about their unwillingness to date bisexual+ men, while others compared a bisexual+ man not disclosing his sexual orientation prior to them having sex to rape, bastardizing talking points about con-sent. In real life, I couldn't exactly be a fly on the wall in the company of groups of women anymore. I became an unintentional target for their ire that they could use as a stand-in for their ex or some man who did them wrong. That or I'd be asked what the male perspective was on a particular issue. Though I could very easily regurgitate unoriginal bio-essentialist tropes about men, I really couldn't explain certain nuances: although I now read like a straight man, I didn't exactly have the decades of down-time with straight men under my belt; I'd spent most of my life around straight women. But I now knew about the subconscious mind. When I would state that based on the actions they'd told me a guy had taken, it sounded like the guy was scared of vulnerability, felt pressured, or likely felt inadequate in some way, my responses were disregarded. They were certain the guy's actions were a power play, a ruse, a sign he didn't care. Nothing more, nothing less. I became hypersensitive to women's criti-cism of men in a way I hadn't before, not even when other queer men would badmouth men.

What had always been a silly way to organize society to me—by assumed gender—was suddenly beginning to make so much sense.

Perhaps aspects of feminism and women's business were really not for the ears of anyone who was not a woman. Perhaps I *should* spend the majority of my time surrounded by and listening to queer and trans men. They, after all, could relate so deeply to my experience, perspectives, fears, needs, and dreams. They were more willing to see me outside of being dubious, even if it was more often than not in a superficial way. These thoughts scared me. Could I truly be practicing Black feminist principles if spending time with Black women had become increasingly uncomfortable and at times intolerable for me? Was this my red pill moment, my manosphere arc at its impetus? Was I really evil at my core after all? This had to be about misogyny, but I'd read the books, listened to the podcasts, gone to therapy, done organizing work. I'd spent most of my life around women; what was the issue? What was happening to me? I thought I was beyond this, *better* than this. But I wasn't better than sexist manosphere men. If I'd taken certain traits on as an identity, hadn't learned how to process my emotions and consider my impact on others, had the same beliefs about men and women, had the same experiences with men and women, and had the same socio-political commitments, I'd be on that same bullshit. It wasn't about being born better; it was about choices, examining beliefs, access to resources, and sociopolitical commitments.

The more I learned about the subconscious mind, the more I realized that my subconscious comfort zone was women who I felt unseen and unheard around. My comfort zone was women I had to earn worth and earn love from. It was biphobic women who thought of themselves as women who kept it real but who were actually mean-spirited. More often than not, they did a lot of the talking, heard what they wanted to, and were likely to pedal misogynistic sentiments when they were angry at another woman as a way of showing they were unbiased. So when they'd get worked up about something that happened, start asking me questions about other men—though they specifically meant straight men—my rising anger was about feeling unseen, unheard, and not considered. I realized it wasn't too much to ask to be considered by friends in conversations that were sensitive for me, to ask not to be put in the position of answering for all men— specifically straight men, and for bi and queer men to be considered when asking me about the *male perspective* instead of straight men being the only legitimate male perspective. As I began to reprogram my subconscious comfort zone and feel better about myself, friendships with women I'd always been drawn to were no longer a match.

Opening up to dating women again was new for me, so of course I'd have certain anxieties that felt prepubescent, of course I'd take friend's criticisms of men personally, and of course I'd have many things to relearn. Dating women again after exclusively dating men for nearly a decade was fascinating. Though the observer that animates humans remained consistent, social conditioning—the rules we agree to play by—and how we see ourselves makes the output different. Men and women have a lot of the same stories about each other: "Men are shallow," "Women are shallow," or "Men can't be trusted in the long run," "Women can't be trusted in the long run," but because of the differences in socioeconomic power in the world, it's a rigged game slotted against women and femininity. It was crystal clear that many people had untreated C-PTSD that came from somewhere. Whether that was attachment figures in childhood, enforced colonial gender, everyday misogyny, adult romantic relationships, or elsewhere, it was noticeably there.

Performing masculinity no longer felt like an act and felt more like another layer of skin. Fatefully, this began to feel like a vehement rejection of who I'd known myself to be for more than twenty-five years. Being fawned over and celebrated because of a perceived masculinity came to be a reminder of all the ways that in trying to survive and have a dynamic acting career I had to betray what came natural to me. What many people miss is that there's an aspect to the masculinity that I now possess that is defeat. I gave up. I had to, for my own wellness and livelihood. Reaching for hegemonic masculinity meant safety for me in my environment and my career as a feminine bisexual+ boy and then man. Being authentic, being human, being soft, being whimsical, being emotional, being kind, being feminine, being anything other than an unfeeling power-hungry individualist meant danger and dying. I don't think I'm the only masculine person who's had that experience. I gave up correcting people after being mislabeled. It was all an act of throwing up my hands metaphorically and saying, *Okay, fuck it, you win.* When it's clear someone is interested in me because of my alleged masculinity, it feels like they're drawn to that resignation and self-rejection.

The more I thought about it, I realized I didn't only want to be believed to be bisexual+ because I appeared more masculine. I didn't want to be showered with praise over my work because of my new adjacency to masculinity. I couldn't tolerate the elevated desirability because it now seemed to be an overt affront to my allegiance and my experiences up until that point. I started heavily relying on aesthetic tells like septum rings, eyeliner, nail polish, and fashion, but in many ways relying on consumerist symbols rather than an ideological, perceptual, or even a communication shift would always leave something to be desired. Complicated, I know. I'm still working through this and occasionally tweet about it.

I would love if you joined in on the X (formerly Twitter) conversation by using the tag #BisexualMenSpeak as frequently as you'd like to ask questions or talk about how being bisexual+ impacts the way you move through the world or whatever you want concerning bisexuality and masculinity. Check out the #BisexualMenSpeak playlist on YouTube where I've gathered over 1,000 videos of bisexual+ men and masculine-identified people speaking about their varied experiences.

NOTES

J.R. Yussuf (@JRYussuf), "I tire of people telling me I don't exist and that I'm lying," Twitter, July 15, 2018, https://twitter.com/JRYussuf/status/1018662930072600576.

J.R. Yussuf, "#BisexualMenSpeak," YouTube video playlist, July 15, 2019, www.youtube.com/playlist?list=PLkMYxg1sLLMW4mn4oLFV-aeL3tVOhxs_w.

Maria S. Tsantani, Pascal Belin, Helena M. Paterson, and Phil McAleer, "Low Vocal Pitch Preference Drives First Impressions Irrespective of Context in Male Voices but Not in Female Voices," *Perception* 45:8 (April 13, 2016), 946–63, https://doi.org/10.1177/0301006616643675.

Da'Shaun L. Harrison, *Belly of the Beast: The Politics of Anti-Fatness as Anti-Blackness* (Berkeley, CA: North Atlantic Books, 2021), 12–13.

Who to Tell, Why to Tell, and How to Tell Them

> But while coming out can be incredibly validating, a way
> to filter out people who are unsafe to be vulnerable around,
> symbolic of personal growth, a mark of acceptance of
> yourself, and can allow people to see you in your totality, the
> reality is not always as poetic, specifically for bisexual people.
>
> —J.R. YUSSUF

WHO TO TELL

Society tries to demand that bisexual+ people come out up front and tell people who we're attracted to, who we think about, who we fantasize about, who we dream about, and who we have crushes on. That's very controlling and downright weird. More importantly, it doesn't always keep us safe if we are disclosing our identity up front, as seen with Josh Ormrod, a nineteen-year-old who was left bloodied and bruised in a horrific unprovoked attack when he was affectionate with a guy, or Greg Ward, who faced an overtly anti-LGBTQ+ workplace environment and hiring discrimination in construction because of being out as bisexual+. There's a lot of risk involved when it comes to disclosing, and you have to decide for yourself if you will disclose, when you will disclose, and who you will disclose to.

SIGNS THAT SOMEONE WILL LIKELY BE SUPPORTIVE OR SAFE TO DISCLOSE TO

- One of the biggest signs that someone will likely be supportive is their willingness to speak positively about marginalized groups they do not belong to, have any familial ties to, or will not benefit from speaking up for.

- Another sign is the level to which they're aware that we've all been conditioned and socialized to prioritize certain groups, topics, and experiences over others.

- If the person has these two traits, I'd say to pay close attention to what they say and how they react to certain things in the news because this is a good sign they may be a safe person to confide in.

- Someone who shows not only a willingness to be taught but also does their own research on marginalized groups they do not belong to.

- Open-minded individuals who seek out the nuances in situations and in life also signal they may potentially be affirming.

- People who aren't stringently attached to gender roles, who don't see things in black and white, who are thoughtful, reflective, and detail-oriented.

- People who you feel a lightness around because they make you feel heard, and like you could tell them anything and it'd be understood.

- People who tend to be kind and accepting of themselves and others.

And at the same time, just because a person is all of these things, they may in fact harbor biphobic attitudes and may not be accepting or supportive of your bisexual+ identity. This is conditioning, this is in our media, this is in our culture, and it has been for a long time. Sometimes disclosing to someone close can be the catalyst for them to educate themselves, start the process of unlearning biphobia and standing in solidarity with bisexual+ communities. Sometimes disclosing to someone close may mean rejection, or them not trying to unlearn biphobia, no matter what you say. I believe that being bisexual+ is a beautiful thing, but the odds are against us. That goes for the larger society and many LGBTQ+ communities, spaces, and organizations. (The reason I use *communities* in the plural rather than the singular is that there are many LGBTQ+ communities, and just because you don't feel particularly liked, comfortable, fully at home, or welcome in a particular one does not mean you will never find one where you do.) Personally I think it's important to take time to gauge someone's potential reaction before disclosing to them, but some people don't.

THINGS TO CONSIDER

- Will this person be supportive of me?

- How relieved will I feel after I just get it out?

- Will this person out me to other people if I tell them?

- How much closer could we be once I share this part of myself with them?

- Do I want to get closer to this person, seeing as how disclosing may create a sense of intimacy that does not exist yet?

- Could they possibly be bisexual+ as well, or queer or trans?

- Is the potential fallout worth it for me?

- Would the emotional labor of educating them about bisexuality and being completely vulnerable be worth it for me?

Sometimes you'll think a person is safe to open up to, and then they're not and they out you to other people, or they sexually harass you. Then other times you'll think someone won't be affirming, and meanwhile they might be bisexual+ themselves, or they might be one of the most supportive people out there. I've felt my loneliest and most suicidal when no one in my life who I was close to *celebrated* my bisexuality. When you disclose to people in your life, you can feel a sense of relief and comfort and intimacy and hope that may not have existed before. Making harmless jokes about your bisexuality and being able to make flirty comments about people of different genders to people you're close to is one of those small things that can have such a positive impact on your mental health and the relationship in question. Letting the right people know can mean you're put in touch with a bisexual+ (or LGBTQ+) community that you didn't previously have access to. You may also be offered resources you didn't know were available. Learning these things about a person does not happen overnight; rather, it's something that takes a while to decipher. What I'm referring to is not a superficial, offhand, performative gesture at the right moments. It is a way of interacting with information and the world. This works in reverse too.

Why Bisexual+ People Don't Owe Anyone Disclosure of Their Sexuality

Choosing to disclose your bisexual+ identity is something many people will try to harass you about, control, obsess over, guilt you over—and the list goes on. Something to keep in mind is that you do not owe anyone disclosure. Not your family, not your partner, not your close friends, not your health care provider, and not LGBTQ+ organizations. Your agency to decline to reveal this information is not compromised in the least by having a bisexual+ orientation. This paramount agency extends beyond disclosure. It also applies to the choice to only engage particular genders, which also doesn't invalidate your bisexuality. There will be no shortage of people who paternalistically encourage coming out, as though it is an eternal salve, and worse still, there will be people who try to guilt bisexual+ people into coming out as though anyone else's curiosity supersedes our right to agency over what we tell to whom.

I've known I was bisexual+ for a long time, yet it hasn't gotten any easier being repeatedly told that I'm actually gay because of my dating history, and that bisexual+ women are actually straight—an overt symptom of the phallocentric cultural climate we live under. I also know firsthand that communicating attraction to more than one gender while in a relationship can be seen by one's partner as a signifier that infidelity has occurred, or a declaration that the relationship has reached its end, which makes me rightfully cautious about disclosing (though I can't exactly take back what I've already put out on the internet, which I discuss further in the "Being Out Online, Being Out in Real Life, Being Out at Work" chapter).

There are many reasons why I do not come out in real life, ranging from not wanting to be attacked to not wanting to be interrogated about my dating and sexual history, not wanting my admission of having a bisexual+ identity mean that everyone has access to my body, not wanting my donated blood to be rejected automatically, not wanting to be harassed about whether I would date a transgender person, or if I'm aware that using the word *bisexual+* invalidates nonbinary people—which it does not. All of this would be worse still if I were a bisexual+ woman, or a trans person, or nonbinary.

In these moments of disclosure, I am also expected to hold space for people to vent their frustrations over some past bisexual+ lover who did them wrong or who they felt insecure next to. I am expected to be inept in explaining the oddity of my own existence, whether or not I am polyamorous, the Kinsey scale, sexual history versus identity versus orientation, gender roles, how gender impacts bisexual+ visibility, and gender fluidity.

This happens on any given day, whether I'm at a bar, a professional event, or a café. It is exhausting and a mood killer, and it is not expected to the same degree of gays and lesbians or straight people if their orientation becomes the topic of conversation.

Bisexual+ people need to be loved and liked just like everyone else, even if certain aspects of ourselves remain hidden. You have a right to privacy. You have a right not to share everything about yourself and every aspect of your experience. Biphobia and bi erasure are not problems for us to solve, as they were not created by us, by offering ourselves up like martyrs time and time again to be killed, violated, interrogated, ignored, gaslit, or discriminated against. Although these are not problems for us to solve, we must survive them.

It is not our personal mandate to convince each person we interact with to believe bisexuality as a valid identity worthy of acknowledgment and respect. Boundaries keep us safe, and withholding personal information about yourself can allow you to be more in control of how the world reacts to you, even though this can come at a sizable cost.

But even if you could be perfectly safe, with no threat of losing your job or relationship or being harmed in any other way, though this is highly unlikely, you still do not have to disclose your sexuality. When Ms. Corey, from the notable documentary *Paris Is Burning,* said she realized that she "didn't have to bend the whole world," that she "just had to get through it," she was really in her proverbial bag. And that sentiment is one that clings to me as I come up with my own changing parameters around disclosing, which does not center anyone outside myself.

People who very strangely demand to have access to this information will make up all kinds of stories about you in order to cope. Let them.

Our sexuality is frequently discussed like it's a menace to society, like we are infectious, like our sexuality is a ball and chain that we must tell our partners about—especially if they are heterosexual women. The onus should not be made ours. We should not be asked to reveal ourselves in a world that is not made safe for us to do so. The eagerness for more bisexual+ people to come out needs to be examined and redirected toward the failings of a larger society that refuses to make space for bisexual+ people to safely exist.

SIGNS SOMEONE WILL LIKELY BE UNSUPPORTIVE OR UNSAFE TO DISCLOSE TO

+ A person who is misogynistic.
+ A person who is rigid in the way they see the world, for example, seeing things in black or white, or gay or straight.
+ A person who is judgmental.
+ A person who is scandalized by or obsessed with men on the down-low, or queer men who they assumed were straight and "tricked them."
+ A person who is preoccupied with bisexual+ men immediately disclosing their sexuality to women and conflating not disclosing with cheating on them with a man.
+ A person who puts a lot of stock into bio-essentialism.
+ A person who fixates on debates about masculinity and dominance versus femininity and submission.
+ A feminine gay or bisexual+ man who sees themselves as less manly or less worthy of respect because of these monikers.
+ A person who expresses ill feelings toward trans people.
+ A person who expresses ill feelings toward vers men.
+ A "masc4masc" guy.

I'd recommend being wary of people who fall into these categories because keeping yourself safe is essential, these individuals likely won't be affirming, and they could potentially become violent toward you. Sometimes when you say you're bisexual+, people think it means you have relinquished your ability to consent, that you've given them the green light to touch you and engage with you in a flirty or sexual manner. To these individuals, being forthcoming about your bisexuality means you are ready to be sexual with any and everyone at any time for any reason. They take you disclosing as an invitation to your body. Many hear *bisexual+* and it subconsciously eclipses your humanity, which is a significant reason many bisexual+ people don't use the label. It's so important to learn who safe people are and what safety looks and feels like.

Keep in mind that according to a Pew Research analysis, roughly 19 percent of bisexual+ people are out to close people in their lives, compared to 75 percent of gay and lesbian people. There's a reason for this.

There is a lot of value in disclosing, but there's also a lot of risk involved. Either way you go, you're not always going to be right, and you should be aware of a myriad of outcomes. Throughout all of this, I recommend being gentle with yourself and being careful, safe, and patient about this entire process because you're not going to always get it right.

WHY TO TELL

The why of disclosing is probably the most important of the three. For years I'd offer up my bisexual+ identity anytime someone mislabeled me as gay or straight in passing conversations. I'd also do it as soon as I was beginning to get to know someone because disclosing was my way of combatting bi erasure and bi invisibility. It was as though I wanted to be the shining example proving that bisexual+ Black men not only exist but that we're honest and up front about our sexuality, against popular opinion. During that time I was my most exhausted since I was constantly in a position where I was *proving* my sexuality, offering up personal information to strangers, doing so without knowing how to stop or disengage, presenting statistics and insights about the bisexual+ experience to people who couldn't actually hear me or care.

The term *sealioning* describes a subtle form of trolling involving bad faith questions. You disingenuously frame your conversation as a sincere request to be enlightened, placing the burden of educating you entirely on the other party. If your bait is successful, the other party may engage, painstakingly laying out their logic and evidence in the false hope of helping someone learn. In fact, you are attempting to harass or waste the time of the other party and have no intention of truly entertaining their point of view. Instead, you react to each piece of information by misinterpreting it or requesting further clarification, ad nauseum. The term *sealioning* comes from a *Wondermark* comic strip. This is what I experienced constantly during the aforementioned period.

Prioritize your safety and peace of mind over trying to prove that bisexuality in men and masculine-identified people is legitimate.

THINGS TO CONSIDER

- Am I doing this to distance myself from being thought of as gay?
- Am I doing this because I think asserting this makes me more acceptable than being thought of as gay would?
- Am I doing this to prove that men can be bisexual+?
- Am I doing this because straight people don't have to worry about who knows their sexuality?
- Am I doing this to frustrate the person?
- Am I doing this because I am proud?
- Am I doing this to get closer to the other person?
- Am I doing this because it's really not that big of a deal?

I proposed these questions so you'd be very clear about your reasons behind disclosing, but at the end of the day, you will make your own decisions that feel right for you, and either way, it is what it is.

HOW

1. Make sure the person you're telling is not operating heavy machinery, for example, while they're driving.

2. Sit them down in a comfortable, perhaps isolated, place, depending on who it is and the circumstances.

3. If it's a family member or someone you're close to, I recommend beginning with why you haven't told them until now. This is

completely up to you and may vary person to person. Any iteration of these will do: "I wasn't sure whether this would change things between us," "because I was afraid you'd throw me out," "because I didn't think I had to; straight people don't have to come out," "because I'm the same person and it's not that big a deal," "because I was afraid you'd judge me," "because I didn't know if you'd still love me," "because I thought it might end the relationship."

4. Next you can discuss how you realized you're bisexual+, or you can just say the words, "I'm bisexual," and see how they receive it. If the label you use is not *bisexual,* you have the option of describing what that word means to you and why it's important. Here's what I say: "Me being bi means that sometimes I have crushes on men and sometimes I have crushes on women." That's how I describe it to people I disclose to of any age or gender or social status. It is easy to understand and immediately gets to the way I like identifying myself.

5. I believe nonbinary people are valid and am very open to engaging with them. If a question comes up about nonbinary people, I say I'm definitely open to dating a nonbinary person and that I'm not leaving them out or invalidating them by identifying as bisexual+ (I discuss this further in the "Questions for Reflection" chapter), or not mentioning them up front, but that most people have not heard of and don't understand nonbinary identities, and I did not want to turn disclosing into an in-depth speech about gender.

6. When I disclosed to my parents, I made sure I said the word *bisexual* at least twice so that they could never pretend like me telling them hadn't happened, or as though I'd said another word entirely, which happens to people quite often. I disclosed over the phone because that's how I felt the safest and most in control. Both my parents were born and raised in Ondo State in Nigeria, raised as devout Christians, and grew up under the very stringent anti-LGBTQ+ law English colonizers enforced beginning in the nineteenth century and the intergenerational violence white missionaries rent on the African continent (and most other parts of the world). As a result, many Nigerians living in Nigeria and

abroad believe being LGBTQ+ is a mental illness, or that you're possessed by a demon or spirit, and the very pronouncement indicates a site of trauma or something gone awry, or is a justification for ostracization, violence, or murder. In high school my best friend's Christian mom, who'd immigrated to the United States, found out she was a lesbian, and soon after my best friend would come to school with black eyes. This persisted for months until my best friend ran away from home and eventually found shelter with Covenant House in Manhattan. Although I was a devout Christian at the time and resolved to identifying as straight indefinitely, deep down I knew I'd never even consider coming out until I was in a position of complete financial independence from my parents so that I couldn't be abused in that way, or have to live in a shelter. I waited until after I moved out at age twenty-six and was sure I was not going to have to move back in. I still wasn't 100 percent sure if coming out in person would lead to me being physically assaulted or disowned from the family or forbidden from seeing my younger siblings, and I preferred to do it over the phone because that felt right for me. I still made sure they weren't driving, that they were alone and seated. This may not work for you. You may want to be face-to-face and see the look in their eyes, and that is completely valid. You may want to send it through a text or a DM or email. That is valid too. I did what felt right for me, and it's completely up to you.

7. You can also disclose very casually by slipping it into an ongoing conversation so that it's not the focus of the conversation. This can greatly help set the tone for how you may feel about your bisexual+ identity, that it is not that big a deal, that it is only one aspect of your experience, and that you want to discuss it in a very casual, non-life-stopping, emotionally charged way. That is completely valid.

The reality is that people you tell may become physically or sexually violent and not want to talk to you anymore. They may maliciously or absentmindedly out you to other people, disown you, tell you they will never accept you or this aspect of your personhood, call it a choice, say they don't agree with it, say they're ashamed of you, ask you not to tell anyone else, pretend like it never happened, show indifference, celebrate you, accept you, thank you for telling them, tell you that they're also bisexual+ or part of the LGBTQ+ community, or simply affirm you. There is risk involved each time you disclose, but there is also great potential for an incredibly liberating experience or simply an opportunity to connect with someone in a deeper way.

Many bisexual+ people do not find disclosing useful or necessary for any relationship. Many don't do labels either, and that is also completely valid. Bisexual+ people do not owe anyone this.

NOTES

Emma Powys Maurice, "Bisexual Student Battered in 'Unprovoked and Completely Random' Homophobic Attack," PinkNews, June 19, 2021, www.pinknews.co.uk/2021/06/19/bisexual-student-josh-ormond-homophobic-attack-liverpool.

Julie Compton, "OutFront: This Advocate Couldn't Find a Bisexual Community, So He Created One," NBC News, May 18, 2017, www.nbcnews.com/feature/nbc-out/outfront-advocate-couldn-t-find-bisexual-community-so-he-created-n761536.

Dillon Couvillon, "10 Things I Learned Six Months after Coming Out," HuffPost, May 30, 2014, www.huffpost.com/entry/ten-things-i-learned-6mon_b_5412788.

Stephen A. Linstead and Garance Maréchal, "How to Overcome Phallus-Obsessed, Toxic Masculinity," The Conversation, November 3, 2017, https://theconversation.com/how-to-overcome-phallus-obsessed-toxic-masculinity-84388.

Cameron Glover, "Not Formally 'Coming Out' Didn't Make Me Less Queer," Glamour, August 22, 2017, www.glamour.com/story/formally-coming-out.

Eliel Cruz, "13 Things Never to Say to Bisexual People," Advocate.com, September 23, 2016, www.advocate.com/bisexuality/2014/06/02/13-things-never-say-bisexual-people.

"BiNet USA, "1990 Anything That Moves Bisexual Manifesto," blog post, January 20, 2014.

Kinsey Institute, "The Kinsey Scale," Indiana University, n.d., https://kinseyinstitute.org/research/publications/kinsey-scale.php.

Natasha Tracy, "What Is Biphobia?" Healthyplace, January 10, 2022, www.healthyplace.com/gender/bisexual/what-is-biphobia.

Diane Anderson-Minshall, "Ending Bi Erasure—on TV and in Our LGBT Worlds," Advocate.com, September 23, 2011, www.advocate.com/news/daily-news/2011/09/23/ending-bi-erasure-tv-and-our-lgbt-worlds.

Human Rights Campaign, "Health Disparities among Bisexual People," September 10, 2015, www.hrc.org/resources/health-disparities-among-bisexual-people.

Clarie Randall, "Coming Out (or Not): A Celebration of Autonomy," Feminist Campus, October 11, 2017, https://feministcampus.org/coming-out-or-not-a-celebration-of-autonomy.

"Performance by Dorian Corey," *Paris Is Burning,* directed by Jennie Livingston, (1990; Academy Entertainment).

David J. Ley, "Where Are All the Bisexuals Hiding?" *Psychology Today,* April 30, 2018, www.psychologytoday.com/us/blog/women-who-stray/201804/where-are-all-the-bisexuals-hiding.

Anna Brown, "Bisexual Adults Are Far Less Likely than Gay Men and Lesbians to Be 'Out' to the People in Their Lives," Pew Research Center, June 18, 2019, www.pewresearch.org/fact-tank/2019/06/18/bisexual-adults-are-far-less-likely-than-gay-men-and-lesbians-to-be-out-to-the-people-in-their-lives.

Being Out Online, Being Out in Real Life, Being Out at Work

Online

Before putting the word *bisexual*+ in your bio or attaching it to your name online, keep a few things in mind:

- What you put on the internet can be used against you if you're using your full name in combination with your picture.

- Being out online essentially means you have no control over who knows, and you should thus assume that everyone who comes across your online profiles will.

- What you put online can have real-world impacts, including being seen as hypersexual, seen as gay and lying, ostracized, overlooked, being fired, pigeonholed, sexually harassed, or something else entirely.

- Not being hired for certain jobs, especially in the worlds of education, or fired if the wrong person in your company finds out are very real potential outcomes.

- There is still a lot of stigma attached to being bisexual+, and the word *bisexual* is often seen as a lewd word that gets some users banned because on many platform it's associated with pornography.

- *Bisexual* is sometimes censored on various platforms so it cannot be searched.

- Creating a profile using an alias and a photo of your favorite animated character is a very common practice.

■ Some people use a bisexual flag twibbon around their profile picture so only other LGBTQ+ people, or people already familiar with the flag, will know. That way, your name or profile is not directly linked with the word *bisexual,* though more and more non-LGBTQ+ people are becoming aware of what this is and means.

Seeing yourself as whole on your own, and viewing your sexuality as equal parts amazing and equal parts mundane, in the way of all human sexuality, is a beautiful aim. While the way you feel about yourself supersedes the way larger society may view you, keeping yourself safe is key. Though I only occasionally receive hate directed at me because I'm out as bisexual+ online, I'm not sure of how people perceive me and how that could or would translate if I were meeting them in real life on a regular basis. I'm not sure about the jobs or networking opportunities I've missed out on. I do, however, receive a lot of unsolicited nudes, sexual advances, people telling me unasked about suspecting their boyfriend or husband is bisexual+, people who ask me to help them understand how a man could be bisexual+, messages telling me about how much god loves me and that unless I repent I will go to hell, offers from sugar daddies looking for company, and more.

I've had a gay Latinx employer who knew I was bisexual+ occasionally make sexual advances and eventually slap my ass while on the clock behind the bar serving patrons. I've had a straight white employer who's a woman constantly rub my lower back, shoulders, and arms. Both found me on social media after being hired, saw that I had *bisexual+* in my bio, and regardless of the intention, or if it was in both cases because I'm bi, I did not like my bosses touching my body or finding me on social media. I do think race as well as sexuality contributed to both bosses feeling like they had access to my body, my receptiveness to it, and the overall ease there was when it came to my personal space. Invading my space is a common thing I notice specifically white people do even before they know for sure that I'm queer. It is in predominantly white, gay spaces that I am often fetishized and approached with no regard for my personal space or autonomy, as though I am a piece of meat, as though I exist to be consumed, as though I exist solely for their pleasure or adoration. It is a feeling I hope no one reading this will make someone else feel or ever experience themselves. Unfortunately, many bars and restaurants do not have HR departments, and even if they did, the HR department functions to protect the company's ass, not yours.

Discussing being completely out is tricky because it is incredibly inconsequential to so many bisexual+ people, but then at the same time it is the biggest of deals to others. It's a strange thing because prior to coming out in real life and online, it can feel so intense and important, and like it will change everything if people know. As someone living in New York City in my thirties, I often find that people are far too preoccupied with their own life, their goals, their jobs, their drama. Many people may see your profile and make a split-second decision to follow or not, to judge or not, to see that it says *bisexual* or not. Many people's attention spans are so short, and the world has demanded it be that way for quite some time now—so people absorb information quickly and move on to the next thing—that so many people in your life as well as strangers may just forget about this detail or not care all that much. Many of these people will see *bisexual* and really see that you're saying you're gay; it's what a lot of people think when they see the LGBTQ+ acronym or any identity that falls under it. On the other hand, there are people who will not follow you, talk about you, and judge you because of this. Let them. If you've gotten to a place where disclosing online is important to you or because you simply want to, you should go for it, and remember it says more about the people who may judge you because of this than it does you. What they think is not your business, although it can affect you.

If you can't tell by now, I do have serious regrets about being so vocal about being bisexual+, both online and in real life. At various points as a young adult, disclosing was a knee-jerk reaction, a way to correct people who insisted I was gay, or at times, straight. It was less a deliberate choice to reveal something intimate about a part of my experience and identity. Then in my mid-twenties, when I finally began to become more comfortable and grounded in my bisexuality, I began to tell people as a personal form of combatting bi erasure, although it does not only operate on a micro level. I'd say I was bisexual+ in every setting I could, to correct and also demand that bisexual+ people—men in particular—be respected and seen. I meant to take on the entire world by myself. This approach put me in many conversations and situations that drained me, some that harmed me and resulted in me being sexually harassed, groped, and on the receiving end of a line of questioning with no real intent from the other party to actually learn, grow, or change.

When you look up my name online, the word *bisexual* quickly comes up, outing me to potential love interests, employers, or anyone who decides to look me up online. I am not saying "Don't come out online" or that you will have the same experiences as I did. I am simply saying that I wish more people in LGBTQ+ communities—bisexual+ ones specifically— were more honest about some of the ramifications that exist for bisexual+ men in particular, instead of pumping the same old "It gets better (once you come out)" message because that's not everyone's experience.

There are more subtle ways to indicate only to bisexual+ people that you are also bisexual+, like putting a blue, pink, and purple heart in your bio to represent the colors of the bisexual flag; it's likely only other bi-sexual+ people would instantly recognize it. Many bisexual+ people simply default to using the laurel twibbons around their avatar picture made up of colors of the bisexual flag. There is also a pansexual flag version of this.

In Real Life

In college I studied abroad in Florence, Italy, for a semester. One night there stands out to me in particular. It was a night I'd spent flirting with a girl who was also part of my program. A group of us from the program had spent the night crammed in someone's apartment drinking wine, laughing too loud, and singing some awful song from the Top 40, as we did back in those days. The night was winding down, people had already split into their groups of twos or threes, and the girl I'd spent the night flirting with had ended up on the balcony with me, looking out at the stars. I eventu-ally went in for a kiss, and she reciprocated. It was magic. I was kissing a beautiful girl I'd liked since we'd met on a balcony in Italy under the stars. Perfect movie moment. When we broke, the first words out of her mouth were, "Why do you have to be gay?" I quickly responded that, "I'm not gay, I'm bi," to which she said, "Yeah . . . but you know what I mean." That really crushed me, and articulated very clearly to me that most straight women didn't believe that a feminine bisexual+ man could actually be bisexual+. There was no amount of flirting, kissing, movie moments, com-pliments, or anything that could convince somebody you're bisexual+ if they're committed to believing bisexuality in men does not exist.

You'll never be able to prove it, as seen with Ray Fuller, a bisexual+ Jamaican man seeking asylum in the United States because of fear of being persecuted and tortured because of his bisexuality. The Seventh Circuit U.S. Court of Appeals dismissed his petition for asylum, convinced that bisexual+ people don't face persecution for being bisexual+ and disbelief as most of Fuller's previous partners were women. Fuller had already had his face sliced for being "gay," had been stoned and mocked at college, and thrown out of his home after being shot at for his sexuality. As also seen with Orashio Edwards, a Jamaican man who was asked to prove his bisexuality by a judge who could grant him asylum on the same basis. He showed the court pictures of him having sex with a man, which was illegal in Jamaica, and the judge still did not believe him. "It was extremely degrading for me to have to do, and still they didn't believe me," Orashio Edwards told *The Independent*. Civil servants in the UK Home Office apparently didn't believe him because he'd been married to a woman before, even though he'd been in a relationship with a man for the past two years, and asserted that he was trying to hoodwink the system.

I recently learned about a term called tribal gaslighting and immediately thought of bisexual+ people. Gaslighting is the denial of another person's reality that happens on an individual basis. This usually causes a person to doubt themselves. Tribal gaslighting is when more than one person, usually many people, support that twist in reality, insisting that your reality and experiences aren't real. The latter has a much more powerful effect, and it happens to bisexual+ people, especially men, especially feminine men, all the time.

TRIBAL GASLIGHTING

Here are some ways to confront and heal from tribal gaslighting from Dr. Ramani Durvasula, a psychologist and narcissism expert:

- The greatest tribal gaslighting repellent is someone from the outside validating your reality.

- To be more gaslighting resistant, you have to be willing to hold onto your own reality and resolve: "This is what I believe."

- Step back from conversations and reshape the relationships you've got, or even step away from them. You don't have to say it out loud because there's no point in engaging a person denying your reality. This person is not at a place in their life for whatever reason to be able to hold your reality alongside theirs. This isn't a healthy space for you.

- Each time you gaslight a person, you diminish them, and what that does is take a relationship that was once somewhat equal and pushes the other person down. By gaslighting a group, you push them down.

- This approach isn't a quick fix. This is a massive shift in how people view human relationships.

I hate that so many bisexual+ people feel responsible for bi erasure when we are the victims of it. This is internalized biphobia. We are not the ones who teach people to see the world in binaries. We are not the ones erasing ourselves. We have to sift through binary thinking and tribal gaslighting in order to understand, embrace, and feel pride about ourselves. I hate that so many bisexual+ people experience anxiety when deciding to express attraction toward a celebrity or a random person. Do we bring up being attracted to another person of a different gender to signal our bisexuality, or do we allow the other person to think we are either gay or straight? Many of us feel like we need to constantly disclose our bisexuality so as to not erase ourselves, or so that we're not labeled dishonest, or that disclosing will somehow put a stop to bi erasure. I tried this approach for roughly a decade and it did not end bi erasure; it launched me into precarity. Visibility without protection or collective education is a trap.

When disclosing in person nowadays, I say I'm "bi" and leave off the *sexual* part. I've noticed that I still encounter questions here and there, but the questions tend to be less sexual in nature. Instead of people who don't know my last name asking me how many women I've had sex with or what age I was when I had my first threesome, I get questions about some of the differences between dating a woman and a man. I say bi very casually and have a change of topic or comment to get myself out of the spotlight and signal that I don't really want to make a big deal about it or talk about it for too long.

Something to keep in mind is that the same treatment exists in many LGBTQ+ spaces and events. Pride is often a site of discomfort for many bisexual+ people, and this is increased if you are dating a woman or someone who is assumed to be a woman and are there with them. Many people in these spaces and at LGBTQ+ events in general make jokes insinuating that bisexual+ men don't truly exist. The sentiment is that we're secretly gay, using women to pretend we're not gay, and are too afraid to come all the way out, that we're confused, that we're trying to deceive ourselves and the women we engage.

Running into people you know at Pride events and LGBTQ+ spaces who think you're straight or have seen you with women in the past or present may be a thing too. They may ask what you're doing there or ask if your girlfriend knows or may assume that you're cheating on them with a man or that you're not so secretly gay. The opposite may happen as well; they may not make a big deal about it and assume you're bisexual+, or they may go about their business because they don't care. People I went to school with or were from where I'm from in Queens would see me at Pride in Manhattan in my early twenties and make comments about how they didn't know I was gay or that they always knew I was gay. As I got more comfortable with being bisexual+ and unlearned homophobia, I've learned to just let it go and keep walking along the parade, but it does suck to never have my sexuality accurately guessed.

HOW TO COMBAT BI ERASURE

- Request that organizations hold seminars or provide resources about the spectrum of sexuality with a marked focus on bisexuality+.

- Remind people that sexuality exists on a spectrum and can be fluid over the course of one's life.

- Make it a point to remember when people or celebrities say they're bisexual+ and correct people who mislabel them.

- Remind people that the single largest group under the LGBTQ+ umbrella are bisexual+ people: pansexual, fluid, no label, and so on.

- Remind people that the reason they may not know of any openly bisexual+ people is because as a society we do not make it safe for bisexual+ people to exist in peace—not because there aren't any.

- Remind people that the sexuality of many bisexual+ historical figures within LGBTQ+ liberation, Black liberation, and social justice have been erased.

- Remind people that bisexual+ individuals are erased on a daily basis when the assumption is that people are either gay or straight.

- Remind others of the importance of self-determination inherent to someone's bisexual+ label and getting people's labels, or lack thereof, right.

At Work

If you come out to one person at work, you've likely come out to everyone at your job. People at work love to gossip generally and even more so when there's downtime or an idle moment. Don't take it personally; any relatively exciting news about anyone who works there is something to discuss. They may not individually tell everyone, but they may let it slip to one or two people who may do the same thing, and so on. There are many exceptions to this rule, and if you preface disclosing by telling them not to tell anyone, that may help—but it may not. Something I had to learn years ago (and still learn again on a daily basis) is that even though you may spend most of your time with your coworkers, and you may develop a friendly relationship with them, they are not your friends. You may share information with one another and learn each other's habits and strengths and weaknesses and about one another's ambitions and the like, but both of you are there for money or to advance your careers. You would not spend as much time with them or know as much about them or feel as comfortable around them if it were not for the money you both earn at that job. If you don't mind this information about you being out there, people potentially gossiping about you or testing out bisexual+ stereotypes on you, then tell whoever, whatever. The bottom line is that coworkers are not your friends. Proceed accordingly.

You may hang a picture of your significant other in your workspace, and based on the assumed gender of that person, people will likely categorize you as gay or straight.

HISTORY

Taking this deep dive into bisexual+ history, and LGBTQ+ history more generally, dug up a myriad of emotions within me, from shock to pride, joy, anger, and finally sadness. So many of our contributions, experiences, and lives were erased beyond human knowing. So many of us have been whittled down so as not to *complicate* things, so that our existence won't *distract,* so as to not *confuse* people, so that the fruits of our efforts won't be ill received, so our mere existence in our totality won't be seen as divisive. Many bisexual+ pioneers and figures are continuously erased or continuously ignored, yet they still showed up and got things done. We're often posed as dishonest interlopers who've jumped onto the LGBTQ+ rights train rather than pioneers present and leading at every leg of the way, and that is incredibly inaccurate, dangerous, and devastating.

Bisexual+ people played a critical role in LGBTQ+ movements for equality, but in addition to being erased, many felt pressured to, or frankly had to, hide their bisexuality and identify as gay. The thinking being that homophobia was at the root of transphobia and biphobia, and if homophobia no longer existed, neither would the other two. Also, the thinking was that *homophobia* was interchangeable with discrimination against sexual minorities and having an atypical experience of gender, and that bisexual+ people would inherently be less committed to the cause. The talking points have largely remained the same about all bisexual+ people having straight-passing privilege and having the ability to enter a relationship with a different gender, be assumed to be straight, that discrimination based on who you partner with is the only legitimate form of sexual oppression, and all their problems would go away. As I discussed earlier, we are not all assumed to be straight. Being assumed to be straight is often conditional, isolating, and painful, and our oppression is not solely in who we love or fuck. In order to contribute to the movement, many bisexual+ people largely had their sexualities erased and were mislabeled as gay. That violence is forgotten, and the result of that violent erasure is weaponized against us to this day. Many gay and lesbian people ask insincere questions about where bisexuals were during all of these significant moments in the fight for equality and justice, and many come up with the story that we were all at home with our wives, or husbands for bisexual+ women, enjoying our straight privilege. No matter how many facts you present, or historical figures, or context surrounding why many bisexual+ people referred to themselves as gay rather than bisexual+, they're not willing or perhaps even able to hear this. Some people are hell-bent on preserving an image of who and what bisexual+ people are, and that sounds like a very sad reality.

It's frustrating that the contributions of bisexual+ people are not readily available in schools and community centers and that more people in the LGBTQ+ community aren't at all aware. I would have had a much easier time knowing that we have an extensive history spanning the centuries in every field of human enterprise; that we have always found a way to make room for ourselves. There is pride that comes with knowing that you're capable of accomplishing things you hadn't imagined, that you have something in common with people who've made a difference or who've simply made it through the obstacle course that life is. I have not listed every piece of bisexual+ history there is, as that would be unexhaustive and impossible since we are so often labeled lesbian, gay, or straight. I've instead decided mainly to focus on recorded contributions of bisexual+ individuals and groups that I could find that stuck out to me. For this and a description of LGBTQ+ culture in different regions of the world, refer to the supplement at www.jryussuf.com/additionals.

NOTES

Nancy Marcus, "Immigration and Seventh Circuit Judges Reject Bisexual Man's Request for Protection; Here's Why They Were Wrong," Lambda Legal, August 19, 2016, www.lambdalegal.org/blog/20160819_ray-fuller -judges-reject-bisexual-mans-request-for-protection.

Thom Senzee, "Bisexual Seeking Asylum Resorts to Photos When Asked to Prove It by UK Officials," Advocate.com, May 11, 2015, www .advocate.com/world/2015/05/10/bisexual-asylum-seeker-humiliated -trying-prove-sexuality-uk-officials-0.

Ramani Durvasula and MedCircle, "Intimate versus Tribal Gaslighting: Differences and How to Spot Them," YouTube video, February 4, 2021, www.youtube.com/watch?v=trh_eTkZLeU.

Andrea Downey, "New Research Finds We're All Bisexual," New York Post, March 14, 2018, https://nypost.com/2018/03/14/new-research-finds -were-all-bisexual.

Health and Wellness

I have to be honest. On editing this chapter, I felt an immense wave of sadness come over me because I was reminded just how much I'd internalized my own oppression and the impossible standards I'd held myself to for years. *Don't be a statistic* and *Pull yourself up by your bootstraps* are lessons that've been drilled into me since before I can remember. Both my parents emigrated from Nigeria, I grew up around other Black people, and I learned early that since I was not heterosexual, societal support or care would be sparse. Being a respectable Black boy, then man, who did not sag his pants or use the N-word or wear baggy clothes or listen to rap or express anger in front of white people or be too loud in front of non-Black people or do poorly in school or associate with certain kinds of Black people was a priority of mine well through undergrad. Being a respectable bisexual+ man who did not have a lot of sex or omit his bisexuality or go on dates with men and women concurrently or have casual sex with more than one gender at a time or have an MMF threesome or consider nonmonogamy or express rage at straight or gay people over bi erasure was a priority of mine until I turned thirty. Respectability was an attempt at accessing social mobility and trying to survive, but it was also an attempt to separate myself from harmful stereotypes, from the communities I belonged to, and in some ways to betray these marginalized groups. I've taken so much individual responsibility for structural failures, and it still hasn't shielded me from anti-Black racism or biphobia. Hyper-independence in the area of health was definitely a trauma response for me that led me to learn as much as I could about wellness, sex, and sexuality so that I'd feel protected, as it was clear I would not be getting that protection from school, my community at the time, or the government. The lengths I went to achieve these things were taxing on my mind and heart, required a lot of numbing and contorting, and I still faced anti-Blackness and biphobia at every turn, though it was not as sharp.

Becoming securely attached at an individual level was not enough, especially because the work does not stop there, as I'm met with environmental and systemic traumas that seek to tell me that I'm shameful, defective, unlovable, untrustworthy, and evil; I don't belong, I'm not enough, I'm rejected, I'm alone, I'm unimportant, I'm unsafe, I'm excluded, I'm misunderstood, I'm disrespected, I'm powerless, and I'm unheard. That's more than enough to create an insecure attachment style, even if my earliest bonds were secure.

In *Belly of the Beast,* Da'Shaun L. Harrison argues:

> *According to the World Health Organization, health is the state of complete physical, mental, and social well-being and not just the absence of disease or infirmity. As I interpret it, this means that for one to be healthy, they must not only be nondisabled but must also be in an environment that allows for them to feel mentally secure, physically safe, and socially well. As such, this means that Black people—especially those of us who exist with multiple marginalized identities—are always already unhealthy because we are always already unsafe.*

In addition, society at large doesn't make it safe to exist along the bisexual+ continuum, outside of a binary it stringently enforces. A huge impetus for leaving Christianity (which I discuss further in the "Bisexuality and Spirituality" chapter), investing in personal growth and mental wellness, learning about race, sexuality, and gender beginning in 2012, centered my own optimal health. Health in every area of my life has been central to my identity since—something I naively thought was neutral and untouched by white supremacy. And it has only been over the last few years that I've come to deeply understand that the foundation of Western psychology in both study and practice is ableism, and the foundation of physical health is fatphobia and the "ascetic aesthetic," as Sabrina Strings mentions in *Fearing the Black Body,* explaining that both are inherently anti-Black. Health as we know it is an aesthetic defined by what whiteness has shown us over and over again, a standard that Black, people of color, LGBTQ+, fat, disabled, and poor people will struggle to, or never be able to, reach. Socioeconomic status has been proven time and again to be a cardinal influence on someone's overall wellness, even though most people still consider BMI—a racist, sexist, unscientific, inadequate measure of health—to be an accurate gauge of well-being. When people are resistant to detangling being fat from being *unhealthy,* I know that it is a similar conundrum that bisexual+ people face in that the bias is one that has been unchallenged and then compounded over time. It's a conundrum that exists on the belief level that white supremacy has targeted in all of us. I didn't realize that chasing health as a Black bisexual+ man living under a white-supremacist society was much like the carrot and stick metaphor. It's a cruel, ceaseless, impossible task.

In this chapter I go over some of the health disparities bisexual+ men and masculine-identified people face, talk about the ways I've maneuvered, resources that exist, preventative measures that may work, and ways to combat these things more broadly. I provide a lot of practical individualistic tips; some are inaccessible and privileged, some cliché yet effective. Take what you need and discard what you don't, keeping in mind that oppression is not the fault of the oppressed. The system is doing its job of maintaining social order, suffocating, and evading, and it will continue to do so until it is destroyed.

HEALTH

When it comes to heart disease, blood pressure levels, cancer, smoking, alcohol abuse, education, poverty, salary, sexual harassment in the workplace, and mental illness, bisexual+ people fare worse than our straight and gay counterparts. California college student Juan Ceballos was fatally shot by a coworker for being bisexual+, and very little news coverage or responses were made by major LGBTQ+ organizations. In reporting of Juan's murder, it was sometimes said to be a hate crime over his sexuality, or he was incorrectly labeled gay, so he was labeled as gay in death. The same violence in life and in death has happened to countless bisexual+ people throughout history and will continue to happen until bi erasure and biphobia are put to an end. Much of the research around bisexual+ people's meager health and wellness shows that this is due to stigma, poor representation in the media, a lack of support in straight communities and LGBTQ+ communities alike, a lack of training by health care providers, and not acknowledging bisexuality+ as its own distinct sexuality requiring specific and immediate attention.

Here's what some of the statistics say:

- Only 28 percent of bisexual+ people say that all the important people in their life know they are bisexual+, compared to 77 percent of gay men and 71 percent of lesbians.

- Nearly half of bisexual+ people report that they are not out to any of their coworkers (49 percent) compared to just 24 percent of lesbian and gay people.

- Approximately 25 percent of bisexual+ men and 30 percent of bisexual+ women live in poverty, compared to 15 percent and 21 percent of non-LGBTQ+ men and women, respectively, and 20 percent and 23 percent of gay men and lesbians.

- 20 percent of bisexual+ people report experiencing a negative employment decision based on their identity, and almost 60 percent of bisexual+ people report hearing anti-bisexual+ jokes and comments on the job.

- When bisexual+ survivors of violence interact with police, however, they are three times more likely to experience police violence than people who are not bisexual+.

- Bisexual+ people have high rates of poor physical and mental health. Physical disparities include higher rates of hypertension, poor or fair physical health, smoking, and risky drinking than non-LGBTQ+ people, lesbians, or gay men. Despite these disparities, and perhaps compounding them, bisexual+ people are less likely than gay men or lesbians to be out to their health care providers.

- Bisexual+ people experience higher rates of sexual and intimate partner violence (rape, physical violence, stalking) than gay, lesbian, and straight people.

- 30 percent of bisexual+ men are smokers compared to 21 percent of gay men and 18 percent of straight men.

- In the 2016 report *Invisible Majority: The Disparities Facing Bisexual People and How to Remedy Them,* the Movement Advancement Project illustrates how, while more than half of the LGBTQ+ community identifies as bisexual+, bisexual people experience alarming rates of invisibility, societal rejection, violence, discrimination, and poor physical and mental health—often at rates higher than their lesbian and gay peers.

- Bisexual+ men and women have the highest smoking rates of any subgroup for which data are readily available. States that have collected data on bisexual+ people via surveys found smoking rates within the population to be between 30 and 40 percent.

- Bisexual+ men who are sexually active with men are at higher risk for anal cancer due to an increased risk of becoming infected with human papillomavirus (HPV), the virus that causes genital and anal warts. Smoking is also among the risk factors for anal cancer.

- Bisexual+ adults (47.4 percent) are significantly more likely to report experiencing intimate partner violence than heterosexual adults (17.2 percent).

- Research has suggested that bisexual+ adults have the lowest level of emotional well-being among people of other sexual orientations.

When it comes to coping, many of us develop destructive habits and coping skills that can offer immediate relief but lead to a harmful cycle or have adverse consequences that can be costly. This knee-jerk impulse to reach for unhealthy things that provide immediate relief is human nature and often continues until people are provided with the right amount of awareness, support, resources, strategies, and motivations to make lasting change. Thus it makes sense that one of the most underserved communities under the LGBTQ+ umbrella would face these challenges at these rates.

Life can be tough even if all your basic needs are met, but when I'm feeling down, I enact these healthy coping skills to pass the time and get me through uncomfortable feelings: taking a walk, exercising regularly, putting on comfortable pajamas and curling up in bed, going to sleep, reading, talking to a friend, journaling, calling my therapist, watching TV or a movie, cleaning, listening to my favorite music, writing about how I'm feeling, recording a voice note about how I'm feeling, redecorating, singing, playing my favorite album, playing an instrument.

There have been studies that show the resonance from pianos reverberates through the nervous system, calms us down, and can make us feel euphoric. I can't stress how far having a balanced diet full of lots of dark leafy greens, fruits, fatty acids, as well as regular exercise and at least seven hours of sleep each night will go. Brushing your teeth at least twice a day dramatically reduces your risk factor for liver cancer and heart disease.

There are so many studies that show making these things a priority will reduce anxiety, depression, and a whole host of other health issues that affect us disproportionately. Approaching your health as a bisexual+ man or masculine-identified person in a multipronged holistic way is nothing short of advisable. Human beings are so strong and full of wonder, and at the same time quite fragile and finicky. One small change to our diet or sleep regimen or lifestyle can make a world of difference, and a whole host of long-lasting lifestyle changes can reverse illnesses and fundamentally change how we see ourselves and move through the world.

What I did:

- Started my healing journey by going to therapy.

- Became vegetarian. There were many studies in 2012 that linked meat consumption to depression, although now conflicting studies render this hypothesis inconclusive.

- Read books about mental wellness, emotional intelligence, stress reduction, and how to be a better communicator.

- Started working out daily, although I will say there are many aspects of fitness culture that are extremely unhealthy and mask eating disorders like orthorexia, anorexia, binging and purging, and body dysmorphia, not to mention normalizing fatphobia, perfectionism, and maintaining a very rigid sense of control over one's body.

- Avoided negative depictions and comments about bisexual+ individuals by blocking people online and unsubscribing from publications who perpetuate this. I am also very careful about who I become close to, and test the waters using the vetting process I went over in the "Who to Tell, Why to Tell, and How to Tell Them" chapter. I also sometimes ask other bisexual+ people about their experience and opinion before I dive into LGBTQ+ shows, movies, events, organizations, and literature.

- Found affirming bisexual+ YouTube channels, people, artists, organizations, podcasts, TV shows, and movies.

■ Eventually found a therapist well-versed in attachment theory and tools to reprogram my subconscious mind and heal my nervous system, which can fuel lifelong change. This has been one of the most impactful things I've ever done for my healing, self-awareness, and altering the trajectory of my life.

Sometimes you just don't have the energy or motivation to do these things; fighting depression is not as simple as willing your way out of it, and you may need professional help. As a preemptive measure, finding a therapist who is bi-friendly is paramount, and asking someone to do this leg work for you may have to be the route you take.

Four Questions Every Bisexual+ Guy Should Ask a Potential Therapist

As a bisexual+ Black man who was drawn to therapy to grow my confidence and understanding of myself, I have not always had positive experiences with therapists surrounding sexuality or race. Between 2011 and 2015, I saw four different therapists, and while each taught me a few valuable life skills—like how to speak up for myself—they also set me back on my mission to embrace my bisexuality. I had to navigate not being believed, not having treatment specifically geared toward supporting my particular needs as a bisexual+ man, and having my already fragile enthusiasm toward engaging with women shot down and redirected.

When it became clear, in 2012, that therapist number four also lacked the knowledge and experience to talk about my bisexuality, I decided to intentionally avoid the topic for the duration of our time together. Instead, I'd talk about work stress, moving back home after college, and mental hygiene. I'd occasionally bring up things I couldn't handle on my own regarding dating men, but I'd keep any fears, insecurities, and challenges I had regarding women to myself—which really sucked.

Looking back, I recognize how much I could have benefited from a bi-friendly therapist. Had I known what I was getting into with that fourth therapist, I could have saved myself a lot of frustration and disappointment. That's why I talked to L'Oréal McCollum, the mental health training manager of the Black Emotional and Mental Health Collective (BEAM), about questions every bi man can ask their therapist during a consultation.

1. Ask them: "What has your experience working with men who are bisexual+ or pansexual been like?"
You want to hear: "That they believe that bisexuality and pansexuality are valid identities," McCollum says, "and that they are aware of the impact that masculinity and its intersections with race, ethnicity, and religion can have on clients' identification with and disclosure of a nonheterosexual orientation, especially bisexuality and pansexuality." It's also important to make sure they've "worked with more than a few bisexual+ men or masculine folk" and are "knowledgeable about various ways in which bisexual+ men and masculine folks' concerns differ from men and masculine folks of other sexualities," McCollum says. If they haven't worked with this group and aren't bisexual+ themselves, then you want to hear that "they are [at the very least] committed to doing the work to expand their proficiency on an ongoing basis," McCollum adds.

Red flags to watch for:

- They have no experience working with bisexual+ men, nor have they done training on how to work with them. "Yes, we health and healing professionals must start somewhere," McCollum says. "However, there are distinct nuances to understanding the experiences of bi+ men and masculine folks that require the professional to be clear on the many ways that these identities and their experiences can differ from others within the LGBTQ+ communities."

- They make assumptions on what *bisexual, pansexual,* or any other label means to you.

- Any attempts at bisexual+ erasure or commentary conflating these identities with the experiences of gay men and masculine folks, "such as suggesting that they have worked with gay men or masculine folks before and therefore are aware of the needs and experiences of bi+ men and masculine folks," McCollum explains.

- Any discomfort in answering the question. "If you sense this, it is possible that the professional may not be adept in their understanding of the unique ways that masculinity and bisexuality or pansexuality can intersect and therefore impact every other aspect of our lives," McCollum says.

2. Ask them: "How do you respond to questions and concerns that come up that may be outside of your area of expertise or lived experience?"

You want to hear: That they are aware of their limitations. "That they regularly seek support, resource-sharing, and professional development opportunities from their peers and clinical supervisors," McCollum says. "And that they respect their clients' decisions to seek a professional who best suits their needs, whenever necessary." You also want to hear that they are happy to refer you to another trusted professional with expertise relevant to your needs, if you request it. "A mindful and self-reflexive therapist has already considered this possibility and will already have a list available of trusted sources," McCollum says.

Red flags to watch for:

- Any indications that the professional cannot consider who they are in relation to others, the impact of this on their worldview, and its impact on the client-therapist dynamic. "They may not be the appropriate person to respond to certain questions and concerns, and that it is okay," McCollum says. "If more clinicians acknowledged these truths and guided their clients in the direction of the person most appropriate to serving their needs, there would be far less harm done within client-therapist relationships."

3. Ask them: "Can you share how you go about addressing bias that may come up in our work?"

You want to hear: "That they attend weekly peer or clinical supervision to talk about, process, and address any issues," such as bias and counter-transference, that may come up in therapeutic sessions, McCollum says. "And that they do their own personal therapy work to process any challenges they may experience in all areas of their life."

Red flags to watch for:

- Any judgments or critiques they may offer within the session. "It is not a matter of how 'we' would do something if we were the ones in our clients' situations—it's about validating their experiences wherever relevant and necessary," McCollum says.

- A lack of consultation with peers or supervisors. "It is imperative that we clinicians do the work to address our relationships to the many 'isms' that exist. It's not a matter of *if* they exist within our personal and professional lives, it's a matter of how they show up, and therefore, impact our perspectives and engagement with others," McCollum says.

- Not being able to accept feedback or work through areas of concern with their clients.

4. Ask them: "Can you please share with me your thoughts on the psychological impact of heterosexism, white supremacy, and oppression?"

You want to hear: That they appreciate you bringing these concepts into the space. "It is commonplace that clinicians provide their areas of expertise particularly because they have direct influence on the ways that we live our lives, how we interact with others, and how our varying identities may be viewed. Bonus points if the clinician understands and can apply said understanding to the harm that heterosexism, white supremacy, and oppression has on the collective," McCollum says. You want to get a sense "that they are aware of how these issues can impact one's well-being and that they've done a lot of work to uncover how these issues affect their own life and well-being."

Red flags to watch for:

- Difficulty with answering the question, which could signal discomfort or even apathy, according to McCollum. "Considering the nature of the question, it would be necessary that the therapist be adept in theoretical knowledge at the minimum, have comfort and confidence addressing the topics, be able to apply their understanding to the circumstances of their clients' lives, as well as validate their experiences."

- Attempts by the therapist to have you explain these concepts to them.

- "Any attempt to deflect from the line of questioning or disengage from the conversation, unless you have reached the end of the session," McCollum says. "In the case of the latter, the onus is on the professional to acknowledge the significance of the question, commend the client on their courage to ask the question, and be sure to address it in a follow-up session."

This was meant to offer guidance on beginning a client-therapist relationship on the right foot, but it's not an exhaustive, foolproof list. It's also worth remembering that a therapist may answer the questions perfectly and still not be the right fit for you.

Unexpectedly, the fourth therapist I worked with has grown and is now quite bi-affirming. Believing in people's ability to grow in an ever-evolving society while not basing decisions on their potential is important. People can educate themselves and grow; just keep in mind this shouldn't be at your expense, especially in a mental health setting. If it's not working out, don't be afraid to look for someone new.

- BiZone (www.bizone.org) is a great resource for finding bisexual-affirming therapists in your state.

- Ayana is a teletherapy app that matches marginalized communities to therapists who share their background.

Something to keep in mind is that the number of bisexual+-affirming therapists may be limited, and not all of them will be easily reachable, affordable, or take your insurance.

A warning about many therapists who say they are LGBTQ+ friendly more generally:

- They sometimes have unchecked bias, especially toward men who are bisexual+.

- Just because a therapist says they are LGBTQ+ friendly or have clients who are LGBTQ+ does not mean they are equipped to be of service to each group in that acronym.

- A therapist who is supportive of gay men might not be equipped to be supportive of a bisexual+ man.

- Don't be afraid to ask questions about how they are committed to or engage the bisexual+ community outside their therapy practice.

■ Having a therapist who does not believe men can be bisexual+ can cause a lot of psychological harm and it is not appropriate to have to educate your therapist on this.

■ Therapists are only human. They do have biases, whether they're aware of and working through them or not. Some have difficulty acknowledging they are not the right fit for you when it comes to supporting your bisexual+ identity specifically. Watch not only their words but also if their behaviors, attitudes, and whether their recommended treatments and tools make you feel more confident, comfortable, validated, or explore your desire with people of more than one gender.

Many, many gay men who are deeply ashamed of their sexuality tell their therapists and other people in their lives they are straight or bisexual+ because they're not ready to face their sexuality, or as if to lessen the blow. Through work, exploration, and self-discovery, they accept that identifying as gay feels true to them when they previously identified as bisexual+. Many places across the country and world are unsafe, and it's not celebrated or seen as normal or valid to be gay; not that being bisexual+ is seen as any more valid. The AIDS epidemic is not distant history, and in many places in the world it is still a very current present crisis blamed on gay and bisexual+ men. In the United States, gay men were painted as the purveyors of the virus and bisexual+ men were depicted as the reason heterosexual people ever contracted it, especially in the Black community. Because of this misinformation, and so much more, many gay men have a hard time admitting that they are gay, and many therapists are far more used to having to go through the process of facilitating them going through this process of self-acceptance than they are helping bisexual+ clients embrace a bisexual+ identity. This is the fault of white-supremacist heteronormative society, not gay men who have this experience—though gay men who assert that all bisexual+ men are not really bisexual+ also have blood on their hands. Many therapists don't have the range, training, sensitivity, or nuance required to support and affirm bisexual+ men, though I am hopeful that this will change soon.

MORE ON THERAPY

People of various abilities can benefit from various forms of therapy in a number of ways. People go to therapy for interview prep, work stress, to get better at negotiating, because they want to get better at communicating with others, because they want to feel happier, because they are feeling overwhelmed with life in general, because they are feeling lost, because they want to be able to connect with others, sexuality and gender struggles, family issues, childhood trauma, trauma in general, depression, anxiety, substance abuse, obsessive compulsive disorder, eating disorders, self-esteem, anger, HIV and AIDS, and the list goes on. All of these reasons for seeking out a therapist are valid. The way I was able to find therapy helpful, even when my therapists had bias or were unequipped to support me, is that I looked at my challenges as if they were an onion with layers I had to peel back and work through one by one. Though I look back on some of that time, and I can recognize some of the ways I was harmed in that environment. I used whatever expertise they did have to peel back other layers that eventually got me to a place where I could do the work on healing my own wounding around my sexuality. There are mental health professionals of various races, genders, and sexualities who have dedicated a part of their lives to learning how to aid and facilitate a space where people address these things in a safe, confidential way. As men and masculine-identified people, we are often taught not to ask for help. As men and masculine-identified people, we oftentimes think that because we have a source of income, have friends, and are in a relationship, we don't need any help, and certainly not the help of a therapist. Seeking help from a therapist does not mean you are incapable, and neither does needing help. It's part of what makes us human. Asking for help means you have the strength and courage to admit where you are in this very moment and recognize that you have the ability to improve in some areas with the right support. There is no shame in that.

Also, I want to make it very clear that talk therapy is not the be-all and end-all. Having access to therapy is a privileged thing, and not having access does not mean you are damned. Therapy only helped me because I wanted to try it, I believed there were areas of my life I wanted to work on, and I could access the kinds of therapy that I found beneficial. I don't think a person can see a therapist and get much from the experience if they're not ready to change, they're not ready to face themselves, or they believe they cannot be helped. In the beginning, I'd come into my therapy sessions, sit down across from my therapist, and think, *Fix me! You're a therapist, aren't you? This is your job, isn't it? Why am I not fixed?* But I learned that I wasn't broken in the first place, and that it doesn't exactly work like that. I had to be active with my own mental health outside of sessions and could not treat my troubles as though they were anyone else's responsibility, even my therapist's. I had to heal myself using the tools I was given. I had to do the work in the interim between therapy sessions: getting at least seven hours of sleep, exercising, practice emotional processing, distancing myself from people who are not good for my mental health, asking for my needs to be met, and setting boundaries, as well as to have a certain willingness to try new things overall. Therapy is simply not accessible for everyone, and not everyone wants to go, but even outside therapy, taking care of your mental and emotional health is paramount, and talk therapy is not the only way. If you're just showing up to a therapist—or to anything, for that matter—and expecting to overcome all your issues immediately, you're in for the same rude awakening that I had. You have to invest in the process and get to know yourself.

Societal norms may be shifting so that mental hygiene and therapy are less stigmatized, but many men and masculine-identified people are still feeling left out of the picture and are instead feeling isolated and unsupported. And while it is clear that some of that is because this is a very personal journey that can be lonely at times, much of that loneliness and lack of support is clearly tied up in racist patriarchal ideas of how men *should* be. The sooner we as bisexual+ men and masculine-identified people divest from those ideals—and the oppression that's inherent to it—the healthier we will be and the sooner we will be able to step out of that isolation to find exactly what works for each of us.

Conversely, many health care professionals don't have the range to facilitate or educate or aid bisexual+ men's specific health needs. Many testing facilities and medical professionals still aren't equipped to discuss sexual health in a way that is not patronizing and shameful, and don't do rectal swabbing to test for STIs in the anus or offer men the option of doing a throat swab to test for STIs in the throat. I get tested regularly but hate it each time because most times their eyes get wide when I answer that I've had sex with men in the last twelve months or that I'm bisexual+. They're often immature and condescending and treat me like I'm a rare inanimate object. Many medical professionals do not provide proper rape kits to lesbian, gay, bisexual+, or transgender people because of bigotry and lack of knowledge and proper training. Many bisexual+ men have to learn the differences between penetrating an anus and a vagina by trial and error and the risks and mechanics of each. How about bisexual+ men who penetrate people with vaginas *and* are penetrated in their anus? How about bisexual+ men who are penetrated in their vagina? They have to learn the mechanics on their own, how much lube to use (a lot), proper hygiene, how to avoid developing hemorrhoids, that the anus is extremely absorbent, increasing the risk of contracting STIs and HIV, and that penetrating the anus can be pleasurable for everyone involved, though it will often take a lot more patience and acute hygienic attention than penetrating a vagina. I go farther in depth on the mechanics in the "Sex and Dating (and Marriage)" chapter.

ENCOUNTERING BIPHOBIA AND CHALLENGING WHITE SUPREMACY IN WESTERN PSYCHOLOGY

I was drawn to therapy with hopes that it would help me become more comfortable with my bisexuality, but I quickly found that would not be a simple task. In an idealized world, therapy is a place where the most up-to-date tools on mental hygiene are provided, where bias does not exist, and there is no risk of harm. As I've learned firsthand many times over, that is simply not true. Western psychology has a history of pathologizing and harming LGBTQ+ individuals, and that continues to exist in the field. Many of its models and practices are rooted in anti-LGBTQ+ sentiment, ableism, and ultimately anti-Black racism.

I have a personal history of being averse to conflict—as the thought often brought up fear of volatility as recourse, and feelings of unworthiness and of abandonment. All things considered, I did not want to have to become my own bisexual+ advocate in the therapy room. But, recently, when I pointed out a therapist's biphobic attitudes and language for the first time, something shifted. I didn't know my healing was on the other side of showing up for myself by having productive conflict.

Seeing my first four therapists set me back on my mission to embrace my bisexuality. I had to navigate not being believed, not having treatment specifically geared toward supporting my particular needs as a bisexual+ man, and having my already fragile enthusiasm toward engaging with women shot down with attempts to redirect it exclusively toward men. As recently as a few months ago, I had to tactfully point out to a fifth therapist how their words and theories they'd learned in their schooling pathologized queerness ("queerness is born from trauma in utero or in childhood") and their language surrounding bisexuality ("changing sexuality from straight to gay") was biphobic and inept. After a bit of time, they came around, apologized, thanked me profusely, implemented change, and got themselves on track to study with a Black queer feminist collective of mental health professionals that I provided them.

Showing up for myself in the moment to say I felt caught off-guard and harmed, then listing exactly what I needed in that moment to the person who caused the harm was one of the hardest things I've ever done. Normally, I'd just get quiet, numb myself, never bring up sexuality again, or perhaps find another therapist. This time I stood my ground, spoke clearly while using as little accusatory language as possible, and allowed myself to be vulnerable. In that moment, I felt my capacity within relationships expand, and shortly after, I cried. I was so overwhelmed by working up the courage to do that, and by being heard, validated, apologized to, and shown a plan for growth and atonement afterward. But this never should have happened in the first place.

It was widely inappropriate for me to have had to be a bisexual+ advocate in that setting, and it was a lot of emotional labor. I was there to heal, receive support, and potentially unlearn internalized biphobia, but was instead pushed into being an "activist"—something that happens to me time and time again. I've talked about the ways therapy is not automatically a good place for bisexual+ men, or Black people in general; at the same time I find this to be a tricky thing to talk about *because* therapy has helped me immensely. It has helped me heal some deep wounds, develop the necessary tools to survive, and work up the courage to advocate for myself, while also feeding me flawed dreams that the country is improving incrementally because of Democrats who are "on the right side." It legitimizes white supremacy, which has created and exacerbates many of the local and global circumstances that have made it necessary for me to seek out therapy in the first place. For a long time, this fostered a desire to cling to neoliberalism for comfort and eventual salvation. And because of this, Western talk therapy that upholds white supremacy must go.

I do not want to make therapy better with my user experience. I do not want to spend another second invested in reforming something so violent, so unconscionable, so depraved. I may use it for now, but I must also remember that it, along with every other oppressive system, must go when the time comes.

I reflect on the ways I've been harmed, and yet I felt a tinge of guilt speaking up for myself and a tinge of guilt writing about it now. Guilt over saying anything bad about therapy—a thing that can be a lifesaving resource, and something people oftentimes put on a pedestal. Guilt over mentioning a therapist's mistakes and shortcomings. I ask myself: Will sharing this help other bisexual+ people? Will it deter them from a potentially lifesaving resource? Will it swallow more LGBTQ+ people whole? And that is the conundrum. Will speaking up deter others and potentially leave them worse off, or will remaining silent usher them into a psychological death grip? The truth is, Western psychology was developed under and exists within a white-supremacist society that more often than not works hard to quell any and every revolutionary bone in your body.

At the beginning of quarantine in March 2020, many people online advocated for mental health professionals and social workers to replace law enforcement after seeing videos of police officers harming people. I could not help but roll my eyes because this assumes that therapy is the solution, as opposed to revolution, that mental health professionals and social workers are one size fits all, and as though many of them are not carceral and lethal themselves.

A huge driving force for my life over the last decade centered on my optimal health. Health in every area of my life has been central to my identity since I began my therapy journey—something I naively thought was a neutral and untouched-by-white-supremacy sector of what it meant to be human. Over the last few years, I've come to deeply understand that the foundation of Western psychology—both in study and in practice (see Mia Mingus's medical industrial complex graphic, cited below in the notes)—is ableism, heterosexism, and anti-Blackness. The resolve I've come to is that Western psychology is a tool with sharp edges that I must keep at arm's length while learning more about and trying to access decolonial therapy, healing justice, and restorative justice. Calling out biphobia in therapy was healing. Justice is in the revolution.

STI AND HIV STIGMA

Sexually transmitted infections (STIs) and HIV are a part of the human experience that do not define a person's value, morality, wisdom, human-ity, or anything else. There is risk involved regarding sex, whether you're getting tested regularly, only having one sexual partner at a time, using condoms, on PrEP or use PEP, or if you're not. The risk level involved may be different for each, but my point is that there is still risk involved no matter what precautions you take or what activity you participate in. There are ways to protect yourself against exposure, like trading STI and HIV results, wearing condoms (finger, vaginal, penis, dental dam), keeping your boxers on during sex while putting your penis through the hole to reduce skin-to-skin contact, and so on. But there is still risk involved. This is not meant to scare or deter you from having sex whatsoever. I spent much of my teens and twenties being celibate for a few reasons that I get into in the "Bisexuality and Spirituality" chapter, but one of them was definitely as a way of trying to avoid contracting STIs and HIV, which is an all-or-nothing approach that left me uninformed when I'd finally cave and have sporadic sex. Long-term, it left me feeling incredibly underde-veloped and inexperienced compared to many of my peers. I am laying out the realities of being a sexual being and challenging the fallacy that having fewer partners or less sex or taking every precaution will eliminate the risk. After accepting this pervasive fact of risk, I strongly encourage you to seek out ways of protecting yourself and to also do the internal work to destigmatize what it means to actually have an STI or HIV. More in depth information regarding protecting oneself needs to be widespread, as do mental and emotional resources to support people who contract STIs, and the criminalization of HIV exposure or transmission needs to end. Contracting an STI or HIV is a reality of being a sexually active adult and it does not have to mean anything about who you are at your core. Stigma around STIs and HIV are real, and you will likely struggle to find people who speak candidly about having an STI or HIV, which helps uphold stigma and an environment where getting tested regularly is met with dread or simply avoided. Antibiotics and vaccines like those for HPV and hepatitis A have come a long way, and you can protect or treat yourself if you contract an STI or HIV. The sooner you know, the better—you can do something about it to treat yourself and not pass it on to others. If you have or contract HIV or an STI, remember that does not make you a bad person, stupid, irresponsible, immoral, unlovable, dirty, or less than, and it's not the end of the world.

In 2019 the American Psychoanalytic Association (APA) apologized for previously treating homosexuality—which also meant bisexuality and being transgender—as a mental illness, saying its past errors contributed to discrimination and trauma for LGBTQ+ people. In the apology, they said they realized nobody had ever offered an official apology. This apology was thirty years late and has not included a plan to rectify the harm and international ripple effects of their actions. If the APA is serious about their apology, rectifying harm, facilitating healing, restoring trust in the APA, and taking part in an accountability process, they will begin by enacting these things:

- The American Psychoanalytic Association ought to hold a nationally televised press conference, annually and as needed, disavowing their former ways that pathologized LGBTQ+ people and psychiatric practices mirroring conversion therapy up until at least 2001 and underscoring the colossal impact this has had on much of the world's understanding of LGBTQ+ people.

- The American Psychoanalytic Association ought to explain how "homosexuality" came to be listed in the *Diagnostic and Statistical Manual of Mental Disorders (DSM)* as a mental disorder and why it was not removed until 1973 after various efforts by LGBTQ+ activists for years.

- The American Psychoanalytic Association ought to look for, acknowledge, and rectify the ways pathologizing, othering, and applying carceral practices toward people deemed to have a mental disorder or be neurodivergent has made an impact in and out of psychological care.

- The American Psychoanalytic Association ought to acknowledge the ways white-supremacist Christian ideals shaped the pathologizing of homosexuality.

- The American Psychoanalytic Association ought to name those who took their lives as a result of these practices.

- The American Psychoanalytic Association ought to hire qualified professionals to describe the difference between a sexual orientation, gender identity, or lack of sexual desire and how that is separate from mental disorders.

- The American Psychoanalytic Association ought to acknowledge that the only reason these practices were formally disavowed was because of the work of the task force comprising bisexual+ activist Ron Fox and other queer people who produced the guidelines.

- The American Psychoanalytic Association ought to provide scholarships to LGBTQ+ people who are interested in careers in psychology and psychiatry.

- The American Psychoanalytic Association ought to look for, acknowledge, and rectify the ways its regressive prejudice still shows up in treatment, psychology classrooms, and educational materials, and how that bias is still alive in many mental health professionals nationwide.

- The American Psychoanalytic Association ought to reach out to all of the LGBTQ+ people that've been exposed to conversion therapy techniques due to their negligence and offer them monetary settlements for pain and suffering, LGBTQ+ therapists of their choosing, an apology, and whatever else they may need.

- The American Psychoanalytic Association ought to underscore the pervasiveness of ableism in our society, within psychology and psychiatry, the psychological effects of living in such a traumatic and bigoted white-supremacist society, and how the *DSM* and Western psychology were founded on racism, misogyny, and ableism that persists throughout practices and the *DSM* to this day.

- The American Psychoanalytic Association ought to discuss how it's model of pathologizing LGBTQ+ people has been used to justify harassment, banishment, corrective rape, and murder domestically and internationally, to name a few.

- The American Psychoanalytic Association ought to describe the impact of their actions as self-proclaimed mental health experts and how many generations they've harmed.

- The American Psychoanalytic Association ought to underscore how the only reason LGBTQ+ people were permitted to receive psychoanalyst training was because they were threatened with a lawsuit in 1991.

- The American Psychoanalytic Association ought to facilitate sensitivity trainings, workshops, and adequate supervision for therapists on the complex and specific needs of each acronym within the LGBTQ+ umbrella, led by qualified LGBTQ+ mental health professionals, long before therapists are allowed to boast being "LGBTQ+-friendly," or that they've had LGBTQ+ clients in the past.

- The American Psychoanalytic Association ought to provide LGBTQ+ people indefinite therapy with an LGBTQ+ provider of their choosing nationwide with a special focus on Black LGBTQ+ people and other LGBTQ+ people who are not white.

- The American Psychoanalytic Association ought to ensure multiple LGBTQ+ people are consistently in influential leadership roles at every level of the APA.

- The American Psychoanalytic Association ought to provide more funding, support, and distinction to the Task Force on Bisexual Issues on Division 44, the gay and lesbian group within the APA.

- And much more.

SURVIVING ABUSE

According to the National Coalition Against Domestic Violence, LGBTQ+ people experience domestic violence at roughly the same or higher rates than our heterosexual counterparts.

- 26 percent of gay men and 37.3 percent of bisexual+ men have experienced rape, physical violence, or stalking by an intimate partner in their lifetime, in comparison to 29 percent of heterosexual men.

- In a study of male same sex relationships, only 26 percent of men called the police for assistance after experiencing near-lethal violence.

- In 2012, fewer than 5 percent of LGBTQ+ survivors of intimate partner violence sought orders of protection.

- Bisexual+ victims are more likely to experience sexual violence compared to people who do not identify as bisexual+.

Types of Domestic Violence Affecting the LGBTQ+ Community

- 20 percent of victims have experienced some form of physical violence.

- 16 percent have been victims to threats and intimidation.

- 15 percent have been verbally harassed.

- 4 percent of survivors have experienced sexual violence.

- 11 percent of intimate violence cases reported in the NCADVP's 2015 report involved a weapon.

Unique Elements of Abuse in LGBTQ+ Community

"Outing" or threatening to reveal one partner's sexual orientation or gender identity may be used as a tool of abuse in violent relationships and may also be a barrier that reduces the likelihood of seeking help for the abuse. Prior experiences of physical or psychological trauma, such as bullying and hate crime, may make LGBTQ+ victims of domestic violence less likely to see help.

LGBTQ+ individuals may experience unique forms of intimate partner violence as well as distinctive barriers to seeking help due to fear of discrimination or bias.

Although the response to LGBTQ+ victims of domestic violence is gradually improving, the LGBTQ+ community if often met with ineffective and victimizing legal responses. Forty-five percent of victims do not report the violence they experience to police because they believe it will not help them. Furthermore, members of the LGBTQ+ community may be denied assistance and domestic violence services as a result of homophobia, transphobia, and biphobia.

Barriers to Seeking Services and Receiving Assistance

- societal beliefs that domestic violence does not occur in LGBTQ+ relationships
- potential homophobia from staff of service providers, or from non-LGBTQ+ domestic violence victims they may come into contact with
- lack of appropriate training regarding LGBTQ+ domestic violence for service providers
- a fear that airing the problems among the LGBTQ+ population will take away from progress toward equality or fuel anti-LGBTQ+ bias
- domestic violence shelters typically being female-only, and transgender individuals may not be allowed entrance due to their gender, genitals, or legal status
- the dangers associated with "outing" oneself and risking rejection from family, friends, and society
- the lack of, or survivors being unaware of, LGBTQ+-friendly assistance resources
- low levels of confidence in the effectiveness of the legal system for LGBTQ+ people

---

NOTES

Mia Mingus, "Medical Industrial Complex Visual," *Leaving Evidence,* blog post, February 6, 2015, https://leavingevidence.wordpress.com/2015/02/06/medical-industrial-complex-visual.

Da'Shaun L. Harrison, *Belly of the Beast: The Politics of Anti-Fatness as Anti-Blackness* (Berkeley, CA: North Atlantic Books, 2021).

Sabrina Strings, *Fearing the Black Body: The Racial Origins of Fat Phobia* (New York: New York University Press, 2019).

Christine Byrne, "The BMI Is Racist and Useless. Here's How to Measure Health Instead," HuffPost, July 20, 2020, www.huffpost.com/entry/bmi-scale-racist-health_l_5f15a8a8c5b6d14c336a43b0.

Eliel Cruz, "Bisexual College Student Shot Dead in Front of His Home," Advocate.com, August 5, 2014, www.advocate.com/bisexuality/2014/08/05/bisexual-college-student-shot-dead-front-his-home.

Movement Advancement Project, BiNet USA, and Bisexual Resource Center, *Understanding Issues Facing Bisexual Americans,* September 2014, www.lgbtmap.org/lgbt-movement-overviews/understanding-issues-facing-bisexual-americans.

Jennifer Kates, Usha Ranji, Adara Beamesderfer, Alina Salganicoff, and Lindsey Dawson, "Health and Access to Care and Coverage for Lesbian, Gay, Bisexual, and Transgender (LGBT) Individuals in the U.S.," KFF Health News, May 3, 2018, www.kff.org/disparities-policy/issue-brief/health-and-access-to-care-and-coverage-for-lesbian-gay-bisexual-and-transgender-individuals-in-the-u-s/view/print.

Movement Advancement Project, "Invisible Majority: The Disparities Facing Bisexual People and How to Remedy Them," 2016, www.lgbtmap.org/policy-and-issue-analysis/invisible-majority.

U.S. Substance Abuse and Mental Health Services Administration, "Top Health Issues for LGBT Populations Information & Resource Kit," March 2012, https://store.samhsa.gov/product/top-health-issues-lgbt-populations/sma12-4684.

Christina R. Wilson, "What Is Self-Sabotage? How to Help Stop the Vicious Cycle," Positive Psychology, April 22, 2021, https://positivepsychology.com/self-sabotage.

Rhonda Rizzo, "5 Ways Playing the Piano Makes Us Healthier in Times of Stress," *Pianist,* blog post, April 15, 2020, www.pianistmagazine.com/blogs/5-ways-playing-the-piano-makes-us-healthier-in-times-of-stress.

Lara DeSanto, "Brushing and Flossing Could Reduce Your Risk of This Cancer," Health Central, November 19, 2020, www.healthcentral.com/article/mouth-health-liver-cancer-risk.

Ana Sandoiu, "Brushing Your Teeth May Keep Your Heart Healthy," Medical News Today, December 3, 2019, www.medicalnewstoday.com /articles/327208.

Monique Tello, "Diet and Depression," *Harvard Health Blog,* February 22, 2018, www.health.harvard.edu/blog/diet-and-depression-2018022213309.

The essay "4 Questions Every Bisexual Guy Should Ask a Potential Therapist" first appeared online in *Men's Health,* September 21, 2021. www .menshealth.com/health/a37612551/bisexual-friendly-therapist.

Bisexual Resource Center, "Reports and Research," 2016, https:// biresource.org/resources/reports-and-research.

Margie Nichols, "The *DSM-5* and LGBT Rights: Still Crazy after All These Years?" Institute for Personal Growth, December 4, 2012, https://ipgcounseling.com/queer-mind/the-dsm-5-and-lgbt-rights-still -crazy-after-all-these-years.

Encyclopedia Britannica, s.v. "Lobotomy." April 6, 2018. www.britannica .com/science/lobotomy.

David Artavia, "Male Bisexuality Is Real, a New Study Confirms Once and for All," Advocate.com, July 21, 2020, www.advocate.com /bisexual/2020/7/21/male-bisexuality-real-new-study-confirms-once -and-all.

Zachary Zane, "10 Things You Should Know before Dating a Bi Guy," Out.com, September 27, 2018, www.out.com/lifestyle/2018 /9/27/10-things-you-should-know-dating-bi-guy.

Christine Fernando, "Collaboration with Police Divides Social Workers across US," AP News, April 20, 2021, https://apnews.com/article /us-news-race-and-ethnicity-police-chicago-racial-injustice -a4753d5ea6b545b40f1e1fe5793d2af4.

Suzy Exposito, "Why Britney Spears' Conservatorship Case Matters for Disability Rights Advocacy," *Los Angeles Times*, July 12, 2021, www.latimes.com/entertainment-arts/music/story/2021-07-12 /britney-spears-conservatorship-hearing-disability-rights.

Daniel Thomas Chung, Christopher James Ryan, Dusan Hadzi-Pavlovic, Swaran Preet Singh, Clive Stanton, and Matthew Michael Large, "Suicide Rates after Discharge from Psychiatric Facilities," *JAMA Psychiatry* 74:7 (July 1, 2017), 694, https://doi.org/10.1001/jamapsychiatry.2017 .1044.

Mia Mingus, "Medical Industrial Complex Visual," *Leaving Evidence,* blog post, February 6, 2015, https://leavingevidence.wordpress.com/2015/02/06/medical-industrial-complex-visual.

Open Society Foundations, "Ten Reasons to Oppose the Criminalization of HIV Exposure or Transmission," December 1, 2008, www.opensocietyfoundations.org/publications/ten-reasons-oppose-criminalization-hiv-exposure-or-transmission.

Daniel Trotta, "U.S. Psychoanalysts Apologize for Labeling Homosexuality an Illness," Reuters, June 21, 2019, www.reuters.com/article/us-usa-lgbt-stonewall-psychoanalysts/u-s-psychoanalysts-apologize-for-labeling-homosexuality-an-illness-idUSKCN1TM169.

National Coalition Against Domestic Violence, "Domestic Violence and the LGBTQ Community," blog post, June 6, 2018, https://ncadv.org/blog/posts/domestic-violence-and-the-lgbtq-community.

Power and Consent

Remember the story I shared in the "Unlearning Biphobia and Homophobia" chapter about some of my problematic desires around being turned off by seeing men in porn be rough with women but extremely aroused seeing it happen between two men? A theme here is understanding consent. These adult performers consented to this type of role-playing, and what makes something okay is a person's ability to consent to something or decline without repercussion. These adult performers (and many women in real life) consent to rough sex. When it comes to participating in rough sex with a particular gender, my aversions matter too, so that may never be something I'm interested in, or I'd have to have more support to become comfortable with it. I think it has a lot to do with the social implications of what it means for a man to hit or be rough with a woman, even in a sexual or role-playing dynamic, and also some lingering sexist beliefs about all women's physical pain tolerance. I also have some work to do surrounding beliefs about all men being naturally rougher and interested in these kinds of dynamics. This belief can lead to sexual violence against men, something that's often overlooked and which I delve into below. It starts with me asking individual partners, not assuming that all men are comfortable with being handled roughly in a sexual or role-playing dynamic.

In a perfect world we would be taught as boys that consent goes far beyond "No means no," that it extends to respecting other people as autonomous human beings at all times. We'd be shown examples of what it means to ask for consent on a moment-to-moment basis and not only for the "big things" like having sex. Too often, men go through our lives without being exposed to in-depth, challenging conversations about sex, power, and consent. It is assumed that everything will work itself out, that we will behave properly, learn the right lessons, and that because no one has overtly told us to sexually assault or harass someone, we won't do it.

But that's not how power works. I wish I'd been shown alternative ways to showing up as a man who is not interested in upholding patriarchy or interested in coercion and other forms of sexual violence. Though I have knowingly and unknowingly participated in upholding patriarchy, I learned that it's not too late to step off that path, and it's not too late to destroy it altogether.

THINGS TO KEEP IN MIND

◆ Under patriarchy, men are centered, protected, coddled, believed, and made to feel like we are more important, more intelligent, more logical, more well-meaning, and more human than any other gender.

◆ Bisexual+ men also have a lot to learn when it comes to consent, not seeing women as our birthright, and objectifying women, to name a few. It's not only cisgender heterosexual men who do this.

It's vital to acknowledge and understand the ways an imbalance of power (race, gender, class, age, height, ability, and more) can influence decisions in various kinds of relationships. Imbalance occurs when one person has the ability to influence things like social capital, money, physical safety, a place to live, a job, or reputation, among other things. What many men fail to realize in real time is how big and physically intimidating many of us can be without meaning to be. Many of us take up a lot of metaphoric and physical space in large part because of conditioning—which does not tell us to shrink ourselves like it tells women—and intentionally using our size and gender to our advantage. I am not saying we should shrink; I am saying we should be aware of this, create space, and sometimes get out of the way.

There are many of us who use our physicality to intimidate, get in front of, influence, block, or hurt people, and a significant part of consent that gets overlooked is the ways someone having more power than someone else can and will change what would normally be a *no* (if the scales were balanced) to a *yes* or an *I don't really have a choice because my choices suck.* This behavior happens every day on a small scale, and every day those small incidents add up to people who are not men being shown they matter less, shown they are less in control of their own safety, less

important, and less significant. Women and nonbinary people find a way
to preserve their agency against all odds. If you've ever been made to feel
any of these things even once, you will know this feeling is gut-wrenching,
can take you to very dark places, and can have an impact on your quality
of life. Imagine that feeling being a constant in your life, exacerbated by
the sun going down, the arrival of warm weather, walking a long distance
alone, and the list goes on.

BEHAVIORS TO AVOID

- Touching people before getting their consent, especially in bars,
  clubs, or crowded areas.

- Coercing and manipulating men, women, and nonbinary people
  into sexual situations or into being less in control by using alcohol
  or introducing drugs.

- Guilting people into being sexual with you or complaining about
  having "blue balls" or saying the other person led you on to get
  them to have sex with you.

- Ensuring the person you're with in a romantic or sexual dynamic
  drinks a lot while you don't drink or drink very little. Same with
  any other drug.

- Using your size, power, or influence to get a desired sexual or
  romantic outcome.

- Assumptions that sex will happen or how it will go.

- These behaviors are manipulative and predatory as fuck.

THINGS TO KEEP IN MIND

- Only engage someone sexually who is just as excited to be sexual with
  you as you are to be sexual with them.

- Don't assume. Aim for clarity. Ask verbally and nonverbally if they're
  interested in being sexual and understand this can change at any point.
  Even if you've started having sex and haven't ejaculated.

- Remember people get to change their minds, and just because they agreed to be sexual before does not mean that cannot change. They have to keep on agreeing to be sexual, moment to moment.

- If someone shows any reluctance at all to being sexual, disengage.

- Enthusiastic sex that comes as a byproduct of enthusiastic consent is the best sex.

- Responding to someone's lack of desire to be sexual with you by becoming visibly upset, complaining about how long it took to get to their place, or mentioning how they wasted your time is inappropriate and manipulative.

- Coercing people into doing what you want them to do is controlling, violent, predatory, and wrong.

- You do not have to try and be sexual with every man, woman, or non-binary person you're attracted to or who flirts with you.

WHAT COULD HELP

- Learning to cope with feeling weak, rejected, or out of control in healthy ways will only lead to a healthier self-esteem and a healthier life.

- Central to having healthy self-esteem is respecting your own humanity and autonomy and being respectful and protective of the same thing in others.

- If everyone prioritized healthy self-esteem, not based on sexual prowess or the ability to control and exert power over others, if there were different societal priorities in place and supports, there would be far less sexual violence and violations of other people's consent and boundaries.

- Doing the work to detangle control and dominance from your attraction to other people is vital.

- Having challenging conversations about consent with other men, ideally run by mental health professionals or consent educators.

If you're in a relationship where the imbalance of power favors you, verbally acknowledge it, and be aware that they may feel like their needs and desires are less likely to be heard. They may fear the consequences of not wanting to be sexual or intimate in some other way, and you must show only thoughtfulness in response, sans the ego. Ask ongoing questions in a way that communicates that their honest answer is imperative—no matter what it is. Explore whether patriarchal aims of wanting to be *dominant* steer who you engage with and how you engage. A lot of us have to do this work especially regarding wanting to have younger, less experienced, less knowledgeable, less assertive partners.

Making Consent Ethical and Clear

- Practicing communication and consent in all areas of one's life makes it easier to emulate when having sexual interactions. Mimicking the harmful patriarchal practice of silence and brute force is whack.

- Ask yourself, would this person likely say yes if I didn't have power, age, or authority over them?

- Being aware of unearned advantages and power dynamics you bring to relationships and being careful not to leverage them as a way of getting what you want is key.

- Developing a clear form of communication between you and your partner, which may not always be verbal but is agreed on and is based on mutual respect and mutual pleasure.

- Many women and nonbinary people have spoken about men using their bodies to masturbate, completely oblivious and uncaring of their pleasure, their desires, or any kind of palatable connectedness. Don't be that guy.

KEEP IN MIND

- If a partner is not as excited as I am to be sexual, that is not the right person for me to be sexual with, and we will not be a good fit.

- In scenarios where the person is just as excited as I am to be sexual, I pay attention to their enthusiasm throughout and check in with them, asking them how they're doing, if they're having fun, if they're comfortable, if they're okay with switching gears or taking things to another level. I do this in both verbal and nonverbal ways and make it sexy.

- Communication *is* sexy if you do it authentically without breaking the energy that's been building.

- A good way to gauge the other party's interest in sexual situations is trading back and forth between taking the lead and encouraging the other person to take the lead.

- Assuming that because you've invited someone to your place or they've invited you to their place that you're entitled to sex (or that they want to have sex) is no good.

- Assuming that because someone flirts with you it means they want to have sex with you is no good.

- Assuming that a person taking care of their appearance or wearing little clothing means they want people to touch or talk to them is no good.

- As men and masculine-identified people, we aren't always warned about our boundaries being violated, experiencing sexual violence, or that us offering enthusiastic consent matters too. That's an injustice because these things do matter, and our boundaries being crossed or infringed on is a common problem, especially when people know you're bisexual+, especially when you're not white, especially when you're fat, especially when you're disabled. Pay attention to the signs that often reveal themselves prior to a physical or sexual boundary being crossed. Some signs are people making assumptions about people who are not wearing many clothes or are sexually active, not prioritizing others' bodily autonomy and comfort in everyday interactions, and someone asking over and over again for something or trying to guilt others into doing something. More subtle signs are people bulldozing over others in conversations, failing to respect people's humanity when they think no one is watching, and how they treat people who they think of as beneath them. Consent is about asking someone before taking an action that will impact them. Imperialist white-supremacist capitalist patriarchy requires violence and coercion, so deeply understanding power imbalances and living with a consent-based politic is both counterculture and a requirement of dismantling it.

SEXUAL VIOLENCE AGAINST BOYS AND MEN

At least 1 in 6 men report having been sexually abused or assaulted, whether as young boys or as adult men. And this is probably a low estimate, since it doesn't include noncontact experiences, which can also have lasting negative effects, and many boys and men are not always taught to recognize them as sexual violence. Men who have such experiences are less likely to disclose them than are women. This problem is common, underreported, underrecognized, and undertreated. In some cases these incidents are encouraged by loved ones and not recognized as abuse by them or their community. Being on the receiving end of sexual abuse is riddled with a particular kind of stigma for boys, men, and people assumed to be men, and a large part of what it is to be a man in many circles is centered around expressing oneself sexually with a woman (and not being gay). Men who've experienced sexual abuse are at much greater risk than those who haven't for serious health problems, including PTSD, depression, alcoholism and drug abuse, suicidal ideation, attempts, and death by suicide, problems in intimate relationships and a distrust of others, underachievement at school and at work, denial, anxiety and social anxiety, and disassociation. The combination of these things creates quite the cocktail for destruction, abuse, and shame to fester.

Thirty-seven percent of bisexual+ men experience rape, physical violence, or stalking by an intimate partner, compared to 26 percent of gay men and 29 percent of straight men. Forty-seven percent of bisexual+ men have experienced sexual violence other than rape, compared to 40 percent of gay men and 21 percent of straight men, and 47 percent of transgender people are sexually assaulted at some point in their lifetime. Also important to mention there are barriers to why bisexual+, gay, and transgender men don't report these instances because of unique forms of intimate partner violence, fear of discrimination or bias, and ineffective and victimizing legal responses that LGBTQ+ individuals experience, especially if they are Black or Brown.

Sexual violence is about aggression, domination, and power and can be performed no matter the gender. Patriarchy calls us to harm and violate one another lest we be harmed and violated—although we will be as long as it stands. Ignore the call. A common form of antagonism many bisexual+ people face is running into partners who take our sexuality as a challenge. Partners who are determined to win us over to their side and change our sexual orientation to no longer desire or be attracted to the other genders. That is not how sexuality works, and that aspiration reeks. These attitudes and more need to be checked long before engaging—sexually or otherwise—with bisexual+ people.

"BISEXUAL MEN ARE THE BEST IN BED" IS FETISHISTIC BIPHOBIA

Trigger warning: mention of fetishization and violence against boys or men.

"Bisexual men are the best in bed" is a comment that continues to gain steam. In 2020 *Cosmopolitan* magazine even featured a personal essay engaging the topic of bisexual+ men being the best in bed—ten years after debuting an egregiously biphobic and homophobic piece. Just like supposedly affirming talking points about bisexual+ (pansexual, fluid, no label) men being less misogynistic, the zinger that is "bisexual+ men are better than straight men in bed" is not always true, and more importantly, it's dangerous to us. It's as if people cannot help but ping-pong between "Bisexual men are cheaters; They are disgusting; They don't exist," and "Bisexual men are the best in bed; Go get yourself one!" Never quite landing on the harried truth, the latter is mistakenly seen as positive, affirming, and a balm for those of us who have experienced rejection and tribal gaslighting surrounding our sexuality. What's missing is that these are two sides of the same biphobic coin which sees someone's bisexuality as the entirety of their being and more relevant than their personhood. Further, the latter contributes to sexual violence against bisexual+ men who already face higher rates of sexual violence than our straight and gay counterparts, especially if they're Black or Brown, especially if they're disabled, and especially if they're transgender. Being fetishized is not a replacement for affirmation, resources, and putting an end to biphobia.

To only be considered because of the promise of good sex, which may not extend to romantic partnership, is a special kind of burn. Fetishization aside, being "good in bed" is extremely subjective and something that can change depending on individual desires and boundaries, or if a person is experiencing a low sex drive, erectile dysfunction, an injury or disability, a change in employment status, mental health challenges, disconnection, and so on. Moreover, every bisexual+ man has a personal, layered relationship with gender, gender roles, sexuality, religion, kink, genitals, and so on. So each bisexual+ man is different—in and out of the bedroom. We can't all be "the best in bed." Somebody lying. Whether you have flesh dick, plasdick, or no dick at all, one's sexual orientation is not enough to determine how one performs in bed. Some of us have trash dick, some of us have dick that can't get hard, some have decent dick, some of us have dick that's A-1. And perhaps most importantly, good sex doesn't have to center or involve dick at all, even if your partner has one. Outside the bedroom, we're just as varied, and many of us are just as problematic as our straight counterparts. We don't all read bell hooks and Vātsyāyana. Not all of us have been to or can afford therapy. Not all of us are aligning our chakras. Some bisexual+ men look at their sexuality with eyes of acceptance and curiosity and are still misogynistic. Some bisexual+ men are not open to dating transgender men or women, don't acknowledge nonbinary identities—or think there are more than two genders, for that matter—while some bisexual+ men are not open to dating cisgender people. Some bisexual+ men are virgins. Some bisexual+ men only engage with women while some only engage with men. Some bisexual+ men are transgender. Some bisexual+ men are intersex.

When our existence goes from being denied completely to then being regarded as though we're the best, most open-minded, most experienced lovers, there will be problems. Neither offers us the opportunity to be individual human beings who are alive, learning and growing in some areas, and drowning or stagnant in others. Many bisexual+ men who have begun the work to unlearning misogyny and getting to know ourselves better can be amazing partners, fathers, friends, and fuck buddies. A lot of us are aware of the way gender impacts our lives in a very different way than our straight and gay counterparts and intimately know the similarities and differences between bodies of all makeups. But we are not a monolith. There are many pressing issues impacting bisexual+ communities that have nothing to do with wanting to fuck us. Being fetishized may even be alluring for some bisexual+ men, but piercing through every bait is a shiny hook that leads to your demise. When society says you don't exist and calls you every name in the book because of your sexuality, being wanted for the very same thing can feel like being seen, but that's not what's happening. Being fetishized is not the same as being seen. If promise of experiencing the best sex is the only way we'll be considered, it'll be more of the same in this biphobic society: more gestures that reinforce the prevailing belief about bisexual+ men's inferiority, which will be exploited for self-serving causes.

WHAT COULD HELP

- Education and awareness around the ways boys and men experience sexual violence, coercion, and how normalized it is in a culture that demands enthusiasm and a particular kind of sexual availability from boys and men.

- Teaching that women can enact sexual violence on boys and men and some of the forms it takes: calling someone "gay" if they turn down sexual advances, performing oral sex on a boy or man while he is asleep or passed out and cannot consent, nonconsensually grabbing the genitals of boys or men, women initiating or participating in sexual acts and predatory conversations with boys, and so on.

- Teaching boys and men that they have a right to their bodies, time, and attention.

- Teaching boys and men about their bodies and that just because they become physically aroused does not mean they should allow someone to touch them or sexually engage with someone.

- Teaching boys and men they can say no to sexual advances even from people they are attracted to.

- Viewing boys and men as vulnerable, complicated human beings who do not deserve harshness or to be "broken in."

- People taking responsibility for their own projections instead of treating random boys and men the way they imagine them to be.

- Warning boys and men that at some point people will likely try to treat them and their body the way patriarchy tells them to.

The reticular activating system (RAS) is a function of the brain that high-lights patterns and has developed in order to ensure the survival of our species. The RAS starts above the spinal cord, is about two inches long, and acts as the gateway of sorts between the conscious and subconscious mind, filtering important information. The subconscious mind collects up to one billion bits of data per second, while the conscious mind collects roughly thirty to forty bits per second. If you've ever thought about buying a particular make, model, and color of a car, you most likely began seeing it more frequently after you began focusing your mind on it and emoting over it. That's your RAS at work. If you've ever experienced some type of acute form of trauma, your brain may have made associations of being in danger to certain details or kinds of people that were present during that acute trauma. It is my belief that tenets of hege-monic masculinity displayed throughout our society in the realms of law, order, government, spirituality, love, interpersonal relationships, and so on become ideas we believe are inherent to men and masculinity, which becomes a self-fulfilling prophecy. As Da'Shaun L. Harrison states in *Belly of the Beast:*

> *Gender, just like health and Desire/ability, is a system forged with the purpose of creating and maintaining a class of subjects designed to be infe-rior to another. The role of "either" gender is achieved through a continued performance. These roles—and these performances—are implied, but also explicitly named, characteristics and duties one must fulfill to be "man" or "woman." They are not inherent to us, meaning we are not born as "boys" or as "girls." In basic sociological terms, we are taught immediately after birth through social institutions like family, media, and school what role we must fulfill if we are to hold on to the gender we are assigned at birth. When we start breaking the rules of those assigned roles, and thus falling outside of gender's hold, we become "sissies" or "tomboys"—depending on which role you were assigned to fulfill from birth. As Judith Butler states in her book* Gender Trouble, *our behaviors that are gendered are not innate to us. We learn them, and then we learn to perform them. And this performance is policed and maintained by cisheteronormativity, or the idea that everyone already is—and therefore all things must be seen as—cisgender and heterosexual. In other words, cisheteronormativity is the "law*

and order" of gender in that it is what determines who is departing from
their assigned role and must therefore be punished because of it.

Just as these things that feel inherent are learned, they can be unlearned
thanks to neuroplasticity. The RAS works with repetition and emotion,
which can be used to reverse-engineer communication dynamics, beliefs,
aspects of life and society, and a collective comfort zone. In spiritual
communities this is known as manifestation, seeing the signs, intention-
setting, or the power of prayer. Left on autopilot with the presiding beliefs
about hegemonic masculinity and men and women in conjunction with
gender policing and hormonal variations, every action or inaction will be
understood as being fatalistic determinants of gender.

LESSONS AS A DOG WALKER

A friend of mine has two dogs that I walk on occasion. One's name is
Marley, a corgi, and the other's is Kali, a Labrador mix. My friend got Marley
first as a puppy, and after a few months began to mention in passing how
a stubborn personality had emerged, which I quickly picked up on during
our walks. A little over a year later, my friend got Kali, whose timid personality began to present itself. It took Kali months before she felt safe enough
to poop outside, and when she did, she needed to have her back to a wall,
tons of encouragement, and to be able to see both ways on the sidewalk.

I noticed Kali could go on really long uninterrupted walks and liked
to run and stretch her long legs without getting tired, whereas Marley
would try to smell every tree or flower or hydrant and insist we stop every
half block. I noticed how jealous Marley became when I poured encouragement into Kali in a way that I didn't think he wanted or needed since
he was so stubborn. Marley would growl or bark incessantly anytime I
gave Kali belly rubs and gentle pets. I'd then start petting him too with
my other hand, which he'd run from after a moment, but then go back
to growling and barking after a moment. It was the strangest thing, but
eventually I started learning about the different needs of dogs according
to breed and how humans often misinterpret the actions of dogs.

I realized that I was easily able to recognize Kali's need for validation
and her fear because she would make herself smaller and give me a look

that I interpreted as fear. What I'd overlooked about Marley was his need for validation and fear because he coped with it by barking and not always doing what I or my friend asked him to do. I interpreted his way of coping to mean that he was stubborn. I overlooked that Marley was tiny as a puppy coming into a big, scary world that he knew very little about and was expected to do things that he might not be able or want to do. I overlooked that Marley was much smaller than most other dogs, and because of his height, he struggled to be able to smell their butts, while they always got to smell his. I overlooked that because of how big I was and how small he was, the pressure behind my petting may have been way too intense, and so when he'd wriggle from me when I'd pet him and Kali and then growl and bark; he was needing to be petted more softly. I overlooked that I already liked going on really long uninterrupted walks, and often communicated more through meaningful looks rather than vocally, making me equipped to be a great walker to Kali and ill equipped to offer the same experience to Marley.

Because of his sex, my understanding of Marley as stubborn, and his coping strategies, I overlooked his needs, which made it easy to write him off as a *bad dog*. When I began to offer Marley softness and nurturing while catering to his size and specific preferences, our walks and interactions got easier, and I was able to see his bids for my attention or his discomfort as what they were. How we interpret people's coping strategies is impacted by gender (and race, sexuality, class, and so on), although the impact of people's coping strategies on others varies. Another friend has a Saint Bernard who would hide under an ottoman in the living room as a puppy after he chewed up shoes or couldn't hold his bladder. As a tiny puppy it was adorable, funny, and harmless. As a full-grown four-foot dog, doing the same meant the ottoman would be flipped and eventually wear down.

THOUGHTS ABOUT RACE AS A BLACK WRITER

Though I haven't exactly shied away from talking about white supremacy and aspects of my experience as a Black man, I feel reluctance approaching this section. I do not enjoy talking about race with people who are not Black. Talking about race is also uncomfortable for me. As a Black person the way I am expected to talk about race, politicians, and police is in a way that centers and is palatable for white people. Or else. And on the other hand my writing, my art, and my ideas are expected to revolve around race, as if that is the only area of merit that I could possess. I couldn't be a better writer or storyteller or thinker in terrain that is not explicitly about race than a white person. As a writer who pitches articles and manuscripts to a wide variety of media outlets, I feel that sharply. Although the United States and the rest of the Western world is built on racism, and my life is profoundly impacted by anti-Black racism, which could not exist without the invention of race, that is not all that I am. I'd be exceptional in many areas even if race did not exist and *because* racism exists I must be exceptional in many areas. I am asked to understand and talk about race at a depth that white people are not.

I find the relationship between gatekeepers and tastemakers in publishing—as well as other forms of media—and Black creators to be racist, predatory, and degenerative. These dealings often say in one way or another that Black people are most valuable as it relates to our pain, our ability to overcome adversity, and for teaching white people how to be "less racist" in an effort to emphasize white people's inherent goodness. I had a white editor a few years ago ask me what the point was of racial-izing (making them anything other than white) one of my characters if I wasn't going to give them a typical background or physical features that are attributed to said racialized group. Why racialize them if I wasn't going to talk about their cultural background or oppression or wide nose? This is a very common experience, believe it or not, for creators who are Black, and it helps support the idea that white people see them-selves as a blank canvas, as the standard, as being without a race, and to *add* race means I must also add cultural context. Black people, and other people of color, cannot simply exist in a particular plot and set of cir-cumstances. It must always be about race and have a racial slant filled with cultural context, but only one that does not ruffle too many white feath-ers; one that never paints white people as villains sans the white savior, lest it won't be published. If I hadn't included certain typical details and refused to change the character's race, my story simply would not have been published. I simply would not have that publishing credit. I simply would be told later on that I needed to get more publishing credits under my belt before I could reach a certain caliber or be allowed to have my first book published.

It is incredibly difficult for me and many other artists to have work that does not revolve around Black trauma or teach white people about racism be published, funded, picked up, preserved, recognized, or celebrated. Even when many Black artists do make work that references race, the work is often stifled and required to be expressed in a sanitized, remedial way so as to not offend or upset or scare white people—though any mention of racial justice often does. That very clearly articulates racism. Racism is structural power, it's suffocating, it's intrusive, it's violent, and it's based on centuries of lies and white terror.

THINGS TO CONSIDER

- Whose norms, values, and perspectives does this society consider to be normal or legitimate? Whose does it silence, marginalize, or delegitimize?

- Who inhabits positions of power within society?

- Whose experiences, norms, values, and perspectives influence society's laws, policies, and systems of evaluation?

- Whose interests does society protect?

- Do I talk about racism, both systemic *and* interpersonal? With people of the same race *and* other races?

- Is my goal not to be called "racist" or to be constantly working toward antiracism?

- Is my goal to quell my guilt?

- Is my goal of having these talks to make me feel like I am doing the work?

- Which groups feel most at home in the societies I take part in—career field, college or alma mater, church or religion, larger society—and which ones feel like unwanted guests?

- Is it possible that I have preconceived notions about people that are based on race?

It is important to think of unlearning racism and problematic ideals and behaviors as a daily hygienic practice rather than a destination. Constantly being reflective about the structures we uphold and participate in, the ideas we hold, the conversations we engage in, everyday interactions, and doing reading on these subjects is vital. Michael Omi and Howard Winant state that racism is a belief system that "creates or reproduces structures of domination based on essential categories of race."

Many white people become extremely defensive when white supremacy, slavery, and white terror are discussed. Behind that defensiveness is a truth many are unwilling to examine. It is palpable daily and shows up occasionally in the form of white people failing up, having generational wealth generated through slave labor or property and businesses that Black people were not permitted to purchase or own. White people have a race but are permitted never to speak about race—at least not in any intelligible sort of way—but that same grace is not extended to me as a writer, and I dislike it intensely. As writer Kelechi Okafor, quoting Robin DiAngelo, states: "White privilege is moving through a racialized world in an unracialized body." All of this is perhaps at the heart of my discomfort approaching this section: feeling the constraints as well as the expectations of this racialized world and not wanting that to be the reality, even though it is. Words to reflect on come from a 1993 Toni Morrison interview with Charlie Rose, a PBS television anchor:

> If the racist white person—I don't mean the person who is examining his consciousness and so on—doesn't understand that he or she is also a race, it's also constructed, it's also made, and it also has some kind of serviceability, but when you take it away—if I take your race away, and there you are, all strung out and all you got is your little self—and what is that? What are you without racism? Are you any good? Are you still strong? Still smart? You still like yourself? I mean, these are the questions, it's part of it, "Yes the victim. How terrible it's been for Black people." . . . If you can only be tall because somebody is on their knees, then you have a serious problem. And my feeling is white people have a very, very serious problem, and they should start thinking about what they can do about it. Take me out of it.

DEMONIZING BLACK MALE BISEXUALITY

When it comes to the earliest depictions of Black male sexuality in America, images of perverse white people in blackface come to mind. These depictions gave voice to the fear, unrest, and obsession many white people had of Black men's bodies, minds, and sexualities. Black men were tirelessly depicted as animalistic predators after any white man's female partner in sight. Black men were pictured as insatiable demons whose sexuality was in and of itself dangerous, deviant, excessive, and reckless. This messaging can still be seen to this day for Black men at large, though it is enhanced when it comes to bisexual+ Black men particularly. This is what racism looks like, and though bisexual+ men of all races face a particular kind of biphobia aimed at men, this layer only exists for Black bisexual+ men in this country. Millions of dollars and eons of racist and biphobic conditioning in the media has gotten us to where we are today. People are rarely aware of or acknowledge the cumulative fruits of those efforts. I hope the gravity of this will be uncovered and explored in years to come.

I always think about how so many non-Black people are quick to point out the overt homophobia and anti-LGBTQ+ sentiments in the Black community but seldom mention the anti-LGBTQ+ sentiment in their communities or colonialism or chattel slavery in tandem as its source. It is impossible to talk about the depths of homophobia and anti-LGBTQ+ sentiments in the Black community without also discussing Christianity being forced onto enslaved people, without also discussing the European anti-sodomy laws first introduced to the African continent in the nineteenth century, without also talking about the demonization of nonwhite sexualities and genders via European conquest, without also discussing the weaponization of sexual violence against enslaved people ("buck breaking," forcing the penetrative rape of a rebellious enslaved man by another enslaved man), and without talking about how legally imposing Christianity and Islam onto a people will deliberately produce a far worse perception of anything outside cisgender heteronormativity and intense anti-LGBTQ+ sentiments opposed to people who have not been colonized but practice that religion.

SOLIDARITY AMONG PEOPLE OF COLOR

There is a long history of solidarity among people of color on this land, dating back to Indigenous people and abducted Africans who were enslaved. White supremacy has led to genocide, erasure, environmental collapse, metaphysical consequence, and layers of harm we do not yet have language for, and those who bear the brunt of that have been people of color. Although relationships to capitalism, imperialism, and the like vary among nonwhite people, especially across class and citizenship lines, white supremacy ensnares and endangers us all. A 2018 U.S. Census projected that white Americans will be a racial minority by 2045. If we survive climate change, racism, biphobia, and capitalism, that projection does little to change the economic and material realities or pervasiveness of white supremacy. You don't have to be white to enact or adopt white-supremacist policies, values, beliefs, or talking points. Unless more opportunities for solidarity, class consciousness, collective learning, and coalition-building are fostered, 2045 will be a colorful, oppressive hell. White supremacy created anti-Black, anti-Indigenous, and anti-Asian racism. The laws against people of color, and broken treaties in the case of Native Americans, are innumerable. The way people of color are disproportionally policed, limited, and accosted are infinite. This will not end—though it will continue to mutate and transform—until white supremacy ends.

There have already been incredibly significant efforts and pivotal moments of solidarity, community building, and radicalization from the country's inception all the way up to the uprisings of 2020 and #StopAsianHate. I have included a growing list online at www.jryussuf .com/additionals.

In *Pedagogy of the Oppressed,* Paulo Freire asserts:

Within an objective situation of oppression, antidialogue is necessary to the oppressor as a means of further oppression—not only economic, but cultural: the vanquished are dispossessed of their word, their expressiveness, their culture. Further, once a situation of oppression has been initiated, antidialogue becomes indispensable to its preservation. Because liberating action is dialogical in nature, dialogue cannot be a posteriori to that action, but must be concomitant with it. And since liberation must be a permanent condition, dialogue becomes a continuing aspect of liberating action. (Once a popular revolution has come to power, the fact that the new power has the ethical duty to repress any attempt to restore the old oppressive power by no means signifies that the revolution is contradicting its dialogical character. Dialogue between the former oppressors and the oppressed as antagonistic classes was not possible before the revolution; it continues to be impossible afterward.)

Additionally, oppressors will continue to intentionally misrepresent dissent while other groups have a vested interest in insisting that the issue is that the oppressed and the oppressors are simply not hearing one another. The oppression is no longer the issue. Hugging agents of the state or sharing pizza at a protest with my enemies is not an interest of mine. When it comes to solidarity among people of color, I am not suggesting we all simply *get over* our traumas, qualms, and differences with one another because I find that to be an incredibly insensitive, immature, and violent retort. I am saying that continuing to collectively heal and thwart white supremacy alongside one another is possible, though it will be challenging. The instances of racial solidarity mentioned at jryussuf .com/additionals aren't meant to be exhaustive. However, these moments and this literature are extremely significant in understanding that solidarity has existed and will always exist across races, though it is not without missteps, grievances, conflict, splintering, atonement, forgiveness, reconciliation, and progress.

NOTES

Arizona Coalition Against Domestic Violence, "Sexual Violence Myths & Misconceptions," 2019, www.acesdv.org/about-sexual-domestic -violence/sexual-violence-myths-misconceptions.

1in6.org, "The 1 in 6 Statistic," 2017, https://1in6.org/statistic.

LexualMedia, "Boosie, Black Boys, and Rape Culture," YouTube video, June 10, 2020, www.youtube.com/watch?v=KHebIPQSJWk.

National Institute of Public Health of Quebec (INSPQ), "Consequences," 2009, www.inspq.qc.ca/en/sexual-assault/understanding-sexual-assault /consequences.

M. L. Walters, J. Chen, and M. J. Breiding, *National Intimate Partner and Sexual Violence Survey: 2010 Findings on Victimization by Sexual Orientation* (Atlanta: U.S. National Center for Injury Prevention and Control, 2010), www.cdc.gov/violenceprevention/pdf/nisvs_sofindings.pdf.

National Coalition Against Domestic Violence, "Domestic Violence and the LGBTQ Community," blog post, June 6, 2018, https://ncadv.org /blog/posts/domestic-violence-and-the-lgbtq-community.

Joe Von Malachowski, "Sleeping with Men Taught Me How to Be a Better Partner to Women," *Cosmopolitan,* September 22, 2020, www.cosmopolitan .com/uk/love-sex/sex/a34107580/bisexual-man-sex.

Nora Hizon, "Is Your Boyfriend Gay?" *Cosmopolitan,* October 26, 2010, www.cosmo.ph/relationships/is-your-boyfriend-gay.

Ramani Durvasula and MedCircle, "Intimate versus Tribal Gaslighting: Differences and How to Spot Them," YouTube video, February 4, 2021, www.youtube.com/watch?v=trh_eTkZLeU.

Human Rights Campaign, "Sexual Assault and the LGBTQ Community," April 10, 2015, www.hrc.org/resources/sexual-assault-and-the-lgbt -community.

Jenifer Kuadli, "32 Disheartening Sexual Assault Statistics for 2021," Legal Jobs, blog post, February 26, 2021, https://legaljobs.io/blog /sexual-assault-statistics.

Lewis Oakley, "Researchers Need to Acknowledge Bi Men's Unique Needs," Bi.org, November 4, 2016, https://bi.org/en/articles/researchers -need-to-acknowledge-bi-mens-unique-needs.

J. R. Yussuf, "Bisexual Virgins & How to Know Which Gender(s) to Date," YouTube video, November 20, 2020, https://youtu.be/yTQIuuMO1fQ.

Roshaante Andersen, "What's It Like to be Intersex?" YouTube video, April 25, 2021, https://youtu.be/0C5hnlCM-j0.

David Artavia, "Male Bisexuality Is Real, a New Study Confirms Once and for All," Advocate.com, July 21, 2020, www.advocate.com /bisexual/2020/7/21/male-bisexuality-real-new-study-confirms -once-and-all.

ANI, "Some May Find It Hard to Believe but Bisexual Men Make Better Lovers, Partners," *Hindustan Times,* April 12, 2017, www .hindustantimes.com/sex-and-relationships/some-may-find-it-hard

-to-believe-but-bisexual-men-make-better-lovers-partners/story-H9k2u0Q0kWXgPiLM6E8Z0J.html.

Rape, Abuse & Incest National Network, "Sexual Assault of Men and Boys," 2000, www.rainn.org/articles/sexual-assault-men-and-boys.

Da'Shaun L. Harrison, *Belly of the Beast: The Politics of Anti-Fatness as Anti-Blackness* (Berkeley, CA: North Atlantic Books, 2021).

Judith Butler, *Gender Trouble: Feminism and the Subversion of Identity* (New York: Routledge, 2006).

Michael Omi and Howard Winant, *Racial Formation in the U.S.: 1969–1900* (New York: Routledge, 1994).

Celeste Headlee, "Racism vs. Discrimination: Why The Distinction Matters," n.d., https://celesteheadlee.com/racism-vs-discrimination-why-the-distinction-matters.

Bedelia Nicola Richards, "Is Your University Racist?" *Inside Higher Ed,* May 25, 2018, www.insidehighered.com/advice/2018/05/25/questions-institutions-should-ask-themselves-determine-if-they-are-operating.

Kelechi Okafor, "The Way to Discuss Racism in the Workplace is to Listen," People Management, July 16, 2020, www.peoplemanagement.co.uk/article/1741923/way-discuss-racism-workplace-listen-kelechi-okafor.

Robin DiAngelo and Michael Eric Dyson, *White Fragility: Why It's So Hard for White People to Talk About Racism* (Boston: Beacon Press, 2018).

Charlie Rose, "Toni Morrison," video, May 7, 1993, https://charlierose.com/videos/18778.

William H. Frey, "The US Will Become 'Minority White' in 2045, Census Projects," Brookings, March 14, 2018, www.brookings.edu/articles/the-us-will-become-minority-white-in-2045-census-projects.

Paulo Freire, *Pedagogy of the Oppressed* (New York: Bloomsbury Academic, 1970), 138–39.

Sex and Dating
(and Marriage)

Up until the age of about fourteen my dad used to shave my head in the bathroom until it was close to my scalp and nearly bald like his. He didn't know how to give me a shape-up, and to be honest, I don't know that I would have wanted him to. My parents didn't have a lot of money, so the clothes and sneakers I had were old, out of style, and cheap. Growing up where I did, your clothes, sneakers, and how you looked meant everything. In addition to getting unrelenting slack because of my femininity, my clothes and bad cut were also things that made me the butt of jokes. So, in middle school, I began shoplifting, then eventually started working summer jobs, and saving as much money as I could to buy clothes. By the end of eighth grade in 2003, I could buy discounted designer clothes from stores like Marshalls, T.J. Maxx, and Burlington Coat Factory. I could get professional haircuts at a popular barbershop in Far Rockaway called Images once in a while, and the shift in how my peers treated me was immediate.

All of a sudden people were nicer to me. They laughed a little louder at my jokes, and the few male friends I had would stick up for me if someone else was trying to get in my face. I was the same person, but because my exterior had changed a bit, my experience had shifted. That was a big lesson that stayed with me and made me internalize the marks of poverty as though superficiality wasn't the problem. It was one of my first major lessons on safety and protection, even if that safety and protection was faulty and tenuous. The lesson: *Teenagers are superficial, and in times of duress and with the right resources, you can use that to your advantage.* Teenagers eventually become adults, and though some of us grow out of superficiality, most do not. That is to be seen in the realms of education, at work, where you live, and with sex and dating.

Eventually, I came to hate comments about my appearance or attention because of it even if it was positive because I knew firsthand how
quickly that could take a turn. Those years imbedded the message that
my appearance is all I am; nothing else mattered. I was my body, which
brought on a feeling of being trapped. When I think back on much of
my life, I notice my spirit gradually folding in on itself, withdrawing,
compartmentalizing, shrinking, and only over the last few years do I find
myself interested in allowing myself to unfold again and be seen. I still
struggle with compliments regarding my appearance because I feel like
I'm being put under a microscope and am being judged, even if it's happening in a positive way. All the way up until high school, I'd randomly
be met with, "Can I ask you a question?" with a knowing look, or the
question, "Are you open-minded?" which would both be followed up
with, "Are you gay?" All were reminders that I didn't belong even if
those questions came from people I'd made friends with. This wound,
this feeling of not belonging, persisted throughout my teens and twenties,
even around the few people who did accept and validate me. It persisted
when I was around straight people and gay people. I pushed many of
these people away. I'd answer "no" to the "Are you gay?" question before
I knew what the word meant because it was clear from their tone that
being gay was bad or too different. I think most people still believe that.
Shortly after I learned what *gay* meant, around ten years old, I learned
what *bi* was. If I felt like it and if I knew it couldn't get back to my parents
or siblings, I'd respond by saying I was bi. Because of this, I often feel like
I was never really in the closet; not really. I resent the idea of *being in the
closet,* and I've never quite had that option because I just didn't blend in.
Eventually I stopped answering these prods because it became clear that
most people who asked didn't care about me or didn't believe me when
I said I was bi. I learned to just walk away when I was asked by people I
didn't know, sometimes giving them a sharp look first.

Throughout my twenties I rarely had the desire to date and occasionally thought I might be asexual because instances of romantic and sexual
desire were few and far between, plus aspects of asexuality resonated with
me. I resonated with romantic connection not being the center of my life,
having a desire to get many of the needs that would normally be met in
a romantic relationship from my career and my chosen family, and with

being interested in solo self-realization. Because of my race, my sexuality, and my gender, I was often completely dismissed when I'd voice this, even with a therapist. Because I'd had sexual contact and fantasies about other people on occasion, I *couldn't* be asexual. It was never an option for me largely because of my identifiers, similar to being bisexual+. As Sherronda J. Brown says in *Refusing Compulsory Sexuality:*

> *Compulsory sexuality is the idea that sex is universally desired as a feature of human nature, that we are essentially obligated to participate in sex at some point in life, and that there is something fundamentally wrong with anyone who does not want to—whether it be perceived as a defect of morality, psychology, or physiology. Therefore, it creates barriers to seeing asexuality as a valid existence. As Kristina Gupta asserts in "Compulsory Sexuality: Evaluating an Emerging Concept," it is an "assumption that all people are sexual and [describes] the social norms and practices that both marginalize various forms of nonsexuality, such as a lack of sexual desire or behavior, and compel people to experience themselves as desiring subjects, take up sexual identities, and engage in sexual activity." And this ideology "regulates the behavior of all people, not just those who identify as asexual."*

There was a lack of genuine curiosity as to why I thought I might be asexual; a lack of curiosity about me. It was about proving that I was not rather than interest and care surrounding why I felt I might be. While it is true that people who identify as asexual are more likely to be women or nonbinary than they are to be men, that does not mean that asexual men do not exist and this does not acknowledge the distinctive barriers there might be for men to identify as such.

Peers seemed obsessed with being in a relationship and wanting to be liked by people they found attractive, and when I wasn't, I was often interpreted as stuck up or too picky. Though I'd be infatuated with people across the gender spectrum, especially TV and film characters— which I later learned was actually limerence—I didn't obsess over being in long-lasting, deep relationships with others. What was modeled to me by caregivers, from friends, and in the media was codependence, enmeshment, and other unhealthy romantic dynamics. When I imagined what my life might look like in a few years, I only saw myself, in part because as a bisexual+ person, envisioning a future had always been a complicated task with few examples to light the way, but also because I've spent most of my life unpartnered and it was hard to imagine that changing. I could see the beauty in many different kinds of people, would occasionally have sex, and would at most obsess about how aesthetically pleasing a person or the idea of a person was, not how much I wanted to intertwine my life with theirs. This resembles experiences along the aromantic spectrum.

Whether or not this is also the case for some who describe themselves as asexual, their label ought to be acknowledged, they should have a right to claim that for as long as they want. They should get to be the drivers of their own understanding of themselves, and Western psychology is wrong about a person landing on an identifier because of trauma, meaning the label is illegitimate or needs to be *fixed*. In the end I realized I wasn't asexual, though I still resonate with many of the ways asexual and aromantic people talk about decentering romantic love, community, relational care, and their gripes about relational depth being withheld unless a romantic or sexual bond is on the table.

In late 2012, I finally found a bisexual+ group at the LGBT Center in New York and felt overjoyed that I'd found a place where I was completely normal. Some of that exuberance came out in odd ways. These groups largely comprised white people in their late forties, fifties, sixties, and beyond. I was in my early twenties at the time and was sometimes the only person in their twenties in the room. There were usually a few other Black people in the room, but they were usually my parents' age. Many of them had been told their whole lives that their bisexual+ feelings were a phase that would go away, and after having children and being married or divorced, many of them were there because those feelings hadn't. In the instances where there were people around my age, I'd be excited to chat with them and try to make friends. Sometimes I'd hit on them. I look back on those experiences and recognize that sometimes I came off as creepy, misogynistic, or flat-out weird.

The sooner you work on your social skills, fears, and wounds, reflect on your behaviors and words, and read the work of Black feminist scholars, the better. This is part of why I don't like the talking point I've seen pop up in recent years, that bisexual+ men are less misogynistic, because

I know being bisexual+ didn't make me automatically "less misogynistic." It took years of conscious unlearning and learning and constant reflection, and that work will never be finished. Misogyny is a system built on the systemic prejudice of women and people assumed to be women. Systems are made up of people with similar beliefs. Misogyny is a vital system in upholding patriarchy. You can support the idea of women working outside of the home and still be misogynistic. You can be nice to women and still be misogynistic. You can love, marry, and have sex with women and still be misogynistic.

There was a time in 2014 when things went pretty well with a woman I met in the bisexual+ groups I frequented. She was sweet, smart, and cute. We went out on a few dates, and though I enjoyed spending time with her, I wasn't sure if I was actually attracted to her, and I definitely didn't feel ready to be moving toward a relationship. She'd experienced various men stringing her along without clarity on where things were headed, and when she posed what I interpreted as an ultimatum on our third date, I split.

At the time I was still in the habit of chronically doubting my own bisexuality, specifically my attraction to women, as had been done to me for most of my life. I'd become like the biphobic people who'd scrutinize my sexuality and disbelieve me no matter what. Though I had fun on our dates, I was left feeling unsure if what I felt for her was attraction or an amicability present in a friendship. It didn't help that the therapist I was seeing at the time also doubted my attraction to women. The woman from the bisexual+ group and I went our separate ways, and for the large part of my twenties after that, I'd brush off any attraction I felt toward women. It felt too uncomfortable to let myself go there, and like work that I didn't really have to do with men—though I still had a lot more homophobia to unlearn. Not wanting to go there with women and not having someone to help me peel back these layers meant that I'd automatically shoot down any romantic thoughts or feelings I'd have about women, because *they won't like me anyway because I'm gay* or I'd simply ignore women when they'd flirt with me. It remained this way until I gained access to tools and made a deliberate choice to start working through my fears rather than letting them dictate my actions. The validity of my sexuality and my personhood had been rejected many times before and I carried that feeling of not belonging wherever I went, even when people were welcoming and celebrated me. I had to offer unconditional acceptance to myself first and truly examine and release what I'd been through.

I did everything I knew to do to identify my deep-seated apprehensions and unfavorable or limiting beliefs about women and men. Next came the hard work of questioning and then undoing those beliefs. One of the more stubborn beliefs I had about women was not being able to view them as fully trustworthy because patriarchy requires them to adopt a facade in order to stay safe, which meant that they were never really being themselves and that I couldn't fully believe them because of this. A similar argument could be made about men not truly knowing who they are because of the ways patriarchy tells them who they must be. Sexist, I know. Hypocritical, I know. Mental gymnastics, I know. Girls were often the only ones willing to be friends with me throughout my life, were the only ones who stood up for me, and I was raised by my sisters and mother. They'd shown up for me in ways I wasn't able to for myself time and time again, but they'd also shown me something else.

Many of the female friends who'd shown me support in middle school, high school, and college would wind up in relationships with overtly homophobic men who they'd eventually desert me for—and though they verbally supported me, in one way or another most let it be known they didn't think men could be bisexual+. My stepmother, who helped raise me, taught me how to cook Nigerian dishes, and has known me since I was eleven years old, recently let slip that she was sure I'd been damaged as a child, which is why I'm bisexual+, and that she does not want her children, my younger siblings, to turn out like me. One of my sisters shared that she'd briefly dated a charming man who had disclosed his bisexual+ identity up front. He was kind and consistent in every other area, but shortly after he disclosed to my sister, she ended things with him. She didn't believe he actually liked her, that bisexual+ men could be faithful or wouldn't eventually leave her for a man. I have plenty of other stories that I will not bore you with but these things really stuck with me, especially because they weren't simply passing comments from strangers on the internet. These instances sent me a clear message that many girls and women can get close to you, watch you grow, be there for you during your toughest moments, be vulnerable with you, teach you things, share laughs, create memories, and the like, and still hold violently biphobic sentiments about who you are at your core.

I've had to look for lots of evidence of the opposite in order to come back to a place of neutrality on this because the impact wouldn't just go away on its own. I had to think of women who had been trustworthy throughout my life, who had expressed romantic interest, sexual interest, and care, and try and communicate that to my subconscious. I still have to reassure myself that I can trust myself to take my time with women to properly gauge how they truly feel about me, bisexual+ men in general, and whether they're trustworthy in other ways.

DATING APPS

You can use apps as a way to hook up, date, or in some cases make friends. Using dating apps was mainly a portal for me to go on dates and occasionally have casual sex. One of the big takeaways from using dating apps is that people gravitate to them for a variety of reasons, and because of that you will likely encounter a variety of people who have similar intentions and vastly different ones. I've had a good time using apps over the years, but I've also put myself in some very risky situations because at times I was deeply lonely and willing to do unwise things in order to feel special or gain approval. Sites like BGCLive and apps like Jack'd were some of the only ways I could talk to gay and bi men when I was a teenager and in my early twenties, and you will find that each app has its own culture and set of norms. Many people of a certain age feel like they're too old to understand or navigate apps and report having an overall negative experience with apps. Being older while online dating is definitely a unique experience filled with unique challenges, however learning how to craft a good dating profile may help. A good dating profile includes many well-lit, non-selfie, solo photos of you doing activities you enjoy that represent aspects of your life. Smiling pics are a major plus. A good dating profile clearly states your romantic or sexual intentions. A good dating profile expresses who you are specifically even if it is polarizing because you do not want to appeal to all people, only people you'll actually connect with. You want people to get a sense of your personality and what you're into based on your profile, even if you only want something casual. Keeping an open mind and keeping your expectations in check while exercising healthy boundaries and clear communication are ways I've found the most success. I cannot stress enough how vital working on your self-esteem, self-love, and confidence are, as evading this work will sabotage all of your relationships in one way or another.

7-DAY CONFIDENCE-BUILDING WORKOUT

Mondays: Focus on what you like about your body, even if it is only something small like your smile or your legs. Too often we focus on our insecurities with our physical body, and we don't give as much energy or attention to the things that we *do* like about our bodies. It's important to note that though you live in your body, you are not *just* your body. There is much more to you. We put heavy emphasis on our bodies and the physical world, but that's not all that there is. There is so much more going on. Don't compare your body to anyone else's today. The moment you find yourself doing so, come back to those things you like about your body. Monday is all about celebrating the unique body you live in.

Tuesdays: Celebrate the self you can't see. Say something that you like about other parts of your being. You may like the fact that you're really in touch with your emotions or that you're a great listener or that you like how good a friend you are or that you like your speaking voice. Don't compare yourself to anyone today. The moment you find yourself doing so, come back to that thing you like about yourself. Tuesday is all about celebrating those things about yourself that you cannot see.

Wednesdays: Give yourself permission to feel. In the West, we focus on masculinity and masculine energy. It's what we praise and celebrate. We tend to punish femininity, talks of emotions, and other things we deem "feminine" and mainly celebrate things we deem "masculine." Wednesday is about trying to bring those things into balance. Celebrate *anything* you feel today, and allow yourself to experience a variety of emotions and see where that takes you.

Thursdays: Live like nobody is watching. This is certainly my favorite on the list. From the moment you wake up until the time you go to sleep, live your life like nobody's watching. Positioned from that mindset, you get a much more authentic, carefree, and attuned version of yourself. I don't like who I am when I care so much about how other people are viewing me. It affects the way I walk and talk and what I wear. It can be toxic and debilitating because it affects too much. When I give myself the permission to be carefree, to just live like nobody else matters besides me regarding how I view myself, I am free. Try it.

Fridays: Practice giving and taking love. Love is giving *and* taking. Some of us are good at one or the other but balance can be elusive here, though it is better. Love is not giving until you're empty, and it is not taking until someone else is empty without any contribution from you; it is both.

Saturdays: Yoga day. I am a huge fan of doing yoga in the living room. Saturday is all about returning to your mat, returning to the body, stretching it, and focusing on the breath. Two awesome YouTubers I recommend are Fightmaster Yoga and Yoga with Tim. Fightmaster Yoga is really good for beginners, as she is really kind and intelligent and giving. Yoga with Tim is an instructor who will challenge you, but sticking with it will be rewarding. Gift yourself this time well spent.

Sundays: Inspirational reading or listening to a podcast. Spend twenty minutes reading an inspirational or self-help book. It is a great day to recharge and start the week off right with a clean slate. Learning about the Homecoming Podcast has been an invaluable asset to my confidence and growth. Sunday is a great time to get in tune with yourself and how you intend to show up during the upcoming week, gather some motivation, and foster inspiration for the week ahead.

Many bisexual+ people would prefer to date other bisexual+ people so they won't have to explain their sexuality or automatically be seen in a less than kind light. For most of the bisexual+ people I know, dating another bisexual+ person sounds like hitting the jackpot. That's not to say that all bisexual+ people are amazing—because they're not—but the idea of not having to face some of the things we constantly face dating people who are not bisexual+ sounds like a reprieve. Whether the person be man, woman, or nonbinary, knowing I was dating another bisexual+

person would lower many of the apprehensions I have around dating, as I have had many negative experiences with straight women and gay men. That said, there is a desperate need for a popular, bug-free dating app specifically for bisexual+ people.

DISCLOSING

Sex and dating can be a lot of fun and a lot of headache, but I will try and focus on the positive. When it comes to disclosing your sexuality, it's helpful to come up with a personal rule (it can certainly change) for engaging in sex and dating. Whether you want to tell people you're having sex with that you're bisexual+ is completely up to you, but just know that they're not entitled to that information, and the stigma does not go away even in such a casual relationship. At the time of writing this, telling a potential sexual partner that you're a bisexual+ man most likely won't be a positive. The other party (man, woman, or nonbinary) or parties may have increased fear because of the work done to stigmatize bisexuality in men and masculine-identified people. My rule for disclosing to people I'm having sex with is that I don't do it. It makes things more unnecessarily complicated and may send the message that I'm interested in developing a more intimate relationship when that may not be the case.

As far as dating goes, I only disclose to people who I feel safe around after getting to know them a bit and people who I connect with in a number of other ways. I disclose to people who I want to intentionally divulge more personal information to in order to bring us closer. This is not something that typically happens after a first or second date. Though there are special cases of meeting people I immediately feel like I've known for a long time, generally I don't disclose until some time has passed, until we've broached the subject of sexuality and gender and I sense they'd be affirming. I do this by using pop culture news or references to test the waters, and if they seem like they'd show acceptance, compassion, or sensitivity to other groups under the LGBTQ+ umbrella who are not gay.

In the three years I was out as bisexual+ on Tinder, from 2015 to 2018, I did not match with a single woman. I matched with men regularly, but it'd often fizzle out or lead to one or two dates at most. Me not matching with a single woman was likely for more reasons than because I was honest about being bisexual+, but I know it was definitely one of them, if not the leading reason. It upset and confused me at first, but eventually I learned not to take it personally and that it was a reflection of attitudes present in larger society. This may or may not be your experience if you're up front about your sexuality; either way, it's important to detach your self-esteem and identity from the access you have to women. I'm not sure if being bisexual+ had a negative impact on my interactions with men online, but dating can be really tricky for everyone, so I chock it up to that.

You may have completely different rules or no rule at all. You may get all of this wrong—and you should bank on it—but as long as you're growing, and you're remaining safe, you're doing something right.

DATING PEOPLE OF TRANS EXPERIENCE

Content warning: If you're transgender or nonbinary, you can skip this.

Transgender is both an umbrella term and an identity marker. It's a way of describing a person whose gender does not align with the gender they were assigned at birth. People who are nonbinary, gender-fluid, and agender fall under this umbrella term as well. Transgender people come in all shapes, sizes, and gender variations. A common misconception is that in order for someone's experience as a transgender person to be valid and have their pronouns and gender affirmed, they must be interested in and begin a transition. This could not be farther from the truth. Like sexuality, gender is not something you can see, and it is not based on genitalia. Gender is something that is felt, innately known, and something that can develop over time with more information and self-discovery.

The gender binary is a norm in our day-to-day lives, and something that's continuously imposed and continues to be a tool of white-supremacist cisgender heteronormative colonial domination. It is there as a way of maintaining social order. Gender outside of white supremacy exists on a spectrum. Gender is complex, varies from individual to individual, and is in many ways a performance. As far as biological sex is concerned, there are at least thirty-six sex variants, so it is not so absurd that there are more than two gender variations or that transgender people exist at all. Unless you have had a chromosome graft, there is no way of being 100 percent sure that your chromosomes are what you might expect them to be, since you were either labeled a male or female at birth based on the doctor's perception of your genitalia.

Here are some tips on interacting with and dating transgender people:

Overfamiliarity. Because of growing representation in news and media, many people, both well-meaning and malicious, can feel a one-sided familiarity toward transgender people they come across online or in person. They forget common decency and etiquette when interacting with a stranger for the first time and cross many boundaries, knowingly and unknowingly. Transgender people are individuals with their own lives, boundaries, and interests. Transgender people do not exist to educate you, and you are not entitled to their attention, information on their genitals or body, or unearned intimacy.

Gender is different from sexuality. Transgender people can be straight, gay, bisexual+ or pansexual, asexual, and so on.

Pronouns. Until you know someone's pronouns, using their name or defaulting to using "they" and "them" for strangers is a step in the right direction, but it's best to ask someone their pronouns and commit them to memory. It gets a lot easier the more you practice and take a step back from defining people by their gender, I promise.

Defending. Educating and pointing out transphobia when transgender people aren't around is a great way to take the burden of education off of transgender people and to help create change. Distancing yourself from people who never make an effort or refuse to learn is also an option.

Supporting. Aiding in fund-raising efforts, offering financial support for hormone replacement therapy (HRT), and offering emotional support are great ways of supporting a transgender person.

Terms. If you're using terms like "trans-attracted" or even "pansexual" as a way to signify that you are open to dating transgender people or that you find them attractive, cut it out. Many transgender people have spoken about how the former does not rub them the right way, is objectifying, sounds like a fetish, and has the effect of othering them. You do not need an additional label to signify that you're interested in transgender people because they are the gender they say they are and not some other combination of genders, unless they specifically say they are. Many people have begun using "pansexual" as a way of signaling that they're willing to engage with trans and nonbinary people. If signaling this is the only reason you're using the pansexual label, rather than because you're attracted to all genders, and you're attracted to people, and their gender doesn't really matter, you may want to rethink that. If the definition of *pansexual* resonates with you, use it. If you are only using "pansexual" to signify that you're open to dating transgender and nonbinary people, reconsider.

Suggesting transgender people are "the best of both worlds" is a big no. Transgender people are the gender they say they are, and this comment completely invalidates their existence and right to self-determination. It is normal to notice some of the differences that may occur when dating or having sex with a transgender person compared to a cisgender person, however statements like this can be objectifying and dehumanizing.

Be sensitive. If you're serious about pursuing a transgender person, tread lightly. Many transgender people avoid bisexuals because of the aforementioned and because they may feel dysphoric with a bisexual+ person who they think may be looking past their gender to find or be attracted to a gender that is not there. Many transgender people have discomfort around their genitals or heightened anxiety around being sexual. You have to be sensitive, patient, and aware.

Sex. Transgender people do not exist to fulfill your sexual fantasies. Do not engage with them as though they're sexual experiments or objects. Transgender people are human beings. Many cisgender bi, pan, and gay men will not let a transgender man top them, even though they are a bottom or vers, and that is transphobic. Many cisgender bi, pan, and gay men assume that all trans women are tops, and that is transphobic. Do not assume what a transgender person likes or does or wants. Always ask.

Genitals ≠ Gender. Some transgender people have surgeries or want to, and some do not. Either way, they are still the gender they say they are, and if the possibility of them having particular genitals makes you uncomfortable or insatiable, do not engage with them. If any of this information is too much for you or too hard to understand right now, I recommend leaving transgender people alone and taking a look at https://transequality.org.

PDA AND SAFETY

Many people are not into public displays of affection (PDA), which is valid and fine because it can get pretty gross and inappropriate for nonpartici-pants. I realized that I was mostly fine with PDAs with women and people assumed to be women, but not fine with PDAs with men and people assumed to be men throughout my teens and twenties. I'd learned early on that expressing any modicum of my desire for men would lead to violence. Many times, even if I was really into a guy who I was out on a date with, I might nudge them playfully or hug them briefly, or on rare occasions give him a quick kiss, but that would really depend on what neighborhood we were in, the time of day, if I felt like he'd also be able to defend himself, if I was in the right headspace to be ready for a potential fight, and so on. With a woman and someone assumed to be a woman, thoughts of safety and reactions from people around us went out the window, and it was more dependent on whether the woman was into me. In the event they were down to make out, grope each other, the works, then so was I.

A Black bisexual+ male friend told me he doesn't engage in PDAs with women anymore because he knew he wouldn't do it with men. Something about that really stuck with me because it's very deliberate and thoughtful. A really damaging aspect of a heteronormative society is that it can be incred-ibly damaging to healthy dynamic relationships for LGBTQ+ people; small acts of affection can be a source of violence, and we can internalize this. Things that our cisgender heterosexual counterparts, and perhaps some of us who are partnered with women and people assumed to be women, take for granted can be life-threatening. Take into consideration where you are, who you're with, and whether or not you're ready to deal with possible backlash.

WOMEN WATCH GAY PORN BUT WON'T DATE BISEXUAL+ MEN

Trigger warning: mention of fetishization of Black men.
    According to the porn website Pornhub:

In our 2016 "Year in Review," we found that Pornhub's proportion of female users had grown to 26 percent worldwide, from 24 percent in 2015.

The gender split viewing gay male porn is actually much higher at 37 per-
cent female. Proportionately, that means women are 69 percent more likely
to be viewing gay porn than their male counterparts. Gay male porn is the
most viewed category by women over forty-five years old, and the second
most viewed category by women eighteen to forty-four years old. Gay
"Black" men are by far the most popular, followed by gay porn involving
"straight guys." Older gay men are more appealing than younger, with
"daddy" ranking six spots above "twink." In our "More of What Women
Want" post, we expanded the demographic statistics and found that 36
percent of Pornhub's female viewers are aged eighteen to twenty-four. The
number of eighteen- to twenty-four-year-old women watching gay male
porn is slightly higher at 40.3 percent. According to Google Analytics.

As a sidebar, people have claimed these statistics are erroneous because
Google Analytics inaccurately assumes gender based on your searches
and its other ways of gathering data about its users, which is important
to name here.

It's also important to name that much like straight and bisexual+ men
who watch lesbian porn, this inverse would make sense. Women who like
men watch gay male porn for a variety of reasons; seeing multiple dicks
is arousing, seeing more androgynous men is a turn-on, and not having
to think about one's own body or gender while watching. What remains
clear and consistent is many women's aversion to bisexual+ men and the
racial fetishization of Black men. Much of the interest and speculation
around Black men is wrapped up in ideas of hypermasculinity that, due
to white supremacy, have been projected onto and forced upon Black
men. An everyday example is images of a male demon or fallen angel
with dark skin and wings who needs saving from himself by a seemingly
innocent female angel with white skin and wings. We are bombarded
with interchangeable imagery and ideas that dark skin is equivalent to
this illusive, inconsistent concept of masculinity and evil while light skin
is synonymous with femininity or good.

Biphobic and homophobic ideals of impurity, carnality, and evil
converge with ideas surrounding Black masculinity as animalistic, scary,
aggressive, and domineering to make the perfect cocktail for many
women of all races to secretly enjoy this at low risk, on their own terms,

and when they're in the mood. The task of interpreting Black bisexual+ men as fully human, unlearning bias, potentially facing proximate social stigma, working through past traumas, and working through fears and wounds is too daunting. It's why I'm able to watch YouTube videos where women say they'd rather be cheated on than date a faithful bisexual+ man and feel sad for those women rather than take that on or turn on my own bisexuality. It reminds me that as a survival-based species, humans will more often than not choose what's familiar because our minds equate familiarity with survival and what's unfamiliar with death.

BI ERASURE IN GAY SPACES AND OUTING CULTURE AMONG GAY MEN

Bi erasure seems to be a rite of passage for many gay men and gay scenes. Being bisexual+ or pansexual—in the rare occasion that it's believed in men—is spoken about in these spaces as if it's a new phenomenon, something only the young kids are or do because they're rambunctious, or a thing too difficult to grasp. Being gay is the *original* LGBTQ+ identity from which we all spawn, and every other moniker should bow down to or gain their approval from in order to be legitimate. It is felt in where the funding goes, the content of the media and seminars, and the attitudes of organizers and attendees. What many gay men get wrong is the ways the conflation of all other identities by white doctors and psychologists into "homosexuals," as well as "degenerates" and "the mentally ill," and how organizers of every gender expression and queer identity rallied around this popular reclaimed term at the time and organized under it—bolstered gay men's influence and visibility. Many gay men do not know, acknowledge, or extend the same solidarity to other identities who carried the gay and homosexual labels in order to help the movement gain steam and signal unity. Sometimes after a series of questions asking how I came to be, explaining that I did not just begin existing or engaging in LGBTQ+ activism or spaces yesterday, gay men will exasperatedly say that being bisexual+, pansexual, or fluid is something we all are and thus does not need societal acknowledgment, restructuring, added language, a modification in funding, or a change in addressed needs by organizations. Those polarities, of either we all are on the bi or pan spectrum so it doesn't need any further attention, or it's just too new to warrant change, is a sliver of conservatism and erasure from a group that experiences that persistently, and this is unacceptable.

Additionally, outing culture among gay men is rampant, vicious, and negatively impacts bisexual+ men tremendously. Outing culture is about violently wielding societal power and intel. Outing culture is telling a straight female friend a guy's bisexual+ sexual or romantic history after an argument as a "gotcha" moment. Outing culture is biphobic jokes, objectification, and problematic language. Outing culture is being inter-rogated or surveilled at Pride. Outing culture is harassment, threats, and blackmail. Outing culture can lead to sexual, physical, emotional, or financial abuse. Outing culture leads to murder. Outing culture is the antithesis of community and yet is often a rite of passage for friendships between gay men and straight women. What is necessary from gay men is solidarity with other queer people that goes beyond lip service and onto learning and action.

MONOGAMY AND NONMONOGAMY

A common misconception about bisexuality is that bisexual+ people have to engage with more than one gender at the same time in order to be satisfied or truly be bisexual+ and that is simply not true.

- A nice way that I have come to reframe that stereotype is by saying that me being bisexual+ means that I can be satisfied by someone of any gender and *that* is what makes me bisexual+.

- This reframing will not work for everyone, and if it does not work for you, that does not invalidate your bisexual+ identity; it simply gives me something witty to say when people recite an iteration of the familiar stereotype. You can come up with something witty to say around nonmonogamy and your own bisexual+ identity.

- Something that really stuck with me that I learned from a polyam-orous friend is that monogamy is a relationship-style choice, but we're all born desiring nonmonogamy; we're all born wanting to experience love or like and a variety of socioemotional interac-tions from more than one person.

- Polyamory is often demonized in society, painted as illegitimate and perverse because it disrupts many of the Christian values American law is built on.

- The individualistic, nuclear, hyper-independent family is a cornerstone of white supremacy.

- Polyamorous people are not afforded the same rights or social status as monogamous people are.

- Marriage via monogamy was invented to be an integral tool of asserting capitalistic enterprise, patriarchal control, and heteronormativity and still principally operates this way.

- Though a lot can be learned about love and being more communal from nonmonogamous people, being nonmonogamous is not synonymous with being progressive or *more evolved*.

As someone who was a devout Christian during very formative years of my life, from age fourteen to twenty-two, I had to do a lot of work to unlearn the myth of *the bad bisexual+ person* and toxic monogamy. Said *bad bisexual+ person* is polyamorous and has lots of sex with men, women, and nonbinary people concurrently and on their terms. This bisexual+ person is messy, jumps from bed to bed, is comfortable with their sexuality, and is even willing to use their wiles to flirt and get what they want from a person of any gender. Said bisexual+ person may end up with a man or a woman or a man *and* a woman. This kind of bisexual+ person is dangerous. Said bisexual+ person is not palatable to people who want to keep bisexual+ people in a box: people who are allegedly okay with us but not in a form they cannot contain or understand or relate to or approve of. I was ignorant, had a lot of internalized biphobia, and was a product of my environment. What I needed was education and to unlearn shame.

Bisexual+ people who are *messy* deserve respect and understanding and love, but they don't need anyone's approval. They may be just as messy as their gay or straight counterparts, or they may somehow be far messier, and that does not negate that they deserve happiness and a good life and not to be written off as being automatically dangerous or sinister. For a long time I shied away from experiencing or enjoying the full breadth of myself sexually because I feared this characterization. I feared my actions would line up with everything that was so wrong about the *down-low brother*. This fear and self-policing impeded on my sex life as well as my romantic endeavors, and the main one harmed by all that was me. Being characterized as the *bad bisexual+ person* came regardless of how many years I was celibate, what I did when I actually was sexual, or how vehemently I rejected it. It's a part of the deal.

> Toxic monogamy, as defined by psychologist Hillary Berry in her since deleted 2018 Medium article "Toxic Monogamy Culture," refers to "monogamy as a cultural institution [that] has been interpreted and practiced in ways that are unhealthy." These ideas are all around us and are often romanticized or perpetuated in media, cultural norms, and social expectations. Prevalent ideas that are examples of toxic monogamy culture are: *If you truly love someone, you will never be attracted to anyone else; The relationship always comes first; Your romantic partner needs to fulfill every single emotional, social, and physical need that you have; Sufficiently passionate and true love will always overcome practical incompatibilities; Jealousy and possessiveness are an indicator of love; Affection and love are in limited supply.*

Nonmonogamy can be beautiful and is a lot more common than you may think. I strongly recommend reading the book *Polysecure: Attachment, Trauma, and Consensual Nonmonogamy,* whether nonmonogamy appeals to you or if it repulses you. It contains vital information that will likely enrich you as a person and will likely strengthen your preexisting relationships. Many of our parents and elders had *understandings* that we were none the wiser to that were part of what made their unions fulfilling, loving, and long-lasting. People are drawn to nonmonogamy for a variety of reasons, and there are various kinds, ranging from monogamish to relationship anarchy. *Relationship anarchy* is most easily defined as applying anarchist principles to intimate relationships and a rejection of a ranking system regarding interpersonal relationships. Important values of relationship anarchy are the absence of state control, autonomy, community interdependence, and anti-hierarchical practices. *Monogamish* is a term coined by Dan Savage to describe couples who are mostly sexually and emotionally exclusive, but periodically—or even only once—engage in extra-relational play or sexual contact. These are brief descriptions of umbrella terms that are much deeper, more personal, coauthored relationship styles that are on two ends of a spectrum. There are many other configurations of nonmonogamy with a lot more nuance than what I've described, and you'd benefit from at least learning about them even if you will never partake.

In general, nonmonogamy requires a lot more conversation, clarity, outlined boundaries, consideration of others, and discipline than monogamy by the lack of cultural normalcy and potential volume of people alone. Nonmonogamy is not a free-for-all, as it requires a lot more emotional bandwidth and potentially money than monogamy does. Nonmonogamy is the opposite of cheating. It is all about honesty with oneself and others, transparency, and consent. If you struggle in any of these areas in monogamy, you will likely fail miserably at nonmonogamy. Either way, there is a lot to be learned from people who practice nonmonogamy when it comes to not treating a partner like a possession, processing jealousy and other emotions that may come up in relationships, and rejecting normativity dictated by patriarchal white supremacy.

Remember: There is a lot of talk of LGBTQ+ people having a delayed or arrested development in the realms of sexual exploration, gender, gender expression, romantic relationships, and a whole host of other things, and one of the reasons for this comes down to safety, heteronormativity, conditioning, and lack of access. When you get to a certain safety level, economic security, and place in your journey, you may be able to explore and express yourself in a variety of ways for the first time. This may make you feel joy but also severely underdeveloped. You may be experiencing things that you feel like you *should* have as a preteen or a teenager, and that is very common and quite a unifying moniker among many LGBTQ+ people. Be gentle with yourself and consider that this is because of the anti-LGBTQ+, heteronormative, patriarchal, white-supremacist society we live under.

MARRIAGE

Many bisexual+ men get married to men, women, or nonbinary people and have amazing, fulfilling marriages. This fact about bisexual+ men living happy lives with families often slips through the cracks, since the world sees people as either gay or straight, and they gather this information from the assumed gender of whoever you're coupled with. Your sexuality and personhood oftentimes becomes congruous with whoever you're married to in the eyes of others. Just because you're bisexual+ doesn't automatically mean you're incapable of being monogamous, doesn't mean you won't get married, and it doesn't mean you will need to engage with more than one gender at the same time to feel fulfilled. Your interests or wants for your life may fall outside the parameters society says are valuable. Not only is that completely valid, it's also admirable, in direct opposition to conformity, and indicative of a strong will. Being in tune with your own desires is something many people do not prize.

Telling your spouse you're bisexual+ can be a difficult but necessary step for your mental health, personhood, and relationship. In no way am I trying to guilt you into doing this or suggest that unless you do your relationship will fall apart; that's simply not true. Getting married does not stop you from being attracted to other people. Conversely, telling your partner about every person you're attracted to is completely unnecessary, and many people think of this as being inconsiderate. I believe it becomes an issue when your bisexual+ orientation is a big secret, something you feel you need to act on, or a site of shame. Love cannot flourish when it is based on secrets and lies. This may sound confusing or even contradictory, but what I am essentially saying is that if being bisexual+ holds significance to you, or is something that you are very deliberately keeping from your spouse, it is likely an indication that the way things are is not sustainable. Biphobia against men and masculine-identified people is extremely common and permeates every facet of society. Nonetheless we are human beings deserving of love, respect, and affection. I know many bisexual+ men who get the love and affection they need from their partners and get their sexuality affirmed by joining bisexual+ support groups or from their queer friends. It is uncommon to find a partner who will understand and provide support for every single facet of your being. That's why people have friends or join teams or are part of organizations independent of their spouse. Knowing this, many bisexual+ men and masculine-identified people don't go into their relationships seeking to find support for their sexuality in their spouse, so they don't disclose, and that makes perfect sense.

Oftentimes, spouses take the news of a bisexual+ man or masculine-identified person disclosing to mean their partner has cheated, or that they're interested in opening up the marriage, or that they're actually gay or straight, and no longer interested in them. You are no less deserving of respect or love if this is you.

THINGS TO KEEP IN MIND

- Make sure to state what your intention is for telling them more than once and make it clear whether or not you're interested in potentially opening up the marriage.

- Open marriages are incredibly common and are not a new phenomenon by any means.

- Being in a nonmonogamous marriage can be an incredible source of joy, love, strength, adventure, fun, and affirmation.

- It is far more common than you think because very few people in open marriages talk about it. This is largely because of societal stigma, heteronormativity, and the overarching Christian influence that touches our sensibilities around sex, gender, love, and relationships.

- For many bisexual+ people, an open marriage will simply not work, now or ever, and is not something they're interested in trying or even considering. That is completely valid.

- You are no less deserving of respect or love.

- Their reaction may completely take you by surprise.

- Their reaction may fill you with so much joy and relief.

- Their reaction may crush you.

- Their reaction has absolutely zero bearing on your character or your value as a man or masculine-identified person.

Here's a passage by Anonymous about being married to a woman as a bisexual+ man from *Rec-Og-Nize: The Voices of Bisexual Men:*

> *I can see nothing but our future, finding new aches and pains together, and it thrills me. You understand my story, you hear every last word and yet you love me. You understand that sometimes I feel the need to go out, and sometimes I need to stay in. And when I say I want to come out, it is the shame in your face that makes me sad. That you would be uncomfortable with the questions of others, their suspicion and confusion. Our love will survive the bump, but it feels like a betrayal. But I will give you that silence just as you give me your personal acceptance.*

Here's a passage from *Rec-Og-Nize* by Ron J. Suresha about disclosing his bisexuality to a male partner as after identifying as gay for more than forty years:

> *Though I feared Rocco would respond negatively to my bisexuality when I came out to him, he completely affirmed, embraced, and supported my identity. Although I've experienced many curious and dubious reactions when I've mentioned my bisexuality, every person in my life who matters has validated me. What ultimately matters, though, is how I perceive and bless my own process.*

Here's a passage from *Rec-Og-Nize* by James Donald Ross about being married to a woman as a bisexual+ man:

> *I came out to my wife and told her my long-held secret. Fortunately she showed how loving a heart and soul can be, accepting me as the bisexual man I truly am. Things improved dramatically from there when in 2011 she too came out as bisexual. We began to share sacred thoughts and dreams together as a bisexual couple, hoping to experience the freedoms we had long wanted.*

Still, some bisexual+ individuals are nonmonogamous and want to have unions with their partners honored and supported by the law, which often elicits strong reactions and is something white supremacy rejects.

Some bisexual+ people reject the idea of marriage altogether, which often elicits strong reactions, making another of the workings, anxieties, and priorities of white supremacy known. Though there is nothing wrong with wanting a single romantic partner in marriage, the nuclear family, individualism, and the rejection of interdependent communal living is a core tenet of white supremacy.

PEGGING

The term *pegging* was first introduced to the mainstream in 2007 via "Savage Love," a sex-advice column where Dan Savage took questions from readers and allowed guest writers to answer. The term was cocreated by readers to describe the act of a woman using a dildo to penetrate a man. Even though from this post it came to be a widely used phrase, that inaugural post is rife with misogyny, biphobia, shaming, and humiliation, and there is a level of cheek that I personally find off-putting but many find playful or endearing. That basically encapsulates how I feel about Dan Savage, though many people would disagree with me. Nevertheless, you can search online for "Is Dan Savage racist?" and see what comes up.

As I go over in the "Man Enough" chapter, being penetrated does not make you any less of a man or *more gay*. According to white supremacy, it does. That kind of thinking is misogynistic and homophobic and steeped in purity and rape culture.

Now let's get into the fun part! Anal stimulation can be top tier. Though being penetrated is not high on my list, having my ass eaten for the first time is an experience I will never forget. I was pretty young and I had no idea there were all those nerve endings back there. When done right, it feels incredible, and I'm always super turned on when someone alternates between eating my ass, licking my balls, and sucking my dick. I personally use Nair to remove hair on my ass, perineum, and balls, but hair removal does not work for everyone. It's my preference for when I'm eating ass, so I try to keep things reciprocal. I also keep my pubic hair trimmed because a mouthful of hair while I'm sucking dick is not my favorite thing and less pubic hair makes my dick look bigger. I've heard great things about Manscaped grooming tools, one of them being little to no itch when hair is growing back, and having shaved balls feels fantastic, but I have not yet used their products. I make sure to shower first, and if I'm in the mood for a finger or tongue inside me, I will use cold water and an anal bulb, using a method I describe in detail in the following section.

Now, on to being penetrated and pegging: First, there is no such thing as too much lube when it comes to anal penetration because the anus is very absorbent and is a pretty strong muscle. Think you used enough? Use more. Silicone-based Shibari is my favorite lube and I recommend it to all my friends who don't already have a favorite brand. Next, for all you guys who get pleasure from seeing your partner be pleased, pegging is not just something that's for your pleasure. Many women and nonbinary people enjoy penetrating or pegging someone else. There are a variety of strap-ons that stimulate the clit so it's not only physically pleasurable for you. Another aspect of the pleasure is knowing your partner is being stimulated and turned on by doing something that turns you on. Many women and nonbinary people also enjoy the rejection of traditional sexual roles that pegging provides. There is a certain vulnerability that comes with being penetrated anally that many women find very attractive, unique, and exhilarating. Lastly, it's something that may bring you closer as it's something that may bring out a different side of you sexually and emotionally. I get into more mechanics below.

Some men find enthusiastic partners during one-night stands by already having an appropriate-size strap-on in a drawer ready to go with condoms and silicone-based lube. If this is something you're interested in, I strongly recommend buying your own strap-ons or dildos of various sizes and figuring out which ones are your favorites so that when you come across someone who'd be into it, the legwork is already done, so to speak, and you're able to lead them in the right direction in case this is unfamiliar terrain for them. Though rejection might happen, the stakes aren't as high with someone you don't know. Some men will wait until they get to know someone, see if they have sexual chemistry, and on seeing they get along as well as show a certain openness and willingness to simply please the other person, they may test the waters and ask if they'd want to try it. In my opinion, this has the potential to be far more hurtful, since you've had the chance to develop a rapport, gotten to know them, and perhaps shared other intimacies.

Using apps, you can make your desire clear before you even meet a potential partner. It's all about putting yourself out there and being prepared for any number of responses. Many women and nonbinary people will not be open to this, and that is a reality you should be aware of, but the right partners for you will be. Apply the same tips on hygiene, lubrication, and taking your time that are outlined in the following section.

BEING PENETRATED DURING SEX

I have to stress hygiene first and foremost. I do not recommend douching because it dries out the anus and thins the already thin layer coating the anus, making you more susceptible to STIs and HIV as well as anal tearing. I recommend filling an anal bulb halfway with cold tap water, putting silicone-based lube on the part you're going to insert and your anus, inserting it and gently squeezing it until a lot of the cold water is inside of your anus. Hold it in for anywhere from one to three minutes, then use the toilet and flush. Repeat each of these steps a few times until the water that comes out of you runs clear. It should take about thirty minutes. Having a diet filled with fiber, leafy greens, and superfoods will make your stools more solid and make your anus contain less fecal matter overall, though it is an anus, after all, so be kind and understanding with yourself and others. In combination with this, I recommend being mindful of the last time you ate and what it was, so that after using an anal bulb the anus is not going to become soiled again before you're going to be penetrated. I recommend waiting two hours after eating, then using the anal bulb, then having anal sex. Immediately after using an anal bulb I recommend taking a warm bath or shower so that the outer part of your anus is also clean and so that your muscles begin to relax.

- Getting a glass dildo prior to interacting with another person in order to practice and get used to the sensation can help you feel a bit more comfortable with the sensation and process. It can also help you explore this part of your body and this particular type of pleasure.

- Using antiretroviral medications often makes stools very watery, so you'll have to take special care about what you eat, at what time, and be mindful about hygiene.

- Porn never shows this happening, but it does when it includes anal play. In order to prepare the anus for penetration, relaxation and lubrication are essential.

- You have to be extremely patient and use a ton of lube on yourself and the person penetrating you. Initially *and* at various points during, there may be a lot of starts and stops.

- The anus is not used to having things enter it, so as a penis, fingers, or dildo is going in, you have to relax and also very gently push out as you're being penetrated.

- There may be lots of awkward moments, and that is okay and perfectly normal.

- Finding the right partner and the right rhythm and positions is essential.

- Many people enjoy getting on top while being penetrated so they're in control of tempo and depth and so they get the right angle, rhythm, or motion. I recommend this position for beginners, or laying on your stomach, as gravity can help.

- Many people of all genders are allergic to latex, seen as swelling, hives, itching, or a full-blown allergic reaction. Women and people assumed female at birth tend to be allergic to latex more often, so you will need to use condoms made of other kinds of materials. Polyurethane condoms, polyisoprene condoms, female condoms, and lambskin condoms are alternatives. Lambskin condoms should only be worn in the prevention of pregnancy and not STIs or HIV, so they should not be used for anal sex. Look into where these can be purchased and the potential risk factors involved with each of these ahead of time.

- After being penetrated, take a warm bath then generously apply olive oil or some other anti-inflammatory balm to your anus to reduce any potential swelling or tearing.

PENETRATING AN ANUS

Assuming the person has excellent hygiene, I recommend lots of oral stimulation before penetrating the anus: intense kissing as well as stimulation of the nipples, perineum, and inner thigh. You have to take your time when going in, even after you've applied generous amounts of lubrication, or you may severely hurt your partner, both physically and mentally. The anus is a very strong muscle that has been developing since youth to keep things in until the body is ready to release waste. Be gentle and go slow. You're likely going to have to slowly insert the head of your penis and then the rest of it, come out, and then after a moment go back in slowly, then come back out slowly. Go back in without pulling all the way out, going slightly deeper in and out with each stroke, gauging your partner's comfort level, applying more silicone-based lubrication each time you come out, kissing them, and trying to get them to feel comfortable and relaxed. Then work up to a rhythm both of you enjoy; I recommend a slower rhythm, especially at first. Sometimes you can attempt to do all of this and it will simply not work. Sometimes your partner will not be able to relax or is sore and you won't be able to penetrate them. Bank on that happening someday and default to oral stimulation, toys, kissing, frotting, watching porn side-by-side while masturbating, and so on.

PENETRATING A VAGINA

So much of man-woman porn is centered around male pleasure, misogyny, dominance, and violence. Unfortunately, it is how most people learn to be sexual, and it is based on lies and fabrication, and derives from the cisheterosexual white-supremacist male gaze. It obsesses over the size of the penis and how hard you can ram into a woman. That is not the key to pleasurable sex with a person with a vagina, or anyone; communication and chemistry are. Porn also delegitimizes sex that does not include a penis penetrating something. You will find many, many women and people with vaginas who do not particularly favor penetration, though it is often propped up as the saving grace and the epicenter of human sexuality. It is not. Most people with vaginas will not be able to orgasm solely from being penetrated. It is largely about the clitoris or outer *and* internal stimulation as well as figuring out preferred positions, their comfort and intimacy level, mental stimulation, and angles and other erogenous zones of the body. I recommend lots of oral stimulation with a special focus on the clitoris, nipples, ears, and inner thigh. I recommend reading *She Comes First* by Ian Kerner, regardless of your experience level.

For some, role-playing will do it; for some, a night of romance will do it; for some, caressing their neck will do it. It's all about communication and acknowledging that every single partner is different. Though the vagina is self-lubricating, I strongly recommend using lubrication every time, as it will help make sex more enjoyable and less risky for the person with the vagina, especially if you're having sex regularly. Many people don't realize their partner has a latex allergy or that they have a latex sensitivity or that the drying-out of the vagina is common for various reasons, namely if lubrication is not being regularly used, as it can become easily irritated, making sex painful and a UTI highly probable. While having sex, you can go from penetrating a vagina to penetrating the anus, but *never* the opposite. The same goes with oral and your fingers. Rectal bacteria should be nowhere near the vagina. Remember many, many people of various genders prefer nonpenetrative sex.

The blog *Sex Ed For Bi Guys* (https://sexedforbiguys.tumblr.com) is an incredible, much more descriptive resource to have on hand.

NOTES

Sherronda J. Brown, *Refusing Compulsory Sexuality: A Black Asexual Lens on Our Sex-Obsessed Culture* (Berkeley, CA: North Atlantic Books, 2022), 7.

Kristina Gupta, "Compulsory Sexuality: Evaluating an Emerging Concept," *Signs* 41:1 (Autumn 2015), https://doi.org/10.1086/681774.

Cora Boyd and The Cut, "A Dating Coach Matches the Dating Profile to the Person," YouTube video, October 15, 2020, www.youtube.com/watch?v=1AoBr9v4MHQ.

The essay "7-Day Confidence Building Workout" first appeared in The Good Men Project as "A 7-Day Mental Health Workout Plan," June 30, 2018, https://goodmenproject.com/health/7-day-mental-health-workout-plan-dg.

Pornhub, "Pornhub's 2016 Year in Review—Pornhub Insights," January 4, 2017, www.pornhub.com/insights/2016-year-in-review.

Pornhub, "Girls Who Like Boys Who Like Boys—Pornhub Insights," October 13, 2017, www.pornhub.com/insights/girls-like-boys-who -like-boys.

Pornhub, "More of What Women Want—Pornhub Insights," July 25, 2015, www.pornhub.com/insights/women-gender-demographics -searches.

Zachary Zane, "Why Some Women Love Watching Gay Porn," *Men's Health,* July 26, 2019, www.menshealth.com/sex-women/a28493364 /why-women-watch-gay-porn.

Jae Lin, "What Is Toxic Monogamy?" *Allgo*, 2020, https://allgo.org/what-is -toxic-monogamy.

Jessica Fern, *Polysecure: Attachment, Trauma and Consensual Nonmonogamy* (Portland, OR: Thorntree Press, 2020).

Robyn Ochs and H. Sharif Williams, *Rec-Og-Nize: The Voices of Bisexual Men: An Anthology* (Boston: Bisexual Resource Center, 2014).

Dan Savage, "Peg, Pegging, Pegged," Savage Love, August 9, 2007, https:// savage.love/savagelove/2007/08/09/peg-pegging-pegged.

Ian Kerner, *She Comes First: The Thinking Man's Guide to Pleasuring a Woman* (New York: HarperCollins, 2010).

Gigi Engle, "The Internal Clitoris, or That Thing You Never Knew You Had," *Glamour,* April 5, 2017, www.glamour.com/story/everything-you -need-to-know-about-the-internal-clitoris.

Bisexuality and Spirituality

From what I understand, humans attach themselves to things that represent or meet their highest personality needs, which is a significant part of how we form our identity. American psychologist Henry Murray developed a theory around personality that is driven by our needs, the foundation of our identity and behaviors. Many of these needs exist on an unconscious level but drive our overall behaviors and play a key role in our personality. There are primary needs, secondary needs, and tertiary needs, with each person having varying levels of fulfillment for each and a specific order or ranking for each. For example, a person whose top three personality needs are belonging, safety, and contribution may get these needs met through family and come to identify as a "family man" or say that family is very important to them. A person whose top three personality needs are autonomy, learning, and validation may get these needs met at work and come to identify as a career-driven person. A person whose top three needs are novelty, structure, and companionship may get these needs met by playing or watching sports and come to identify as a sports fan. People usually come to these identifiers based on repeated positive experiences with these identifiers meeting their needs and because the positives outweigh any fears or bad experiences the person may have.

When we are unaware of our individual personality needs and the ways identifiers meet our personality needs, we can feel as though identifiers are who we are, and we can tether ourselves to them as though they are keeping us alive. When these identifiers are called into question or critiqued, it can feel like an assault on our being, like we are facing attack, and our mortal safety is in danger because we've identified our sense of self with the things that get our needs met rather than the needs themselves. When we have an awareness of our personality needs, we can get creative about how we can meet these needs in various forms, not be tethered to identifiers to a self-effacing degree, and examine if the identifiers we currently hold are still serving us and truly align with our morals and values.

A person's relationship to spirituality is one of the seven areas of life that can make them feel fulfilled or chronically drained. The seven areas of life are career, financial, relationships, mental, emotional, physical, and spiritual or moral. If we're getting our personality needs met in each of the seven areas of our lives, if there's balance across these areas of life, and if the things we deeply value align with the lives we've created for ourselves, we are likely to feel content and have lots of energy. If you're getting a sense of certainty, belonging, love and connection, community, feeling seen, growth, peace, stability, trust, validation, discovery, inspiration, self-development, self-realization, awareness, understanding, nurturing, support, certainty, meaning, contribution, significance, participation, validation, and integrity from belonging to a particular religion or spiritual community, the consequences of said religion's ideologies and practices being discussed explicitly can make you want to fight, run away, become defensive, shut down, or gaslight others. This is my way of telling you this chapter may be challenging to get through, especially if you're Christian.

I believe that the more people know about personality needs, how they interact with the seven areas of life, and how we get needs met through identifiers like being religious, the more people would be able to be more flexible about the methods used to get needs met and not be so bound to the identifier, especially if those identifiers cause harm or are no longer serving in one way or another. Let me make something clear: I am not trying to convert anyone. I believe that to be an egregious violation of spiritual boundaries and something I hated about Christianity when I was still a Christian. The Christian faith remains alive, has spread across the globe, and depends on violating people's spiritual boundaries as well as other forms of violence. You will figure out what works for you, though it would be naive to pretend as though every religion and nontheism have equal footing or publicity as Christianity and Catholicism does in the world we live in. I am laying out personal experiences and critiques of an institution that was and is an integral arm of white-supremacist patriarchal capitalistic colonialism that has had an undeniable impact on much of the world's values, cultural norms, ideas around sexuality and gender, laws and governments, and families. I understand and respect that spirituality is an important area of most people's lives, but I want to discuss this topic explicitly as more and more people conflate sexuality and immorality and muse whether someone can actually be an LGBTQ+ person of faith.

I was raised by two conservative Christian parents who migrated to New York from Ondo State, Nigeria. We occasionally went to church on Sundays, though there were periods of my younger life where we didn't go for months at a time. Then as a preteen, I'd have the option of whether I'd want to tag along or not. I'd opt out as often as I could in large part because going to these Nigerian churches was another reminder of the ways I didn't measure up to being a masculine boy and because I didn't feel Nigerian enough. Feeling caught between two worlds is not solely reserved to me being bisexual+; it seems to be in my very DNA, and learning how to be fluent in various social circles is a skill that I had to master to survive.

I became a born-again Christian toward the end of my freshman year of high school and remained devout for the next seven years. During that time I read roughly 95 percent of the bible, exclusively surrounded myself with other Christians, sang in the choir and praise team every Sunday, was the treasurer's assistant, helped usher on occasion, helped clean the church weekly, started a traveling gospel group, prayed, fasted and tithed regularly, rarely if ever listened to music that was not explicitly Christian, didn't drink or do drugs, curse or have sex, and would go to church anywhere from two to four times a week. I was *devout*. Christianity was my life during some very formative years, and though I'd been clear about being attracted to more than one gender early on, I didn't feel like I could be a Christian and call myself anything other than straight. I was led to believe simply acknowledging my attraction to men meant I was sinning; openly identifying as bisexual+ was unthinkable.

Back then I had no resources as a bisexual+ Black boy who knew he wanted to be Christian and also knew he was attracted to more than one gender. I thought I had to push down my attraction to other boys and young men, and because of that I placed great importance on my attraction to girls. All that repression and pressure actually made my attraction to girls wane and my attraction to boys go into overdrive. When you're not processing your emotions, rejecting parts of yourself, and feel like you're being restricted, it can be lethal. Ironically, my bisexuality wasn't why I left Christianity in the end. It had a lot more to do with my values no longer aligning with the religion, how deeply sexist Christianity is, introspecting and realizing practicing was not healthy for me, my hunger for knowledge, and the clarity I got because of the distance I had from my church family going away to college. Looking back on it all, I don't know how I made it through all that pressure, and I recognize it as deeply harmful and a common symptom of global issues that can be traced back to white supremacy. Thankfully, resources to help people reconcile their LGBTQ+ identity with their faith are more accessible, and more people know they don't have to choose between spirituality and bisexuality. You can engage both.

In 2020, I was also asked by the Bi Resource Center to coauthor a pamphlet with Rachel Siden about bisexuality+ and Christianity. One of the main reasons I participated was because I was going to have the opportunity to provide some sort of intermediary consolation to people who were transitioning out of Christianity. When I was leaving Christianity in 2012, those were some of the loneliest and darkest times of my life. The only real support I had was from my therapist at the time. I felt as though I was the only person in all of humanity to be going through that, and struggled to find community and support outside the therapy room. Below are a few of my favorite passages from the pamphlet I coauthored. You can find the pamphlet in its entirety at https://biresource.org:

RECOGNIZING ABUSE OR REJECTION

Faith communities, especially ones that believe that any LGBTQ+ identity is a severe sin in the moral hierarchy, may reject or mistreat their bisexual members. This behavior may be so normalized to us that we may not immediately recognize how it may have harmed us.

Have you ever experienced . . .

- being verbally harassed or outed by someone in your faith community to leadership or the congregation?

- trying to change your sexuality through prayer sessions, counselling, "conversion therapy," or even exorcisms?

- heard constant comments about your "sinful nature," God's displeasure, or others fixating on your "spiritual health" more than anyone else's?

- being forced to leave your congregation or shunned by members of your family or faith community?

Even if you have never experienced any of the above, receiving religious-based messages that LGBTQ+ people are immoral or less-than can still impact us. Do you ever struggle with . . .

- feeling ashamed, guilty, or dirty in regard to your sexuality?
- feeling like you should only date the "opposite" gender?
- forming healthy relationships or friendships with other LGBTQ+ people?
- believing that when something bad happens, it was because of your sexuality?
- feeling uncomfortable or experiencing panic attacks when attending religious ceremonies or functions?

If you are struggling, remember that you are not alone, that there is always hope, and that many resources and support groups exist that can help you heal and get help. If you are currently experiencing abuse, contact a hotline to assist you in getting help.

Leaving Christianity

If you start to feel that a Christian context isn't healthy or authentic for you as a bi+ person, you may choose to leave your church, denomination, or even Christianity itself, and that is understandable. This transition can feel very difficult, or cause feelings of loss, pain, or guilt, because faith communities are often very tightly knit. Your faith may be so completely entwined with other aspects of your identity, especially an ethnic or cultural identity, that it can feel difficult or even impossible to separate.

- Call on affirming friends or family that can support you in making this transition.
- Engage with the parts of your religion that added something good to your life as you leave behind the parts that are damaging.

- Look for support groups, online communities, or forums where you can talk to others who have left Christianity, particularly ones with LGBTQ people or people that share your cultural identity.

- Learn about recovery from religious trauma syndrome at www .journeyfree.org.

I have to be completely transparent about what drew me to the Christian faith in the first place. It wasn't necessarily some desire to be kinder to people or my parents' prods finally wearing me down—it was born out of my disgust for myself and my sexuality. I loathed my attraction to men and felt that I was dirty, shameful at my core, evil, and unlovable. Then I was presented with the idea that there is a god who loves even the most *unlovable* of us. It was a match made in hell. Even when I dated girls or had crushes on them, I felt tainted because I'd had fantasies about boys my age and had even done some fooling around. I remember weeping the night I gave my life to Christ. I was overcome with emotion over the fact that some perfect, omnipotent being could love me—even though I was so disgusting, so corrupted, so impure—and that was the hook, line, and sinker.

When I briefly go over my religious history with people, they often assume the reason I left Christianity was because of my bisexuality, and once again, that's not the case. My self-esteem and bisexual+ politic was nonexistent then, and I thought I deserved to be regarded as a walking sin throughout my time as a Christian. I wanted my attraction to men to disappear, and if someone outright said or insinuated that I was less manly or actively sinning, I either agreed or shrugged it off while quietly believing my desires, my thoughts, and my existence to be wretched. I thought I was despicable up to the time I was leaving the religion. Leaving wasn't some act of budding bisexual+ pride. I left because I no longer believed that god existed. If this god that I spent so much time investing in didn't exist, what was the point of adopting and performing from a value system that was at odds with what I felt was right deep down inside? Christianity seemed intensely unfair, and I sensed the damage it'd been doing to my psyche and self-esteem, even though I couldn't exactly articulate it.

I'd witnessed the unfairness of gender expectations up close, the ways it affected my congregation as well as women in the Christian faith at large. It sincerely upset me that no matter how devout, no matter how proficient, no matter how passionate a woman was, being the sole pastor of a congregation was controversial, and in many churches, not allowed. The pastor who ushered me into Christianity was a newly widowed woman I'd witness be doubted, lied about, and more severely judged than male pastors were. There were rumors that she'd killed her husband—though he'd died of cancer—and that she was secretly a witch. Many people attending our church for the first time would listen to her preaching, but look around uneasily, waiting expectantly for the senior pastor, *a man,* to show up. A man would elevate and validate her stature. Even people who'd previously attended and people in the congregation found ways to voice their discomfort with a woman leading the congregation, and recommended a number of things to remedy this; one of them was closing down the church and having us join the ranks of a nearby congregation.

This situation is but a microcosm of the ways I saw gender expectations act as a creeping poison under the supervision of Christianity, and it made me take notice of the stark inequality among the sexes that is so blatant in the Christian faith and larger society. It was not uncommon to hear sermons about women who have Jezebel spirits or seek to take on manly roles; sermons badmouthing women who wear makeup, tight-fitting clothes whose purpose was to tempt men, especially men of god. I'd hear these sermons preached by women and men alike at all kinds of churches and events, and this promotes rape culture, purity culture, and biological essentialism, all integral parts of patriarchy.

The congregation I belonged to was made up of an overwhelming majority of Black women. The few men that were part of the congregation were hastily placed in leadership positions regardless of their skill, commitment, or interest, and were already married to women in the congregation. Though single women were the most consistent in every way, that was expected without acknowledgment or the reward of being offered a leadership role for years, if at all. But if a single man began to attend regularly, he'd often be offered a leadership position as a way of getting him to stay and encouraging him to join the congregation.

Another startling thing I witnessed was the expectation for the single women to either be virgins or "born-again virgins" who practiced abstinence until god led them to the right man of god. The expectation and the response were not consistent across genders. This left the worst taste in my mouth, the inequality of it all.

Nowadays, I see people resisting analysis surrounding the ways religious and spiritual communities have caused harm and can nurture mob mentality. I see this as an inability to separate their sense of self from their identifier and from the dissent taking place. Because they are in defense mode, they refuse claims that their respective religious and spiritual communities have historically and currently led to harm, materially and otherwise. They struggle to accept that something that meets so many of their own needs and brings them fulfillment and peace has been and continues to be a site of great violence for many and they personalize this as an attack on who they are. I see many LGBTQ+ Christians pointing out the English word *homosexual* was not in any bible until 1946, when it appeared in the Revised Standard Version. The RSV team admitted that the Greek word *arsenokoitai* was not condemning homosexuals, but instead those who were abusive in their pursuit of sexual encounters, and that it was an inaccurate translation, but they'd signed a ten-year contract that did not allow revisions. Others point out an older mistranslation that occurred in 1893 when the American company Biblica paid for an updated German bible that used the word *homosexual* instead of *knabenschander,* which means "boy molester." This was later put into English bibles, which read, "Man shall not lie with man, for it is an abomination." There are other historians and LGBTQ+ Christians committed to doing the work of righting this wrong, but making the church LGBTQ+ friendly does not rectify the generations of genocide, sexism, misinformation, destruction, and devastation Christianity and Catholicism have rent on the globe. The correct position for beginning to rectify this is aiding in decolonization efforts and adopting an anti-imperialist politic. What many people would benefit from realizing is that by refining their own ethics and personal convictions, and seeking out people with a compatible ethos, they'd get many of the same needs met as belonging to an organized religion, though it would not come with as many of the societal benefits or protections.

NOTES

Kendra Cherry, "How Different Types of Needs Might Influence Your Personality," Verywell Mind, September 17, 2020, www.verywellmind.com/murrays-theory-of-psychogenic-needs-2795952.

J.R. Yussuf and Rachel Siden, "Bisexuality+ and Christianity," Bi Resource Center, 2021, https://biresource.org/bi-info/bisexuality-and-christianity.

Ed Oxford, "My Quest to Find the Word 'Homosexual' in the Bible," Baptist News Global, August 10, 2020, https://baptistnews.com/article/my-quest-to-find-the-word-homosexual-in-the-bible/#.Ya_1DS2ZPq0.

Schuyler Bailar, "Homosexuality & the Bible," Pinkmantaray, March 15, 2021, https://pinkmantaray.com/bible.

Bisexuality as a Politic

Let me begin by reiterating that an identity is not a politic and that marginalized groups are not a monolith. I will elaborate on what I mean by naming this chapter "Bisexuality as a Politic" throughout this chapter.

As I mentioned in the "Unlearning Biphobia and Homophobia" chapter, talks of a gay agenda have been used to vilify and ostracize LGBTQ+ people. Since then, I've come to prioritize the company, perspective, politicization, and radicalism of others under the LGBTQ+ umbrella. As a way of protecting myself, and as a show of my appreciation and solidarity, I significantly limit the access cisgender heterosexual people take up in my mind and my life and center Black LGBTQ+ feminist politics. This is not possible for everyone, is not a perfect salve for me, and is not meant to be a stand-alone of what bisexuality is as a politic.

As Shiri Eisner writes in *Bi: Notes for a Bisexual Revolution:*

In the face of biphobia, and sexism, bisexual men have a "way out" of patriarchy, and a "way in" to creating new, "post patriarchal" masculinities. Male bisexuality gives them the opportunity to step away from dominant masculinity, to refuse to be oppressors and to instead participate in the deconstruction of patriarchy. Instead of trying to "do better" at being men, bisexual men have the opportunity to create a sexual and gender revolution.

I believe we can use our various positions not only to safely intervene in overt sexism and transphobia, if we are cisgender, but also to correct and point out everyday misogyny and transphobia. Because we are men and masculine-identified folk, people are inclined listen to us and consider what we have to say. This is not always true if you are a feminine man, and because growing up as a feminine boy is a defining part of my experience, this severely affected my confidence in my ability and at times my voice being heard. Some men do not intentionally mean to perpetuate misogyny,

although many do because it is advantageous, but they live in the same
sexist society that we do with few, if any, examples of other men correcting, challenging, and eradicating everyday misogyny, facets of rape culture,
institutional marginalization, and gender bias. Talk of a sexual and gender
revolution being possible at the hands of bisexual+ men is not hyperbole.
We're at a tremendously significant intersection in society, ranging across
lines of race, class, ability, ingenuity, and access, and together we can upend
ideas about gender and sexuality that marginalize some and favor others.

In "Pansies Against Patriarchy," Sunfrog writes:

> *Bisexual men have an important choice and responsibility. If we can tran-
> scend heterosexist power dynamics in our gay relationships, does this enable
> us to have truly liberatory relationships with women? We can begin by
> deconstructing the macho straightjacket of mainstream masculinity. [Many
> bisexual men] espouse a self-congratulatory stance. [They mistake the]
> gender-neutral utopia for which many of us strive . . . as a given reality
> in the present. They get defensive at the mere suggestion that they may
> harbor . . . internalized sexism or homophobia.*

We *must* work to be more honest than our predecessors who do not
acknowledge our own vested interest in misogyny and homophobia as
a way to assert our manhood and distance ourselves from ideas of being
perceived as weak by proximity to femininity and being seen as anything
outside a heterosexual man. Sometimes doing the right thing will mean
you will suffer to some extent or give up certain privileges. Reckoning
with this and how necessary sacrifice will be to transforming the world
into a safe, just place for everyone is key.

In an essay, therapist Dave Matteson writes, "Like all change, the process
was slow. But the rewards were many. I felt more whole. Some feminine
parts I'd learned from my mother were now consciously accepted and
integrated. . . . I no longer felt as protective of [my wife]; she learned to
care for herself better, instead of focusing her care on others."

Sunfrog also writes:

> *Because the nature of desire is so pervasive, and at times frighteningly
> subtle in our society, it is dangerous to deny these realities [of internalized*

sexism and homophobia]. The first step for any man, regardless of class, race, or sexual orientation in the fight against sexism and homophobia, is to find those seeds of oppression rooted in his own consciousness and to confront them. Disinvesting ourselves from the litany of power afforded to heterosexual men in our culture will not be easy. It includes accepting how we as men have consistently used that power to our advantage and have hurt our friends and lovers in the process. . . . Let's do it, brothers. We have human liberation to gain. We have a world of pleasure to win.

And while this sentiment likely came from good intention and comradery, and it resonates deeply, the final line could be improved. It becomes about what we can gain rather than an ethical conviction; a belief that doing the right thing because we believe it is the right thing to do is important regardless of whether or not we are *rewarded* by being the recipients of something to gain or "a world of pleasure to win"—though rim jobs are wonderful.

Saki Benibo and Joshua Briond state in their essay "'Good Men' and the Mythological Dichotomy between Toxic Masculinity and Masculinity":

Of course, there are racial implications when it comes to the conversation of masculinity and patriarchy as a whole. Its most dominant forms, as we know it, is absolutely a white-supremacist construct. And with that, racialized and colonized people do not experience or benefit from gender, patriarchy, and masculinities as white people do. It was not intended or created for us. It is crucial that we recognize this nuance. But that doesn't negate the material reality that many of us do align ourselves with these gendered and sexual structures and hierarchies.

Nonwhite men often go out of their way to prove their "manhood" in violent and oppressive ways (specifically against the women and non-cis-het men in their communities). While that can be explained by the ways we're all socialized under white-supremacist patriarchy, an explanation is not an excuse. Saying "toxic masculinity" is like saying "toxic whiteness," "toxic capitalism," or "toxic police state." It's redundant. If a system or structure is created for the purpose of maintaining power through the sub-jugation and domination of the most vulnerable and marginalized of our society, then the system or structure as a whole is the issue.

It is nothing more than arrogant and inefficacious to subject young boys and men to the teaching of masculinity as an individual struggle that you can simply opt out of through a minimal change in behavior and personality patterns. This supplants truly interrogating masculinity and manhood as a hegemonic structure that only exists to maintain gendered and sexual hierarchies and dominance.

What boys and men learn is a less overt, subtle expression of hegemonic masculinity that maintains their dominance as men. For "good men," the opposite of "toxic masculinity" is a benevolent and respectable patriarchy. Both are damaging, but the latter is dangerous because it masks itself as an alternative or reprieve. At the end of the day, these programs (summits, panels, speeches, discussions, what have you) create "good men" who are nice, but not kind. Men who have baseline emotional intelligence but lack basic empathy; men who will say and maybe even performatively do the "right" things but will relinquish none of their structural power. Because he is a "good man" who is trying, any rebuke seems unreasonably harsh or unforgiving. Liberal notions of just simply "acknowledging" and "being aware of one's privilege" is seen as substantial and "good enough" for "allies" to do toward the fight to end sexual and gendered oppression— when in reality, it does nothing materially to end structural oppression.

If we are serious about this bisexual+ revolution thing, it must include betraying masculinity, patriarchal structures, and divesting from being *one of the good ones* at a minimum. We must go on to cocreate new realities and designs not rooted in domination or ego or distortion or emotional illiteracy but in partnership with those who experience marginalization because of their gender to create harmony. I'm no longer invested in trying to rehabilitate masculinity or give alternatives to it because I understand that its design and its function is inequity. I see it in the areas children are corrected depending on their assumed gender, in how proficiency in certain areas is expected and enforced depending on someone's gender (or assumed gender), in how people romanticize codependency based on gender roles, and so on. I want to be rid of these designs so there is more space. I want freedom. I want the whole pie.

POLITICAL-ORIENTED BISEXUALITY

Many radicals crucial to political movements across history have been bisexual+, and whether their bisexuality in all its subversive nature was central to why they rebelled or not is difficult to prove in every case. Using bisexual+ identity as a defiant political statement and as active resistance to systems, however, can create change. In *Bi: Notes for a Bisexual Revolution*, Shiri Eisner writes:

> *According to [Mizrahi feminist] Vicky Shiran, the power of feminist and Mizrahi identifications stems from the threat that they hold against existing patriarchal and Ashkenazi order. Identifying by these terms means reversing the system that privileges certain groups over everyone else and using their own power against them. Taking a militant, subversive stance exposes the power structure by proudly taking on an identity that, to the existing order, should be trodden and erased. This position is defiant precisely because it dares to create a counterpoint in the face of hegemony, to intentionally reverse the values of the oppressive system.*
>
> *Seen from this perspective, it's of little surprise that Mizrahi and feminist identities provoke such intense reactions. Privileged people can feel the way these identities threaten their privileged status and the benefits that they receive as a result. For this reason also, trying to reassure hegemony that those identities are not a threat to it (for the purpose of being "accepted" into society) is moot. Hegemony is right to feel threatened, because there's no way one could change social order without deconstructing power.*
>
> *This defiant journey of subversion, however, doesn't end with the external world. According to Shiran, a woman taking on these political identities has also taken upon herself to be accountable to her own privileges and oppressor status. This means that her attempt to deconstruct power isn't only limited to the types of power that oppress her but requires an ability to examine oneself honestly and then to work on taking apart one's privileges and internalized oppression. This comes from the understanding that deconstructing only one patch of power while preserving others only creates a different kind of hegemony and oppression. Since the goal of these politics is to create another world, we could be satisfied with nothing less than everything. . . .*

Likewise, bisexuality can be used as a defiant political tactic for destroying existing order and subverting power structures. It can be used as a political tool to communicate our understanding of the social power structure as monosexist, acknowledging that the collective one belongs to has been marginalized and erased. Just like Mizrahi or feminist identities can symbolize a personal and political journey of liberation, so can bisexual identity. . . .

It means understanding that different kinds of oppression are interlinked, and that one can't liberate only one group without the others. It means acknowledging kyriarchy and intersectionality—the fact that along different axes, we're both oppressed and oppressors, privileged and without privilege. In this way taking on a bisexual identity also means taking on the responsibility for taking apart all oppression, starting with our very selves. . . .

Using bisexuality like this also means acknowledging that identities alone can't create a revolution. Rather, it means being committed to acting on the political statement borne by bisexual identity, and actively working to dismantle systems of oppression by doing activist, community, and personal work. It means being willing to look at all the dirty details and work on addressing these issues specifically and radically.

Of course, using bisexuality in this way also means acknowledging the source of this suggestion, respecting and being accountable to feminism and Mizrahi-ness. It means not only being committed to resisting all oppression in general, but also being specifically committed to supporting women and racialized people.

Bi: Notes for a Bisexual Revolution had a tremendous impact on me because I hadn't been able to connect the dots between my sexuality and my politics in my early twenties and had actively resisted it up until then. The text is rich, and the work to build this new world is plentiful, but coming up with a new design is possible. Because I see inequality as a web made strong by who else it ensnares and feeds is why Black feminist principles are a part of my foundation and politic and world view and conversations around bisexuality. It is why I no longer resist when people politicize my bisexuality and try to assign me to the post of bisexuality professor. I witness the terror behind people's eyes as they consider the collapsing of other concepts they thought of as binary and potentially their understanding of themselves. Then I make them aware of the fear and discomfort they project onto me and my sexuality and I move on. I've had to develop firm boundaries around this so that I do not fall into getting emotionally escalated or into playing the role of bisexuality professor. Instead I tell people to look up their questions online, or I simply say, "I'm not in the mood to talk about this."

On the "Straight, Bisexual & Queer Identities with Dr. Jane Ward" episode of the *Two Bi Guys* podcast, professor Jane Ward, feminist and author of *Not Gay: Sex Between Straight White Men*, argues:

> *Sexuality is not necessarily about the bodies you're attracted to or the specific gender or people but more so the types and circumstances around it and the way you want to identify politically.*
>
> *First, going to a seedy queer bar [and meeting] people of all kinds of genders. [I thought,] this is it! This is what turns me on, the profound juiciness of not really knowing what they were into or what kinds of bodies were under their clothes or just the sexual and gender creativity was dazzling to me. This is not about how I was born with a desire for vaginas. This is about that I am excited about queer life, queer spaces, the unpredictable, the unexpected; people with really smart analysis of gender and sex, creativity with their gender and sexuality. Radical politics is hot. All that context matters more to me than bodies. What we've been given is so, so narrow. It is precisely because queerness refuses normalization that it is meaningful to me and other queers. The subversion is where the romance lies.*

Ward's belief is that everyone has the capacity to be bisexual+, and thus bringing that to light and saying that the mere capacity alone is not a helpful measure of *who* is bisexual+ because it's already built into the human experience.

> *These identities are not identities built into a vacuum; it's a whole cultural experience. It's part of why people fear it [because] once you identify, then a whole landslide of cultural meanings get assigned to you. How do individual people understand their sexual desires? Do they think it has some*

bearing on their identity? Where is their cultural home? Where do they feel the most fit? Is it within queer culture or is it within straight culture? I know a lot of straight-identified women who love to hook up with other women, but they have no interest whatsoever in identifying as bi. They love heteronormativity. They love the way straightness feels in their lives and on them. They love being perceived as straight. That would be a prison for me, if I had to identify as straight. . . . It feels like such a profound misrecognition of who I am, but that's not true for them. So for me to be like no, no, no, you've had sex with women and enjoyed it, so you've got to identify as bi, at least, really feels like missing the most important point.

Following this, one of the hosts posits, "Is this a form of bi erasure?"

It's precisely because I take the bi community, bi identity, and bi politics so seriously that I don't want to say that every guy who has touched a dick during fraternity hazing is bi. Because I think of bisexuality as a political orientation and as a thoughtful sexual orientation that is at least in my social circle claimed by people who have really thought through the complexity of their sexual identity. So to say that everybody who has ever engaged in a single homosexual sex act is bi, to me just casts so wide a net as to become meaningless. So for me it's about spotlighting bisexuality, preserving bisexuality, recognizing the legitimacy of bisexuality. These are the reasons I'm not interested in calling straight-identified men "bisexual" unless they do themselves.

I absolutely love the points Ward and Eisner make here, and I find a lot of value in them. They really helped expand my mind and look at things from different angles, which I sincerely appreciate. I find issue with the double standard that seems to exist within this line of thinking, which is, in order to be or identify as bisexual+ it must be this radical, well thought out, deeply contemplated thing. The default in this society is heterosexuality, and that is seen as apolitical. To identify as anything else is automatically seen as forcefully political, though for decades there have been many gay and lesbian people who have sought to remove the political overtone from their sexuality and simply *be normal*, so much so that queer scholar Lisa Duggan helped popularize the term *homonormativity*. The term refers to a trend in queer politics that upholds and sustains "dominant hetero-normative assumptions and institutions" and endorses "a privatized, depoliticized gay culture anchored in domesticity and consumption." A stance that harps, *We're gay but we're just like you.* Enter same sex marriage as the be-all end-all.

I resent that being and identifying as bisexual+ is innately subversive and political and is often met with such intense reactions. Obviously Eisner and Ward are not responsible for this and are merely pointing things out from their research and respective angles, but it still is upset-ting that my sexual orientation is so politicized and fundamentally radical because we live in such an oppressive society. It doesn't seem fair that my existence is at such odds with the foundation of the world. A binary world founded by and deeply invested in imperialist white-supremacist capitalist patriarchy could never be *fair,* and if I hope to dissolve this resentment for good, white supremacy must fall.

I think about Steven Underwood's essay "Black Boys and Bird-Chests, or the Racialized Legacy of Body Dysmorphia in African-American Men," in which he talks about the disappointment, abuse, and criti-cism his frail Black pubescent body was met with, his experiences with body dysmorphia as a Black man, and the world's obsession with the Black male physique, masculinity, and conditional power. I think about Kimberly N. Foster of For Harriet and her video titled "WAP and the Spectacle of Sexual Liberation," where she aptly critiques Black women being coerced into displaying a very particular kind of sexual expression in order to be marketable as musicians and on social media and how it is mislabeled as "sexual liberation" far too often. Big Black men are celebrated for their accomplishments in sports while constantly being taken advantage of, seen as property in the case of Colin Kaepernick and J. R. Smith and his "Supreme" tattoo, and being commanded to leave politics out of sports. Black women are coerced to perform a sexuality that appeals to the male gaze in music and entertainment in order to be successful while marred by the very same thing. I think about how these sanctions of white supremacy are used to make a case for Black people as more primal, animalistic, less evolved. I think about fat Black women's bodies and their minds and their spirits and their will and their liberation and their joy.

BINARY SEXUALITY AS A COLONIAL PROJECT

Most people do not want to push the limits of their ideas about sexuality, and the same is true for gender. Bisexuality+ and being transgender are similar in certain regards—although sexuality is not the same as gender— in that they upend, directly threaten, and call into question this idea of the fixed, Western, colonial binary that we are told from very early on is truth. Because we live under such a constructed binary fallacy, bisexuality as well as being transgender have inherently revolutionary, disruptive potential; however, not all bisexual+ people are revolutionaries, and neither are all transgender people. Bisexuality is a threat to white supremacy in that it can illustrate how the distinct line between women and men, gay and straight, undesirables and the ideal aren't as severe as white supremacy would lead us to believe. I believe this to be part of why bisexual+ people get the question, "But which do you prefer?" so often. People are trying to mentally categorize us as one or the other.

Perhaps this is the crux of why so many bisexual+ people dislike or take issue with being labeled. And even when landing on a label like bisexual+ or pansexual or fluid, it can sometimes be a site of distress, frustration, or irritation because it's all about the possibility and circum- stances, not the box, not the labels. In the grand scheme of things, these labels were only very recently created, whereas this uncontainable pos- sibility is a moniker of what it is to be human. At best, labels are but the visible tip of the iceberg. Many bisexual+ people and transgender people feel quite significantly this limitation inherent to white supremacy, espe- cially around sexuality and gender, especially while using colonial lan- guages. Bisexuality has the potential to point out binary sexuality and binary gender as a colonial project and that without white supremacy, there'd be far more people—perhaps most—engaging romantically with or having sex with various genders and gender presentations.

Can we reconsider human sexuality actually being predominantly sit- uated along the bisexual+ spectrum, with only a small percentage existing at polar opposites, instead of heterosexuality being the predominant human sexuality? Can we look at all the ways attraction begins and ends, and how it's not always about penetrative sex but often about close- ness, admiration, familiarity, resolution, and trait variety? Can we look at nonsexual attraction, and more specifically asexuality, as valid? What would society look like if everyone along the bisexual+ spectrum was protected and had their needs met? What would society look like with an end to biphobia, homophobia, and transphobia? What would society look like with an end to sexism, purity culture, and rape culture? What would society look like with an end to ableism, fatphobia, and racism? What would we need to make that a reality?

Imagine and embrace the possibility bisexuality+ offers. This uncertainty can be rattling to some, but there is bravery in being open to the possibility of your life looking a myriad of ways depending on who you're with, and there's certainty in knowing that who you're with does not determine who you are. You can also know exactly how you want your life to look, and the only unknown is the person or gender of your partner or partners. Further, nonmonogamy may be another thing that disrupts the individualistic nuclear family model that's been prescribed by white supremacy as the only valid form of love or family or society. Even if nonmonogamy is not for you, many relationship anarchist principles center community, care, and cultivating deep relationships whether they be familial, platonic, or romantic. That is a direct challenge to the individualistic white supremacy model. We must kill our god if we are to experience true revolution as a society. Our god is white imperialist capitalist patriarchy, which centers domination and withholding.

I do not think it's enough to simply become more comfortable with our bisexuality and exist under this current system of white-supremacist capitalist cisheteropatriarchy. You are more than welcome to do that. You can take what you will from this book, find your community and partners, and go about your life. This system is so incredibly insidious, overbearing, and violent, however, and not everyone will be able to heal and reconcile their identities in all these different ways. The system must be dismantled, destroyed, and replaced, and I think it's more daring, more sound, to upend it.

MENTORING AND THE GAY AGENDA

Ideas that get flung around about the gay agenda can seep into how you see yourself and how you show up in the world. Viewing yourself through this lens, another's lens, as though you are damaged or infected and can spread said infection, can do lasting damage to your psyche. Years ago, I remember getting myself ready to have *the talk* with my eleven-year-old brother and getting this intense fear that me talking to him about safer sex, consent, and sexuality in general would turn him bisexual+ or gay. I didn't want to infect him with my queerness. This is a very exclusive yet revealing example of the ways these societal ideas manifest in many queer people. Many gay and bisexual+ men and masculine-identified people think the information we have about safe sex is tainted or inadequate in the face of presenting this to a cisgender heterosexual boy or young man. Many of us feel like our experience as queer or feminine men might not be enough, and this manifests in many ways.

THINGS TO KEEP IN MIND

- I asked myself, What does an eleven-year-old boy need to know about safer sex and consent?
- Taking myself out of it helped, and though the talk can be awkward regardless, it doesn't have to be.
- I had to remind myself that being bisexual+ or gay is not contagious and it is not an illness; it's beautiful.
- A lot of times, if you don't make talking about sex and sexuality such a big deal, the young men in your life may not either.
- The talk doesn't have to be one long monologue where you cover all the bases regarding sex and dating and sexuality. Sex and gender are vast and complex and deserve many conversations.
- It should be an ongoing conversation where you're sharing information as you learn it in an age-appropriate way.
- The young people in our lives can teach us many things.

BISEXUAL+ HEALING

There's an aspect of being marginalized and ridiculed in greater society as well as within many LGBTQ+ organizations and communities that is central to many bisexual+ people's experience. What gets less recognition are the dangers present in many bisexual+ communities and organizations as a result of the stigma, erasure, and conditions we're often subjected to. In many bisexual+ communities people live with mental illness or chronic pain, are neurodivergent, live in poverty, are abuse survivors, are sexual assault survivors, have poor boundaries, are abusive, are predatory, and so on. Because these things shape people's reality and the way they communicate with the world around them, trauma and dysfunctional communication often become commonplace. How do we thrive and heal as a bisexual+ community—and more widely as the LGBTQ+ community—if so many of us are living with unaddressed trauma and in turn are in a perpetual state of retraumatizing ourselves and traumatizing one another?

THINGS TO CONSIDER

- This question might be unqualified pathological bullshit that is unfair, banally pessimistic, and may not apply to your life or experience whatsoever.

- Someone being bisexual+ does not automatically mean they're a safe open-minded person.

- Every bisexual+ support group is not created equal, *and* there are people and personalities who linger in support groups for various reasons.

- Every bisexual+ person does not have the interests of all bisexual+ people of all socioeconomic and political affiliations in mind.

- You can be empathetic to people's trauma without allowing yourself to become a punching bag, or get reeled in to their lives, or allow your relationship with them to be dictated by that trauma.

- Asserting healthy boundaries in a respectful way is a skill you can develop and get better at.

- You can speak up about your apprehension to being in contact with certain people.

- You can ask others about someone else's patterns of treating people.

- Modeling appropriate behavior may not be enough. Sometimes you may have to verbally tell people their behavior is inappropriate or let them know that if they engage with you in a way you do not like, you will no longer speak to them.

◆ Sometimes you may have to find community outside major bisexual+ and LGBTQ+ groups and organizations, whether that be one or two healthy bisexual+ friends or monosexual people who are healthy and supportive.

◆ Healing myself by doing the work in therapy (cognitive behavioral therapy, EMDR, IFS, and so on); reading self-help books; writing about my experiences; watching YouTube videos; daily meditation to let my body and mind know I am safe to relax, to get in touch with my emotions, to observe my patterns, fears, and insecurities, to offer myself approval, to come up with strategies to get my needs met in the future; exploring Eastern healing methods such as acupuncture, yoga, and chakra work; joining the Personal Development School to learn about attachment theory and understanding the subconscious mind; and coming up with tailored regimens that work for me is how I make sure I show up to bisexual+ communities and the world without causing harm.

◆ I recognize that this is incredibly inaccessible and cannot keep up with the rates of bisexual+ people frequently facing violence and surviving trauma.

Hopefully someone reading this will be able to come up with solutions to this pressing problem of trying to find safety within marginalized, and oftentimes traumatized, communities.

NOTES

Shiri Eisner, *Bi: Notes for a Bisexual Revolution* (Berkeley, CA: Seal Press, 2013), 234.

Sunfrog, "Pansies Against Patriarchy: Gender Blur, Bisexual Men, and Queer Liberation," in *Bi-Sexual Politics: Theories, Queries and Visions,* ed. Naomi Tucker (New York: Harrington Park, 1996), 319–24.

Dave Matteson, "Bisexual Feminist Man," in *Bi Any Other Name: Bisexual People Speak Out,* 2nd ed., eds. Lani Ka'ahumanu and Loraine Hutchins (Riverdale, NY: Riverdale Avenue Books, 2015).

Saki Benibo and Joshua Briond, "'Good Men' and the Mythological Dichotomy between Toxic Masculinity and Masculinity," RaceBaitr, March 21, 2019, https://racebaitr.com/2019/03/21/good-men-and-the -mythological-dichotomy-between-toxic-masculinity-and-masculinity.

Rob Cohen and Alex Boyd, "Straight, Bisexual & Queer Identities with Dr. Jane Ward," *Two Bi Guys,* podcast, October 21, 2019, https://podcasts.apple .com/us/podcast/straight-bisexual-queer-identities-with-dr-jane-ward /id1480131653?i=1000454287221.

Steven Underwood, "Black Boys and Bird-Chests, or the Racialized Legacy of Body Dysmorphia in African-American Men," Medium, February 22, 2019, https://blaqueword.medium.com/black-boys-and-body -dysmorphia-b85cf97dd32c.

Kimberly N. Foster, "WAP and the Spectacle of Sexual Liberation," For Harriet, YouTube video, August 30, 2020, https://youtu.be /ILApR36KgQw.

Cam Wolf, "NBA Tells J. R. Smith to Cover Up His Supreme Tattoo Or Else," *GQ,* October 1, 2018, www.gq.com/story/jr-smith-supreme -tattoo-nba.

Emily Moss, Kriston McIntosh, Wendy Edelberg, and Kristen E. Broady, "The Black-White Wealth Gap Left Black Households More Vulnerable," Brookings, December 8, 2020, www.brookings.edu/blog /up-front/2020/12/08/the-black-white-wealth-gap-left-black -households-more-vulnerable.

Stephen Miller, "Black Workers Still Earn Less than Their White Counterparts," SHRM, June 11, 2020, www.shrm.org/ResourcesAndTools /hr-topics/compensation/Pages/racial-wage-gaps-persistence-poses -challenge.aspx.

Francesca Gino, "Another Reason Top Managers Are Disproportionally White Men," *Scientific American*, September 12, 2017, www .scientificamerican.com/article/another-reason-top-managers-are -disproportionally-white-men.

Olivia Pavco-Giaccia, Martha Fitch Little, Jason Stanley, and Yarrow Dunham, "Rationality Is Gendered," *Collabra: Psychology* 5:1 (January 1, 2019), 54, https://doi.org/10.1525/collabra.274.

Lauren Rouse, "Suicide Rates Are on the Rise among Older White Men in Rural Areas," Vital Record, March 29, 2021, https://vitalrecord.tamhsc

.edu/suicide-rates-are-on-the-rise-among-older-white-men-in -rural-areas.

Ashley Nellis, "The Color of Justice: Racial and Ethnic Disparity in State Prisons," The Sentencing Project, October 13, 2021, www.sentencing project.org/publications/color-of-justice-racial-and-ethnic-disparity -in-state-prisons.

Questions for Reflection

Something that I still find intriguing to this day is just how much negative, critical self-talk can diminish experiencing attraction to a particular gender. I realized if I was constantly doubting the legitimacy of my own sexuality, or thinking of all the ways things could go wrong, or how unequipped I was, or how much I didn't want to be betrayed by or made to look stupid by a particular gender, it impacted overall attraction. That is mind-blowing to me because I'd previously thought of attraction as something that was completely unconscious, innate, and sedentary. I'd internalized so much disbelief, stigma, fear, and inadequacy around my attraction to women during my teens that for the large part of my twenties, I only occasionally found myself drawn to women. I'd avert my eyes when I came across attractive women, judge desires I had for women as creepy, find some way to brush off budding attraction, or talk myself out of any possibility that it could ever work. Eventually my attraction to women spoke to me less and less. For many of you, this may sound familiar, only it may be this way for you with men. I learned to have more compassionate self-talk, free of judgment and expectation, and to completely accept and celebrate my attractions across the gender spectrum. I learned to work on the fears I had surrounding being attracted to, dating, and having sex with women. I intentionally showed my sexuality unconditional love by setting thought boundaries, boundaries with friends and family, and boundaries around the media I consume. After pouring time and love into the relationship I had with myself and my sexuality, I began to experience relief and more consistent attraction to women. Because I have worked through a lot of my major fears surrounding women, men, nonbinary people, my needs, boundaries, nonmonogamy, commitment, relationships, vulnerability, giving and receiving, trust, and sex, I am able to be far more present in my day-to-day life and during interactions with people I'm attracted to of various genders. This is the picture of what my most realized bisexual+ self looks like, and I am looking forward to seeing what the rest of my life has in store for me.

Questions You May Get from Others

What are you? Are you gay? When people who I haven't made up my mind about disclosing to yet ask me about my sexuality, or I do not feel safe, I default to saying that I don't do labels. It usually works, but if someone is pressuring me or asks other questions to try to get an answer out of me or to put my sexuality together for themselves, I usually turn it back around on them and ask why they're questioning me. What do they hope to gain from knowing this detail about me? Sometimes it will be because they're attracted to me and don't know how to say it, because they are working through their own sexuality or because they have some unresolved feelings about sexuality or bisexuality from some past lover or circumstance. Regardless of whether they mean well or not, it is important to have boundaries in this regard and to enforce them respectfully and firmly even if a person seems to mean well.

Can bisexual+ men be bottoms? Yes. Remember the type of pleasure you want to experience in your body is not the same as who you want to experience that pleasure with. The submissive versus dominant role, especially in the BDSM sex arena, has no bearings on the genders you find attractive and actually speaks to *what* turns you on rather than *who* turns you on. Through all of this we have to keep in mind that the cisgender male G-spot is located in the anus, and it's an enormous site of nerve endings, a.k.a. a pleasure center.

Why aren't more bisexual+ men honest? This is a leading question that's disparaging toward the character of bisexual+ men. Many bisexual+ men are honest about their sexuality, although stigma and archaic ideas around manhood and masculinity makes this incredibly difficult. It's important to note that bisexual+ men don't owe people information about who they find attractive.

How many women have you had sex with? Why are you asking? What does it matter? This is an inappropriate question. Regardless of what the answer is, that does not make me any more or less bisexual+.

How many men have you had sex with? Why are you asking? What does it matter? This is an inappropriate question. Regardless of what the answer is, that does not make me any more or less bisexual+.

Being with a transgender person is like dating both genders, right? No. Transgender people are the gender they say they are. Transgender people are not more than one gender, unless they say they are.

How is it coming out to other members of the LGBTQ+ community? Personally I am not a big fan of it. In my experience, announcing my bisexuality can come off as though I am trying to put distance between myself and the LGBTQ+ person. As though I am trying to say I'm still part of the straight world and haven't fully embraced my queerness. For me, meeting another LGBTQ+ person does not automatically ensure that I will be accepted or supported, and I often gauge to see how much they know about gender *and* sexuality being a spectrum.

How do you know you're bisexual+ if you haven't had sex with a particular gender? Being bisexual+ is about desire, as is being gay or straight. You don't need to kiss or hug or be close to or fuck a person of a particular gender to know that you'd like to. Lastly, bisexual+ virgins exist.

Are bisexual+ men less misogynistic? Are bisexual+ men better at sex? No. Each bisexual+ man has their own complicated relationship with misogyny, gender, sexuality, religion, feminism, culture, tradition, and so on, and someone being bisexual+ does not necessarily mean they will be any more or less misogynistic. Some bisexual+ men have had to think about traditional gender roles in a way our straight counterparts never will, and thus can sometimes take an active interest in challenging widely accepted beliefs about gender. Every bisexual+ man is different.

I find that a lot of bisexual+ men, especially in the beginning of their journey of accepting their bisexual+ identity, are intensely tied to ideas of Eurocentric gender roles, which say only a hyperfeminine woman is the ideal type of woman and only a hypermasculine man is the ideal type of man. A lot of bisexual+ men don't want to date trans women, trans men, or nonbinary trans people; many bisexual+ men don't believe that there are more than two genders.

So when the conversation goes from denying our very existence to the opposite, which is that bisexual+ men are not misogynistic at all, once again bisexual+ men are not allowed to exist as complex, distinct human beings.

Many bisexual+ men who have been out for a while or who do the work to continuously challenge sexism can be really healthy, supportive, loving partners and fathers who listen and consider their partner's feelings and consider certain things their partner's face because they're aware of the way gender impacts people's lives in a way that is very different from our gay and straight counterparts.

Have I internalized homophobia if I'm not into the gay scene? When you're first coming out or are beginning to accept your attraction to the same gender, it can be terrifying and the cause of an identity crisis or a time filled with uncomfortable moments, and in some cases, uncomfortable years. Therapy can help this process along greatly, and so can joining a bisexual+ support group or LGBTQ+ support groups more generally. Being around other people who were like me helped a lot with my confidence and self-assurance because it was infallible confirmation that I wasn't the only one. But even still, it was very uncomfortable for quite some time.

Being exposed to gay/LGBTQ+ culture can be incredibly overwhelming. Perhaps you grew up being the only LGBTQ+ person in your neighborhood, or you haven't had many in-depth relationships with a variety of LGBTQ+ people; either way, suddenly being around so many LGBTQ+ people can take some getting used to. LGBTQ+ spaces can be dramatically different in that they sometimes display penetrative sex and openly discuss physical pleasure, sex, and sexuality in a very overt way that can be very jarring. I remember my first time in a large gay club, and there were go-go boys—akin to strippers who can become naked or not, or give private dances or not—walking around, hanging out, and dancing on people in thongs. They dance at highly visible spots in the club and help energize the room. That is a norm for many large gay clubs, and so is same-sex porn playing on TV screens at clubs or bars, which can be a lot to get used to. If you are still working through your phobias, self-esteem, and being comfortable in your own skin, these environments might bring all sorts of feelings to the surface and cause a strong reaction to being in these spaces. When you talk about queer nightlife, a lot of it is about exploring sexuality, trying to take some of the stigma away from it, and acknowledging that we're all human beings with varying sex drives, and there's nothing wrong with desiring men sexually. It confronts this head-on in a very direct, oftentimes crude way. Though that may be part of the intention, there's room for a lot of critique because it is a bit one-dimensional to reduce sexuality and your interest in men to solely body parts and sex. Sex can be a site of liberation, really beautiful, fun, and quite healing. It's about experiencing pleasure in your body, and that's amazing, but that is not the full scope of my own sexuality. It's oftentimes about connection, it's oftentimes about being able to joke, bond, share affection, and my romantic imaginings of people.

What kinds of body parts are allowed to be shown in these spaces? It's almost always white, cisgender, muscled or thin, and able-bodied. I find a lot of the critique valid, though at the same time I think there is a lot of strength looking directly at your sexual attractions and trying to let go of the shame or whatever you feel around it. There's nothing wrong with sex, but there is something wrong with what has been applied to sex, specifically between people of the same gender, by the larger society and major religions that encourage shame.

Also in larger society, rigid ideas around gender are extremely significant, especially regarding how you address and interact with people, which dictates the quality of people's lives. In many LGBTQ+ spaces, that is intentionally fucked with, and is often a fluid or flipped thing. Calling another man "sis," "girl," "ma'am," "bitch," and so on is not uncommon in many LGBTQ+ spaces. Some of it is a play on what so many of us have been told all our lives, that we're not *really* men, according to white supremacy, and that we're not man enough, so the lingo often confronts that and tries to make light of something that may be a site of pain for you. Some of it is also just very playful and tongue-in-cheek, with very little thought put into it, and occasionally it can be used as pejorative, depending on the context. Also, some gay and bisexual+ men have a hard time respecting boundaries in terms of how others would like to be referred to. Many trans men and trans masculine people have talked about how triggering being referred to as "sis," "ma'am," and the like is, and everyone, whether trans or cis, ought to be referred to the way they would like to be.

Another thing is assumptions. When entering gay or LGBTQ+ spaces for the first time, some people don't want others to make assumptions about them that play into stereotypes about gay men, but no matter what you wear or do or who you hang out with, people are going to make assumptions about you. You don't have to live up to those; you don't have to allow those assumptions to define you; and you don't have to fight so hard to distance yourself from them. Working to become more confident in your sexuality and who you are at your core will help make the assumptions people make about you become incredibly insignificant. If you're clear about who you are, it won't matter all that much. You just have to be you while being open to trying new things without judgment and go about your business.

I felt very uncomfortable around drag queens when I first started frequenting LGBTQ+ spaces. A lot of that had to do with the rigid ideas about gender I'd been taught, which said men shouldn't wear dresses or wigs or makeup. It was also because I thought they were mocking cisgender women, or were trans women with egotistical personalities. What helped me was doing a bit more research and learning that though drag performance may be associated with the trans umbrella, they are the opposite of what it is to be a transgender person—unless they actually are transgender. Drag is about the show, the creativity, and the performance of gender to an exaggerated degree in that it can often critique the rigidity assigned to gender, clothes, and gender roles. Gender roles times ten, whereas being a person of trans experience is all about being a real person of the particular gender they know themselves to be. Hearing it framed that way allowed something within me to click. What also helped was being aware that drag performers are actors who are there to entertain, host, and put on a show.

It's important to mention that not all drag performers see it the way I've described, and to them it's just fun. It's a character they're putting on. They're just having a good time being a host and taking on a larger than life persona as a job. It reminds me of being a kid sitting in front of the fan, singing with a T-shirt fixed on my head so that it acted as my hair that blew in the wind the fan made. I'd do it by myself or with my sisters, and it was fun and silly and harmless. Drag shows are not really my thing, but they don't bother me like they did in the beginning, and sometimes they help improve my weekend experience.

In the beginning I shied away from drag queens because I didn't want to be associated with them or be seen as *that kind of gay*. Though I grew up assumed to be gay, I'd always policed myself, never allowed myself to really relish in my femininity, and I was terrified to be seen as *that kind of gay* by straight people. I didn't want to live up to the stereotype of the feminine queer man; it really bothered me. I didn't want people to think I was like that. Part of the work was going there and evaluating what I thought was so bad about being a feminine man or a drag queen. I had to answer, *What do I think all feminine gay or bi+ men are like?* Firstly acknowledging that they're not all the same, and then asking, *Well, what's so wrong with the way they present their gender or behave?* They're just living their lives. They're doing what they want to do, having fun or being silly or doing a job or whatever. What is so bad about that? We all should be allowed that agency to express ourselves and present our own unique expression of our gender with it not being that big of a deal. There is a problem that exists in society where the ways someone is marginalized becomes their entire personhood, as though they don't have interests, ideas, and skills that don't revolve around their marginalization. As a society we have a hard time seeing people who are not white, cisgender, heterosexual, thin or muscled, and abled as layered human beings with range. They're pictured in snapshots.

Even though I've done this internal work, in many gay spaces I do feel uncomfortable but for very different reasons. Biphobia is rampant in many gay and LGBTQ+ spaces, and I often feel like we're just one or two more drinks away from someone making a joke rooted in biphobia. I do feel uncomfortable walking into a bar or club and there being porn on all of the TV screens because for me it creates this sex-driven and sexually charged atmosphere where connection and autonomy is not a priority. That does make me uncomfortable, and I know what bars and clubs feature porn, and I try to stay away from them unless I'm in a particular mood. Being in an environment with go-go boys is not uncomfortable for me anymore because I've educated myself on various forms of sex work. It's no longer a big deal for me and occasionally I patronize go-go boys.

There's often groping happening in gay clubs, and some men don't practice consent. I always gauge the room or space when I enter it because not
every space is the same. When I go out, I see what the vibe is, and see how
drunk people are, which will often exacerbate some of the negative things I
mentioned. From that I decide how long I'm going to stay and how I feel.

Also, when it comes to the ways the LGBTQ+ community is displayed at large, and our spaces, it does glorify nudity, alcohol, muscles,
defying gender norms, and partying; however, there are many gay and
bisexual+ men who are into gaming, sports, cars, music festivals, the out-
doors, alternative or Goth scenes, and so on. There are many LGBTQ+
communities that center those things, where you might feel more at
home than the places described above. You've just got to go where your
curiosity and interests take you without passing judgment on certain
LGBTQ+ communities that may not feel good for you at the present
moment. These other interests aren't often attributed to what it means
to be LGBTQ+, and I think more work should be done to change that
without looking down on or further demonizing popular LGBTQ+
images. You have to find *people* you gel with.

**How do I know if I'm bisexual+? How'd you know you were
bisexual+?** Everyone is different, and some people don't realize they're
bisexual+ until much later in life or after their first romantic or sexual
encounter with a person of a gender they don't normally engage with.
I knew very early on because I would easily become infatuated with
people of more than one gender. I'd want to be around said individuals
often, for them to like me and think I was impressive in some way. For
me, infatuation begins with me thinking someone is admirable or proficient in some way, with some curiosity about them, and then it grows
if we have positive interactions or I allow my mind to dwell on them.
I didn't start to have sexual fantasies about my crushes until the end
of middle school. Nowadays my fantasies aren't usually sexual; they're
usually very G-rated, involving hugging, kissing, and verbal validation.
Everyone is different, though, and your attraction and experience of this
is valid. The way your attraction works can and will change over time.

How do I stop being afraid of dating women? For me, my feeling of fear surrounding dating women lasted for years, but during that
time I was working on my confidence and doing work to unlearn the

things I'd learned about gender and patriarchy, which itemizes women and turns them into a notch on your belt, proving that you're truly bisexual+, that you're truly a man. Another one was that it would invalidate my bisexual+ identity, separate me from my queer identity, and mean that I was straight. I did a lot of healing work by going to therapy, doing attachment theory work, doing a ton of reading and watching YouTube videos, and confronting my biases, both conscious and unconscious. I was consuming more media created by women with feminist themes either weaved in or at the forefront of the narrative in order to learn about and absorb more perspectives outside my own with absolutely no attachment to the idea that doing this would allow me more access to women. I cannot stress that part enough. I went into this because I wanted to heal *and* because I believed it was the right thing to do. That's it.

Honestly speaking, I was really scared of women for most of my twenties, and I didn't want to be rejected by them anymore because I'd had quite a bit of rejection based on me being feminine, being assumed to be gay, because I acted like a creep, because they weren't attracted to me, because we weren't compatible. I had no desire to be rejected in a romantic sense by a woman anymore and had completely given up on the idea of engaging with women at all. I was doing this work because I thought it was the right thing to do, not because I was trying to end up in a relationship with a woman or trying to prove to people that because I'm in a relationship with a woman, that means I am truly bisexual+. We have to fight really hard against these urges because they're steeped in misogyny, steeped in viewing women as items and trophies and not as real human beings with agency and autonomy and gravitas. You're not fully valuing the other person in front of you when you're prizing them as their gender. "Yeah, I'm with a woman!" Well, how do you feel about her? How does she feel about you? How does she feel about herself? Is this relationship worthwhile? Are they the right person for you either for right now or for a long time?

Take your time. Take a break from the idea of even trying to engage women. Try to work on yourself, heal, and work on that misogyny. If there's one thing I hope you gain from this book, it is perspective on the ways you uphold patriarchy and the part you play in it. Spend more time trying to bring patriarchy down.

Many bisexual+ men fear engaging with women for entirely different reasons that revolve around gender expectations, experience, and sexual performance. Many bisexual+ men have more experience with men or feel as though in order to be attractive to women, they have to shrink themselves or step into the role of being a masculine, heterosexual, alpha male. I would say that in those cases it is important to find the right women, possibly bisexual+ women, who would find your sense of humor, your references, your gender expression and presentation desirable and not like something that needs to be hidden or toned down. It may take a lot longer or may not happen altogether, but what's important to absorb here is that changing things about yourself because of this may not be healthy and may do damage to your self-esteem. You can lose yourself trying to be liked.

If you have hesitation about engaging with women due to being less sexually experienced with women, do more to educate yourself. Search online for different sexual techniques for clitoral stimulation and penetration so that you're more confident and it's not such a scary unknown.

A valuable question I learned to ask myself when I'm experiencing distress is, *What do I need to feel relief?* For a large part of my twenties, what I needed was to take dating women off the table and understand what some of the underlying things causing me so much distress were. Now what I need to feel relief concerning engaging with women is to remind myself to trust in my ability to investigate how a woman truly feels about bisexual+ men, determine whether or not I feel safe around her, and trust that I'll leave if it's anything but affirming.

How do I stop being afraid of dating men? Part of this may be the fear of negative reactions from family, friends, and society at large, which is a well-founded fear that you do have to consider. Referring back to the "Who to Tell, Why to Tell, and How to Tell Them" and "Being Out Online, Being Out in Real Life, Being Out at Work" chapters may come in handy. There's also the aspect of being afraid that dating a man will make you gay, people will think you're gay, and that it will invalidate your bisexual+ identity. Remember that being bisexual+ means that you are attracted to, open to, or capable of being satisfied with a person of any gender, and you are still bisexual+ regardless of the gender of the person you're dating, unless your bisexual+ identity is not exactly this.

I've found it incredibly helpful to interrogate whatever negative ideas I have about being gay or being perceived as gay and what would be so bad about people thinking I'm gay. That was a major area of work that I had to do. Bi erasure is real, and it's deadly, and that is important to name and address. However, it was important for my wellness that I unlearn the homophobia that I'd internalized.

Also, many people are afraid of dating men because so many men are rough, emotionally unintelligent, macho, and downright mean. That is a very real societal norm, and it can be incredibly scary to open oneself up to the possibility of dating someone who may possess some or all of these qualities. What helped me was knowing that even though many men are like this, not all of them are. Finding value in the parts of myself that are feminine helped me see value in femininity as a whole that I hadn't seen growing up, as did understanding that everyone is on a spectrum and is a balance between what we deem masculine and feminine. Remember, you don't have to be with someone who's a jerk, and you can always leave or call out their behavior as it happens. You can also take dating men off the table completely for yourself and still be bisexual+. You do not have to engage with a particular gender if you do not want to. On reflection, I found that I was less scared of dating men than I was of dating women in my twenties, but at first I was scared of opening up and being truly vulnerable with men. I did a lot of healing work by going to therapy, doing attachment theory work, unlearning femmephobia, leaning into and valuing my own femininity, and confronting my biases, both conscious and unconscious.

A valuable question I learned to ask myself when I'm experiencing distress is, *What do I need to feel relief?* For most of my teenage years and early twenties, what I needed was to take engaging with boys and men off the table and understanding what some of the underlying things causing me so much distress were. Now what I need to feel relief concerning engaging with men is to remind myself that I'm still bi regardless of who I engage with, and that I can trust myself to take my time getting to know them and learning what they have the capacity for in the relationship department, while managing my expectations.

My partner reacted poorly to me telling them about my bisexual+ identity. What do I do? This might be the beginning of the end. Unfortunately this is a very common reaction to men coming out as bisexual+, especially when they're in a relationship with a woman. Many women hear that a man is bisexual+ and automatically think it means they've cheated or that they're actually being told the guy is gay and no longer interested in them. Some hear that their partner plans to cheat or wants to be in an open relationship, or that they'll never be satisfied with only one gender. Unfortunately, because of conditioning and the demonization of bisexual+ men, especially Black bisexual+ men, they do not hear that the guy simply finds more than one gender attractive; they hear that he wants a threesome, that he's actively having sex with more than one gender, and that he's actually gay.

It sucks when someone responds this way. It sucks to be rejected for being honest about your sexuality. What I've learned over the years is to not take other people's projections personally because it has nothing to do with me and everything to do with what they've learned about the world around them. It has everything to do with the lack of information they have and the bias and stigma around bisexuality. This is easier said than done, especially if it happens with someone you've been with for a while who has gotten to know you on a deep level, or if it's happened multiple times. Remember that their bias is present because of conditioning. Nearly every time we see bisexual+ men in the media, they're associated with cheating, lying, secretly being gay, and transmitting HIV.

It's important to let your partner know what being bisexual+ means specifically for you, and let them know the ways society conditions all of us. Let them know you waited because you wanted to get to know them without this label hanging over you, that you wanted to be honest and share another part of your experience with them because you thought they'd be supportive.

With many gay men, what can happen is erasure. They may dismiss your sexuality, and say that you're really gay, and try to minimize your attraction to women, or point out that since you're with them, your bisexuality doesn't matter, and you're gay. They may refer to you as "gay" to their friends and online. All these things are damaging and harmful because they do not show support and are blatant acts of bi erasure. Let them know how hurtful this is, and that you need them to get your sexuality right, and respect your label and identity when you're present and when you're not.

Honestly speaking, this person does not sound like they'd be the most supportive, and while there are other ways of finding support around your sexuality, such as support groups, seeking out a community and friends, therapy, and YouTube, it is important to be with someone who you feel supports and validates you, not someone who is ashamed of a part of you. There are some people who discourage their partner from being out as bisexual+ while they're in a relationship because they don't want to face ridicule or because they're embarrassed. Anybody who does not want to be with you solely because you are bisexual+ may not be the right person for you long-term. It's important to prioritize your self-esteem because the relationship you have with yourself is the most important relationship you could ever have. You deserve better, but the world around us also needs to radically change.

Do we have a duty to be visible for the next generation of LGBTQ+ youth? You do not have a duty, but it is an opportunity. It's not a must that you out yourself to let the next generation know that they're not alone, but it does present an opportunity to do so. You do not have to do anything that inconveniences you or goes against your personal decision to keep personal things personal. It's an opportunity to learn and share some experiences, but it's not all fairy tales, it's not all great, and it does come with risk and vulnerability. Sometimes sharing yourself in this way can be draining, not only in confronting and reliving certain things through conversation with the younger generation, but it can be very challenging.

It is an *opportunity* for the next generation to know that there is someone they can look up to, that there's an example of what their life could look like. I didn't know what my life could look like in my twenties and thirties because I didn't know of a Black bisexual+ man who was just living his life on his own terms. That would have helped open up a world of possibility for me where there was just a blank slate in my imagination.

A lot of bisexual+ people feel guilty for being assumed to be straight, and often feel like they're not queer enough, or that their identity is constantly being erased, or that they are hiding. This is completely understandable, and there are many parallels between this and being in a relationship with someone of the same gender. Ways people combat bi erasure is by wearing a bisexual+ or pansexual pride pin, or putting the flag on your car, or other tame ways of letting people know that your identity is still your identity even though you're in a monogamous relationship.

Do bisexual+ people have an easier time coming out than gay and lesbian people do? No. Many bisexual+ people experience homophobia and the added layer of biphobia. For example, many parents, family members, and friends will disregard the disclosure of a bisexual+ identity, pretend as though it didn't happen, and assert that it is a phase, or that they'll end up with a gender different than their own, and then they'll be straight. Many loved ones will suggest bisexual+ people hide their sexuality in the hopes they'll end up with a gender different than their own, or pressure them to be with someone of a different gender and disregard, disrespect, and invalidate any relationship they're in with a person of the same gender. This puts an unhealthy pressure on the bisexual+ person to be with a particular *gender* over their interest in a particular *person*. This almost always will affect their romantic relationships, even if subconsciously. This can make a bisexual+ person internalize homophobic and biphobic ideas and cause them to view same-gender partnerships as illegitimate, only good for sex (although only wanting sexual relations with a particular gender does not automatically mean someone thinks this). Bisexual+ people are often groped or experience other forms of sexual violence when they come out in the workplace or in social settings. They face disbelief and discrimination from straight and gay people alike.

I've never done anything with another man so I can't be bisexual+, right? Bisexual virgins exist, as do bisexual+ people who have only been with a particular gender. That does not make them any less bisexual+. Being bisexual+ is about who you have romantic or sexual desire for. Even though you've never done anything with another man, you can still be and identify as bisexual+.

You can expect iterations of these questions and more, but here's the thing: you don't have to provide an answer. You don't owe anyone an answer to any of these questions for any reason. These questions can be intrusive, rude, and draining. You are not obligated to provide anyone with the answers, and it is not your responsibility to educate others on this. The internet exists. Books exist. YouTube exists. By always being the only point person someone has to source knowledge, you can actually enable codependency, which disempowers people to develop their own learning and proficiency in a particular area. I wish someone would have stressed this to me because it would have saved me so much stress and pointless conversations throughout my twenties, where I left them feeling drained. Oftentimes, the other person would ask question after question without really accepting what I was saying or without care for the toll having a conversation about my sexuality took on me. If you do choose to educate, remember in those moments that you'll often be expected to hold space for people to vent their frustrations over some past bisexual+ lover who did them wrong or who they felt insecure next to. You may be expected to be inept in explaining the *oddity* of your own existence, whether or not you are polyamorous, the Kinsey scale, sexual history versus identity versus orientation, gender roles, how gender impacts bisexual+ visibility, gender fluidity, transgender people, and your dating and sexual history, to name a few.

For more robust self-reflection questions, check out the online supplement at www.jryussuf.com/additionals.

EPILOGUE

Now that you've reached the end, you may be wondering—what now? What are you going to do with all of this information? What are you going to do about your bisexual+ identity? Well, that's totally up to you. As you know by now I am not big on pressuring anyone to disclose their bisexual+ identity, so whether or not you disclose and who you disclose to is completely up to you.

Ultimately, who you tell what and how you live your life is in your hands, and whether or not the things in this book will be of use will largely depend on access, where you are in your journey, and willingness. I wanted to offer examples of how to navigate the world, sharing things I've learned along the way that've helped me, and host it all in one place. I love learning about people's mistakes or shortcomings as well as where they excel because in doing this I get to absorb things I like and discard what I don't. I learn how to navigate particular challenges without actually having to experience them myself, and that's what I hoped to offer with this book.

It's important that I point out the question, *What are you going to do about your bisexual+ identity?* You may have been asking yourself this or may be asked in the future. It insinuates that simply acknowledging your bisexual+ identity is not enough, as though you have to *do* something about it or prove it, as though you have to date or have sex in order for your bisexual+ identity to be legitimate; this could not be farther from the truth. So many men and masculine-identified people would have so much more peace if they simply acknowledged that they've felt attraction for people of more than one gender. Also, bisexual+ virgins exist, and in the same way our gay and straight counterparts knew they were gay or straight before they had a sexual experience, the same is true for bisexual+ virgins. Bisexual+ people who are celibate also exist. Being bisexual+ is about desire, not your history, and you don't have to *do* anything if you're not ready, don't have the ability, or if you don't want to.

Up to the age of about nine, I was a 1 ("predominantly heterosexual, only incidentally homosexual") on the Kinsey scale, then I became a 2 ("predominantly heterosexual, but more than incidentally homosexual") until puberty. Once puberty hit, I was a 3 ("equally heterosexual and homosexual") and then toward my late teens hovered around a 4 or 5 ("predominantly homosexual, but more than incidentally heterosexual" and "predominantly homosexual, only incidentally heterosexual" respectively) for a while. When I was repetitively shown that women I liked weren't into me or thought I was gay, it stayed at a 5. Over the last few years as I've worked through my fears, experiences, and started to put myself out there again, and it sits at a 4. I think once I have more positive experiences with women it could hover around a 3 or 4 again, but either way, the most important thing is that I make peace with wherever it currently sits and continue being curious about my internal world.

The amount of access you have to LGBTQ+ communities versus cisgender heterosexual ones will likely dictate the experiences you may be able to have, but nothing can affect the validity of your bisexuality. Either way, I'd say try familiarizing yourself with and incrementally venture into circles you don't normally frequent and give it an honest shot. If you're normally in LGBTQ+ communities, give straight circles a try, if you can do so safely. Or if you're normally in straight circles, give LGBTQ+ communities, or bisexual+ communities more specifically, a try. Your first few times in spaces you don't normally frequent will almost certainly have their share of awkward moments, but what you will find as time goes on is that you may have a good time, you may make a friend, and there will likely be people there who are looking to meet people and are a bit nervous too.

As usual I'm going to say that safety comes first, and I am a big proponent of testing the waters rather than jumping headfirst into unnerving situations. When things seem like they'll be okay, I wade in a bit farther, granting myself permission to bail at any time but acknowledging that the discomfort won't last forever, and just because discomfort is present, that does not mean I don't belong. Going outside what is comfortable can be the space where you find like-minded people who you have other things in common with.

PUTTING YOURSELF OUT THERE

Many bisexual+ people often have a preference regarding gender, which can certainly change with experience and time, and even further, many of us feel our sexuality and experiences are lopsided, like Charles M. Blow describes in *Shut Up Fire in My Bones*.

> *While the word "bisexual" was technically correct, I would only slowly come to use it to refer to myself in part because of the derisive connotations. But, in addition, it would seem to me woefully inadequate and impressionistically inaccurate. It reduced a range of identities, unbelievably wide and splendidly varied, in which same-gender attraction presented in graduated measures—from a pinch to a pound—to a single expression. To me it seemed too narrowly drawn in the collective consciousness, suggesting an identity fixed precisely in the middle between straight and gay, giving equal weight to each, bearing no resemblance to what I felt. In me, the attraction to men would never be equal to the attraction to women—in men it was also closer to the pinch—but it would always be in flux.*

Your history may at times feel like a prison or as though you've already "picked a side," but that is simply not true. Love and sex and dating and sexuality are about finding the person or people you're compatible with, not necessarily the genders. Life is nonlinear. It's complex and beautiful, and finding the right approach to communicating with anyone is a skill that can most certainly be developed.

Even if you only find yourself attracted to a particular gender occasionally, I do recommend putting yourself out there in a measured, self-respecting way. In this scenario, you're not necessarily attached to the outcome that you end up falling madly in love or having sex, but that you simply tried to strike up a conversation. That's it. Stepping outside your own fantasies and desires of what you want to happen in order to be present momentarily and see if you can listen and contribute to what is happening right in front of you is an important skill. Even if the conversation fizzles out, falls flat, ends abruptly, takes an unexpected turn, ends on a weird note, or ends with you two determining to be friends, it's a win. By doing this, it means that you're not only acknowledging your attractions but also affirming them by doing something active by trying to meet a new person, putting yourself out there, and getting experience. Be kind and patient with yourself.

Something I wish I'd known as I was first venturing into this territory was how weak doing much of this would make me feel initially. My reality was mismatched with the ideas I'd prescribed for a person my age and my experience level. How could I be so wholly developed in so many other areas and yet underdeveloped in this one? Especially when it seemed to come so easily to my peers, especially when navigating a sexual or romantic relationship had been doable for me with men. I remember feeling very childlike, in the worst way, like a fish out of water, although I was already an adult. I was punishing myself with how good I *should* have been at starting conversations and engaging women. I had little compassion or empathy for where I was in my journey. I didn't take into account that if I'd already spent hundreds of hours developing skills with a particular gender, I'd need to spend more time developing other skills with other genders before it was fair to even compare them. Having compassion for myself was something else I'd have to learn to develop.

Choosing to never engage with women I was attracted to was something I definitely considered as a way to avoid the truth of where I was at in my journey. I hated stumbling through awkward first encounters. I hated feeling like I didn't measure up to other men, specifically cisgender heterosexual men. I struggle to fully put into words what made me stick with it, but I think it had something to do with no longer being content with not doing anything about my attraction to women. I was no longer content having butterflies in my stomach while interacting with a woman but talking myself out of actually flirting because I was sure she'd think I was gay or not masculine enough. I was no longer content contemplating all the reasons it'd go nowhere and why I wasn't enough; putting myself down and doing little about it. I was no longer content with my negative self-talk or my worldview; I wanted a different experience, so I tried something new.

Only over the past few years have I considered engaging with women again in a romantic or sexual way after nearly a decade of swearing off women, though I think it would only work with a bisexual+

or queer woman. The truth of the matter is that most bisexual+ women prefer bisexual+ men who are working on their own misogyny over straight men with extreme prejudice. I just happen to have some wounding in that area that I'm still working through. More often than not, I encounter women who refuse to see my sexuality and do what my friend Alan Hill refers to as "euthanizing you to fit better into their lives and understanding of the world" and men in general. I am not on PrEP, though my physician recommends it like it's a breath mint, even though I never have unprotected sex and taking it, specifically Truvada, for long periods can have an impact on your liver and kidneys, cause bone loss, and have other negative side effects. The brand Descovy, on the other hand, is not reported to have these complications but was not yet available when my doctor initially recommended this years ago. Descovy contains a newer form of tenofovir called tenofovir alafenamide (TAF), and Truvada contains the original form of tenofovir as tenofovir disoproxil fumarate (TDF).

PrEP and PEP are remarkable groundbreaking medications that prevent transmission of HIV, but I am rebuffed by condescension among health care professionals considering the negligence I've already mentioned, and that they rarely recommend it to cisgender heterosexual people unless they engage in sex work, share needles, or have sex with men who have sex with men. I routinely go through periods of celibacy, as that is my default, having grown up a devout Christian and undoing the remnants of religious trauma syndrome (a form of PTSD). I've also begun to consider nonmonogamy and being a unicorn (a person who is willing to join an existing couple either for sex or a more involved relationship) for a man-woman pairing—a thought I never really allowed myself to entertain even in my fantasies—which is quite a departure from my upbringing. I am also reading up on unicorn horror stories from bisexual+ women and recognizing what the appeal is for me, how to navigate safely, and if there are other ways to get the same feeling or experience I'm looking for from being a unicorn. I am far less uptight than I used to be and more willing to explore different kinds of sexual and relationship dynamics that I can have even if they exist outside of dominance and submission or monogamy, as I mentioned earlier. Since so much of the work I've done centers bisexuality, and it can be quite a loaded topic, I rarely talk about it in my day-to-day life and tend to avoid it completely during the first few dates. I don't enjoy becoming the bisexuality professor in real life. I take my time getting to know friends and lovers and try and gauge how accepting, open-minded, and potentially supportive they'd be without putting myself in the line of fire. It mostly works unless they look me up online.

When shooting your shot and dating in general, you'll find very quickly that just because you're attracted to someone doesn't mean you'll be a good fit in any capacity. You will not always have access to the people you're attracted to. You may find that whatever spark you feel initially may quickly fade once you begin communicating. Or you may hit it off from the start. You never know, and that is perhaps what I want to impress upon you, that there's no way to prepare for every single scenario, but you have to trust yourself to do the right thing for you in the moment. Whatever feelings come up for you while embarking on this are to be expected and are incredibly common and acceptable. It's important and healthy that you're acknowledging your desires and emotions and working through them instead of suppressing or avoiding them.

MEDICAL PROFESSIONALS

Finding the right medical professionals who will affirm and educate you might not be a luxury you get to enjoy, or may take some time, or you may get it right away. Either way I'd say putting the entirety of this part of your life in any one person's hands is unwise. By taking initiative with your mental, emotional, and physical health, you will not only become a more knowledgeable person but you will be healthier and better off so that the full weight of your health will not lean solely on flawed— oftentimes bigoted—medical professionals. By becoming more invested in a variety of healing and preventative measures, hopefully the bias against bisexual+ individuals in the medical world and the holes in medical professional's knowledge will affect you less. Sad, I know. Organizing around this and demanding more from our medical system is imperative to ending hyper-independence in this area.

WRAPPING UP: RACE, MASCULINITY, AND REVOLUTION

A critical understanding of race, gender, LGBTQ+, and radical politics based in theory and praxis is how I'm able to imagine tools of revolution. I am not interested in absorbing things currently deemed feminine into the fold of masculinity into a *new masculinity* of sorts. This repackaging of masculinity is hollow and does not solve the issue of devaluing femininity and women, systemically and interpersonally. It does not eliminate expectations posited around gender or the way it actually functions. The connections I've made between race, sexuality, gender, gender expression, and desirability is where I begin the work of revolution set exactly where I'm at.

EVERYDAY ACTIVISM

Joining the fight for bisexual+ visibility is a well-meaning ambition that signals bravery and selflessness, but it can also be a severely draining one. I've also critiqued calls for bisexual+, and LGBTQ+ people as a whole, to simply reveal themselves as being dangerous, inaccessible, and something that alone will not solve oppression. Visibility alone cannot end oppression. Putting an end to oppressive structures, erecting new ones where power is shared, having vigilance around power hoarding and the forming of hierarchies, and understanding how cyclical this all can be is the goal.

Advocating for more bisexual+ and generally LGBTQ+ characters in children's cartoons, adult animation, literature, and media at large, championing those that already exist, and leaving constructive reviews also helps *immensely*. When someone's sexuality is being guessed or assumed, casually introducing the idea of them possibly being bisexual+ or pansexual instead of either gay or straight is one of my favorite ways of getting people to consider bisexuality in everyday life. Making videos about your experience available online, writing essays, articles, and literature, starting podcasts or listening to bisexual+ podcasts that already exist are also options. Getting a bisexual+ or pansexual flag or pin or sign is an option, as is getting involved with a local bisexual+ group or starting one of your own. Excelling or simply being a reliable, sound-minded, kind person in whatever field you're in, or whichever hobbies you have while being visible, or supporting other visible bisexual+ people where you can, are extremely valuable and perhaps more impactful on an interpersonal level. Decentering heteronormativity in conversation so it is not always propped up as being normal, instead that it merely exists as one other experience among many, is incredibly important work.

Though I've talked a lot about doing the right thing because you believe it to be the right thing to do, that is somewhat fallible. Many of us severely harm others because we believe it is the right thing to do or because we can't see beyond our own perspective or pain to consider someone else. Neither our moral compasses nor a "lesser of two evils" model will take us the whole way. The way we show up in the world must go beyond moral conviction to impact, consent, ethics, and justice. The relationship bill of rights and the equality wheel are evergreen north stars commonly used in domestic violence resource centers. Both prop up nonnegotiable rights and signposts that we all should have in healthy relationships. There have been, currently are, and will continue to be bisexual+ people in the trenches organizing, in government, across class lines, and around the globe advocating, organizing, and pioneering new models for the betterment of bisexual+ individuals. You are not alone.

Subconsciously, I may have known my kindergarten crush on the girl who was nice to me and smelled good would be celebrated yet my crush on the boy with the shiny sneakers who shared his toys would not. I somehow knew to keep the latter to myself. That wouldn't be the first time I'd try to bury a crush I had on a boy, though it did set a precedent that was hard to shake well into my twenties. I did everything I could to be masculine, suppress being attracted to men, and beef up my attraction to women for so long, which caused me worlds of suffering. Self-loathing over my femininity coupled with the fact that many women I interacted with were disgusted by bisexual+ men affected the way I saw myself. I am not alone in this, as many bisexual+ men see themselves as less manly, less worthy of respect, attention, love, and appeal; worse still if they're feminine. These ideas come from experience as well as larger society as a product of white supremacy, and until white supremacy is destroyed, many of us will continue to face violence on multiple levels and internalize this messaging. Let me just say that straight women do not get to decide who we are. Gay men do not get to decide who we are. We do not need their approval to be valid. We get to decide who we are. When bisexual+ men speak our piece, it's not always well received, but that does not make it any less true or significant. When bisexual+ men speak, we affirm ourselves to ourselves. When bisexual+ men speak, we get closer to the truth of human sexuality. This goes beyond visibility, dignity, or having crushes validated and rather stands on justice, revolution and, finally, rethinking and reimagining sexuality and gender as a society.

NOTES

Charles M. Blow, *Shut Up Fire in My Bones* (Boston: Mariner, 2014).

Lindsay Slowiczek, "Truvada," Medical News Today, October 26, 2018, www.medicalnewstoday.com/articles/325820.

Ariana Resnik, "What Is Unicorn Polyamory?" Very Well Mind, February 5, 2022, www.verywellmind.com/what-is-unicorn-polyamory-5215473 #:~:text=A%20unicorn%20is%20a%20person,nonsexual%2C %20companionship%20time%20together%20too.

StrongHearts Native Helpline, "Healthy Relationship Bill of Rights," December 10, 2022, https://strongheartshelpline.org/abuse/healthy -relationship-bill-of-rights.

Edita Stiborova, "The Equality Wheel (The Duluth Method)," Social Workers Toolbox.com, 2016, www.socialworkerstoolbox.com/the-equality -wheel-the-duluth-model.

RESOURCES

- #BisexualMenSpeak on X (formerly Twitter): a place for bisexual+ men and masculine-identified people to speak for ourselves and get answers on a variety of topics.

- #bisexualmenexist on X (formerly Twitter): Post a selfie and connect with other bisexual+ men.

- #BiTwitter on X (formerly Twitter): Connect with a larger bisexual+ community.

- r/BisexualMen—Official on Discord: Connect with a community of bisexual+ men.

- The blog *Sex Ed For Bi Guys* (https://sexedforbiguys.tumblr.com) is an incredible descriptive resource to have on hand.

- *Primed: A Sex Guide for Trans Men Into Men* (www.scribd.com /document/461670086), a PDF. The first sexual health resource written by and for gay, bi, and queer trans men. It was first published in 2007 and updated in 2015. Described as the back pocket guide for trans men and the men who dig them.

- *Larker Anthology* (https://larkeranthology.com) is a yearly publication that comes out on September 23rd for Bi Visibility Day, celebrating the richness and diversity of the bisexual+ community.

- Use the Meetup app or website (www.meetup.com) to find local bisexual+ or LGBTQ+ groups and activities.

- *Slutever* on Vice (www.vicetv.com/en_us/show/slutever-tv) is a great show that helps detangle shame from sex, from a white "mostly straight" woman's point of view. They even have an episode on bisexuality in men, which I'm on!

- The Expansive Group (https://theexpansivegroup.com) is a collective of therapists who've been trained to center and empower clients who are queer, trans, nonmonogamous, pleasure-positive, curious, exploring, sex nerds, therapists, educators, aspiring therapists, and so on. It's a great resource for finding a bisexual+-affirming virtual therapist.

- BiZone (www.bizone.org) is a great resource for finding bisexual+-affirming therapists in your state.

- A directory to help Black men in their search for a therapist: https://therapyforblackmen.org.

- Ayana: a teletherapy app that matches marginalized communities to therapists who share their background.

- RAINN (https://rainn.org) is the nation's largest anti–sexual violence organization that offers 24-7 confidential crisis support.

- MenKIND (#fluidbidesign on X, formerly Twitter) is a network for fluid and bisexual+ men of African descent.

BOOKS I'VE LOVED

Nnanna Ikpo, *Fimí Sílè Forever: Heaven Gave It to Me* (London: Team Angelica, 2017).

Marina Peralta, *Barriers to Love: Embracing a Bisexual Identity* (Los Angeles: Barriers, 2013).

Shiri Eisner, *Bi: Notes for a Bisexual Revolution* (Berkeley, CA: Seal Press, 2013).

Charles M. Blow, *Shut Up Fire in My Bones* (Boston: Mariner, 2014).

Robyn Ochs and H. Sharif Williams, *Rec-Og-Nize: The Voices of Bisexual Men: An Anthology* (Boston: Bisexual Resource Center, 2014).

Aaron H. Aceves, *This Is Why They Hate Us* (New York: Simon & Schuster, 2022).

Bill Konigsberg, *Openly Straight* (New York: Scholastic, 2015).

Deborah Harkness's All Souls Trilogy: *A Discovery of Witches, Shadow of Night,* and *The Book of Life* (New York: Penguin, 2011–2014). Although these books are about sexy vampires and witches and not bisexuality explicitly, the author intentionally used these characters as metaphors for the prejudices and contradictions present in the United States surrounding Proposition 8, California's 2008 anti–same-sex marriage ballot measure, which was eventually ruled unconstitutional. This is where I got the idea to see bisexuality as the unaltered source and expression of human love and connection instead of as a derivative of straight or gay.

PODCASTS I LOVE

FRUIT, a podcast by Issa Rae Productions: A professional football player, X, recounts his journey of self-discovery and sexual exploration both on and off the field in this first-person narrative. *FRUIT* chronicles X's relationship with his friends, teammates, and family as they impose their own perceptions of his role in an alpha male–dominated industry of professional sports. Amid questioning for a larger league-related scandal, X must ultimately decide how he wants his story to be told, for himself and for others like him.

Two Bi Guys: a podcast about fluid sexuality, gender, masculinity and femininity, intimacy, relationships, and more, hosted by two bi guys.

Non-Monogamy Help

Let's Talk Bruh

Bad in Bed

Bisexual Brunch

Black Fluidity: Bi Black Men Talk

Bisexual Real Talk

GETTING HELP

Hotlines

- Depression Hotline: (630) 482-9696
- Suicide Prevention Lifeline: (800) 273-8255
- Trans Crisis Line: (800) 273-8255
- Rape and sexual assault: (800) 656-4673
- Domestic violence: (800) 799-7233

- Trevor Project Lifeline: (866) 488-7386

- Sexuality support: (800) 246-7743

- Eating disorders: (800) 931-2237

- Grief counseling: (415) 499-1195

- Runaway Safeline: (800) 786-2929

- Planned Parenthood: (800) 230-7526

- STD hotline: (800) 227-8922

- Substance mental health: (800) 662-4357

- ACA health marketplace: (800) 318-2596

Websites

- The Trevor Project: www.thetrevorproject.org

- LGBT Nation Help Center: www.glbtnationalhelpcenter.org

- Pride Counseling: www.pridecounseling.com

- Bisexual Resource Center: www.biresource.org

LGBTQ+ RELIGION

- #FaithfullyLGBT: a network of religious LGBTQ+ people.

- The Elm Foundation (www.elmfoundation.art) is a Unitarian organization that believes in mending hearts through art.

- At the Spiritualist church of New York City (https://spiritualist churchnyc.com), everyone is welcome regardless of color, name, or origin. They're LGBTQ+ friendly.

- Queer Theology (www.queertheology.com/resources): uncovering and celebrating the gifts that LGBTQ+ people bring to the Christian church and the world.

- QueerTheology Christian bible podcast: www.queertheology.com /listen.

- Believe Out Loud: www.believeoutloud.com.

Finding an Affirming Church Community

- Church Clarity: www.churchclarity.org
- Gaychurch.org Find a Church: www.gaychurch.org/find_a_church

POPULAR BISEXUAL+-FRIENDLY DATING APPS AND WEBSITES

- Feeld: an app that is very bisexual+ positive, sex positive, kink positive, threesome and group sex positive, and nonmonogamous positive.
- #Open: a dating app.
- 3Fun: an app that's very threesome and group sex positive.
- Taimi: a dating app.
- BisexualPrideDating.com.
- Bisexual Dating Site: a dating app.
- BiCupid: a dating app.
- BiChat: a dating app.
- Bisexual Amino: a social community.

OTHER HELPFUL LINKS

- HRC bisexual resources guide: www.hrc.org/resources/resource -guide-to-coming-out-as-bisexual.
- Bisexual Resource Center, "Bi+ 101": https://bi.org/en/101.
- Bisexual Resource Center, "How to Be an Ally": https://biresource .org/bi-info/for-allies.
- Bisexual Resource Center, "Mental Health in the Bi+ Community": http://biresource.org/wp-content/uploads/2019/03/Mental -Health-Brochure-2019.pdf.
- University of Southern California Library, "LGBTQ+ Terminol-ogy and Definitions": https://libguides.usc.edu/healthsciences /LGBTQhealth/terminology.

- Bisexual Resource Center: https://biresource.org.
- New York City LGBT Center resources list: https://gaycenter.org /resources.
- New York Bisexual Network bulletin board: http://nyabn.org.
- New York City's Thrive Program: https://thrivenyc.cityofnew york.us/wp-content/uploads/2021/02/ThriveNYC-ProgressReport -2021.pdf.

ACKNOWLEDGMENTS

Hats off to my editor, Amber Williams, who took a look at all of the thoughts I've ever had on this subject and helped find the right places for them. Thank you for believing in my writing and pushing me. To Gillian and the entire team at North Atlantic Books, thank you so much for your belief in my work and being the perfect home for this book. To all the men and masculine people in the Bi Black Men's group chat, thank you for saving my life. I hope I made y'all proud. To Gabby, Steven, and Juwan, thanks for the laughs, sharing so much with me, and giving me permission to explore just by living. Much thanks to Alan Hill for being so supportive and encouraging, and my Black feminism reading partner. To AdrianXpression, thank you for consistently using your voice to support bisexual+ men and for being your wonderful self. To Ryan Douglass, thank you for the rich feedback on my writing and support overall. I appreciate you. To Sherronda Brown, thank you for your apt edits over the years and for taking a look at this and giving thoughtful feedback. To Tyson, thank you for being so encouraging over the years and taking a look at this for me; I appreciate you. To Shaheem, thanks for encouraging me to keep this thing going and letting me know that I had a right to speak about masculinity. To Jewel, Rob, Benji, John, Tash, and Omar, thank y'all for keeping me accountable and not letting me back out of putting this out. Thank you for being an important part of my life. To Paris, thank you for being there from the beginning when this was just an idea I was spitballing all the way up to this point. Thank you for letting me turn most of our conversations into gender-studies forums. To Ola, Abi, and Mo, thanks for helping raise me and showing me how to stand up for myself.

BIBLIOGRAPHY

1in6.org. "The 1 in 6 Statistic." 2017. https://1in6.org/statistic.

Abgarian, Almara. "It's National Orgasm Day, So Here Are Seven Different Types of Male Orgasms." *Metro,* July 31, 2019. https://metro.co.uk/2019/07/31/national -orgasm-day-seven-different-types-male-orgasms-10495431.

Aceves, Aaron H. *This Is Why They Hate Us.* New York: Simon & Schuster, 2022.

American Civil Liberties Union. "Trans Rights under Attack in 2020." 2020. www .aclu.org/issues/lgbtq-rights/transgender-rights/trans-rights-under-attack-2020.

Andersen, Roshaante. "What's It Like to be Intersex?" YouTube video. April 25, 2021. https://youtu.be/0C5hnlCM-j0.

Anderson-Minshall, Diane. "Ending Bi Erasure—on TV and in Our LGBT Worlds." Advocate.com, September 23, 2011. www.advocate.com/news/daily-news/2011 /09/23/ending-bi-erasure-tv-and-our-lgbt-worlds.

Andre, Amy. "Show Us the Money: Funding for Bisexual Community Lacking." Huff- Post, January 4, 2012. www.huffpost.com/entry/bisexual-funding_b_1178932.

ANI. "Some May Find It Hard to Believe but Bisexual Men Make Better Lovers, Partners." *Hindustan Times,* April 12, 2017. www.hindustantimes.com/sex-and -relationships/some-may-find-it-hard-to-believe-but-bisexual-men-make-better -lovers-partners/story-H9k2u0Q0kWXgPiLM6E8Z0J.html.

Arizona Coalition Against Domestic Violence. "Sexual Violence Myths & Miscon- ceptions." 2019. www.acesdv.org/about-sexual-domestic-violence/sexual-violence -myths-misconceptions.

Artavia, David. "Male Bisexuality Is Real, a New Study Confirms Once and for All." Advocate.com, July 21, 2020. www.advocate.com/bisexual/2020/7/21/male -bisexuality-real-new-study-confirms-once-and-all.

Bachand, Charles, and Nikki Djak. "Stockholm Syndrome in Athletics: A Paradox." *Chil- dren Australia* 43:3 (June 20, 2018), 175–80. https://doi.org/10.1017/cha.2018.31.

Bailar, Schuyler. "Homosexuality & the Bible." Pinkmantaray. March 15, 2021. https:// pinkmantaray.com/bible.

Baldoni, Justin. *Man Enough.* Podcast series. 2021. www.youtube.com/channel/ UC2MbPazrSLEbgiHT3yQ4DnQ.

Bederman, Gail. *Manliness and Civilization: A Cultural History of Gender and Race in the United States, 1880–1917.* Chicago: University of Chicago Press, 1997.

Benibo, Saki, and Joshua Briond. "'Good Men' and the Mythological Dichotomy between Toxic Masculinity and Masculinity." RaceBaitr, March 21, 2019. https:// racebaitr.com/2019/03/21/good-men-and-the-mythological-dichotomy -between-toxic-masculinity-and-masculinity.

Bhattacharjee, Puja. "The Complicated Gender History of Pink." CNN Health, January 12, 2018. www.cnn.com/2018/01/12/health/colorscope-pink-boy-girl-gender/index.html.

BiNet USA. "1990 Anything That Moves Bisexual Manifesto." Blog post. January 20, 2014.

Bisexual Resource Center. "Bisexual Resource Center Celebrates 5th Annual Bisexual Health Awareness Month in March." February 20, 2018. https://bihealthmonth.org/2018/02/20/bisexual-resource-center-celebrates-5th-annual-bisexual-health-awareness-month-in-march.

Bisexual Resource Center. "Reports and Research." 2016. https://biresource.org/resources/reports-and-research.

Black Youth Project. "How Biphobia Impacts Black Bisexual Men's Health." April 30, 2019. http://blackyouthproject.com/how-biphobia-impacts-black-bisexual-mens-health.

Black Youth Project. "How *Black Mirror*'s 'Striking Vipers' Episode Failed Bisexual Men & Trans Women." June 21, 2019. http://blackyouthproject.com/how-black-mirrors-striking-vipers-episode-failed-bisexual-men-trans-women-1.

Blow, Charles M. *Shut Up Fire in My Bones.* Boston: Mariner, 2014.

Boyd, Cora, and The Cut. "A Dating Coach Matches the Dating Profile to the Person." YouTube video. October 15, 2020. www.youtube.com/watch?v=1AoBr9v4MHQ.

Brown, Anna. "Bisexual Adults Are Far Less Likely than Gay Men and Lesbians to Be 'Out' to the People in Their Lives." Pew Research Center. June 18, 2019. www.pewresearch.org/fact-tank/2019/06/18/bisexual-adults-are-far-less-likely-than-gay-men-and-lesbians-to-be-out-to-the-people-in-their-lives.

Brown, Sherronda J. *Refusing Compulsory Sexuality: A Black Asexual Lens on Our Sex-Obsessed Culture.* Berkeley, CA: North Atlantic Books, 2022.

Burke, Tarana, and Brené Brown, eds. *You Are Your Best Thing: Vulnerability, Shame Resistance, and the Black Experience.* New York: Random House, 2021.

Butler, Judith. *Gender Trouble: Feminism and the Subversion of Identity.* New York: Routledge, 2006.

Byrne, Christine. "The BMI Is Racist and Useless. Here's How to Measure Health Instead." HuffPost, July 20, 2020. www.huffpost.com/entry/bmi-scale-racist-health_l_5f15a8a8c5b6d14c336a43b0.

Cairns, Gus. "New PEP Studies Revive Interest in Post-Exposure Prevention." Aidsmap.com, March 11, 2020. www.aidsmap.com/news/mar-2020/new-pep-studies-revive-interest-post-exposure-prevention.

Cherry, Kendra. "How Different Types of Needs Might Influence Your Personality." Verywell Mind, September 17, 2020. www.verywellmind.com/murrays-theory-of-psychogenic-needs-2795952.

Chung, Daniel Thomas, Christopher James Ryan, Dusan Hadzi-Pavlovic, Swaran Preet Singh, Clive Stanton, and Matthew Michael Large. "Suicide Rates after

Discharge from Psychiatric Facilities." *JAMA Psychiatry* 74:7 (July 1, 2017), 694. https://doi.org/10.1001/jamapsychiatry.2017.1044.

Coates, Ta-Nehisi. "A Low-Down Crying Shame: Why the Myth of the "On the Down Low" Brother Refuses to Die." Slate, March 9, 2007. https://slate.com /technology/2007/03/why-the-myth-of-on-the-down-low-refuses-to-die.html.

Cohen, Jon. "A Silent Epidemic: Why Is There Such a High Percentage of HIV and AIDS among Black Women?" Slate, October 27, 2004. https://slate.com/technology /2004/10/black-women-and-aids.html.

Cohen, Rob, and Alex Boyd. "Straight, Bisexual & Queer Identities with Dr. Jane Ward." *Two Bi Guys.* Podcast. October 21, 2019. https://podcasts.apple.com /us/podcast/straight-bisexual-queer-identities-with-dr-jane-ward/id1480131653 ?i=1000454287221.

Compton, Julie. "OutFront: This Advocate Couldn't Find a Bisexual Community, So He Created One." NBC News, May 18, 2017. www.nbcnews.com/feature /nbc-out/outfront-advocate-couldn-t-find-bisexual-community-so-he-created -n761536.

Couvillon, Dillon. "10 Things I Learned Six Months after Coming Out." HuffPost, May 30, 2014. www.huffpost.com/entry/ten-things-i-learned-6mon_b _5412788.

Cruz, Eliel. "Bisexual College Student Shot Dead in Front of His Home." Advocate .com, August 5, 2014. ww.advocate.com/bisexuality/2014/08/05/bisexual -college-student-shot-dead-front-his-home.

Cruz, Eliel. "MTV's 'Faking It' Big Bisexual Blunder." HuffPost, October 30, 2015. www.huffpost.com/entry/mtvs-faking-it-big-bisexu_b_8413276.

Cruz, Eliel. "13 Things Never to Say to Bisexual People." Advocate.com, September 23, 2016. www.advocate.com/bisexuality/2014/06/02/13-things-never-say -bisexual-people.

Dastagir, Alia E. "LGBTQ Definitions Every Ally Should Know for Pride Month (and All Year Long)." *USA Today,* June 2, 2022. www.usatoday.com/story/news /nation/2022/06/02/lgbtq-glossary-ally-learn-language/7469059001.

DeSanto, Lara. "Brushing and Flossing Could Reduce Your Risk of This Cancer." Health Central, November 19, 2020. www.healthcentral.com/article/mouth -health-liver-cancer-risk.

DiAngelo, Robin, and Michael Eric Dyson. *White Fragility: Why It's So Hard for White People to Talk About Racism.* Boston: Beacon Press, 2018.

Dispenza, Joe. *You Are the Placebo: Making Your Mind Matter.* Carlsbad, CA: Hay House, 2014.

Downey, Andrea. "New Research Finds We're All Bisexual." New York Post, March 14, 2018. https://nypost.com/2018/03/14/new-research-finds-were-all-bisexual.

Durvasula, Ramani, and MedCircle. "Intimate versus Tribal Gaslighting: Differences and How to Spot Them." YouTube video. February 4, 2021. www.youtube.com /watch?v=trh_eTkZLeU.

Durvasula, Ramani, and MedCircle. "The Magic of Therapy: Indulge in Your Fantasies. Here's Why." YouTube video. May 24, 2021. www.youtube.com/watch?v=909dpQTCwB0.

Eisner, Shiri. *Bi: Notes for a Bisexual Revolution*. Berkeley, CA: Seal Press, 2013.

Elemental, Chai. "Things You Didn't Know Were Acemisic." *That Weird Ace Woman*. Blog post. June 24, 2022. https://thatweirdacewoman.wordpress.com/2022/06/24/things-you-didnt-know-were-acemisic.

Engle, Gigi. "The Internal Clitoris, or That Thing You Never Knew You Had." *Glamour*, April 5, 2017. www.glamour.com/story/everything-you-need-to-know-about-the-internal-clitoris.

Exposito, Suzy. "Why Britney Spears' Conservatorship Case Matters for Disability Rights Advocacy." *Los Angeles Times*, July 12, 2021. www.latimes.com/entertainment-arts/music/story/2021-07-12/britney-spears-conservatorship-hearing-disability-rights.

Fabrar. "Dan Levy as David Rose in Schitt's Creek Is One of the Best Comedy Performances in a Long Time." Reddit r/television, August 7, 2020. www.reddit.com/r/television/comments/i57cw8/dan_levy_as_david_rose_in_schitts_creek_is_one_of.

Fern, Jessica. *Polysecure: Attachment, Trauma and Consensual Nonmonogamy*. Portland, OR: Thorntree Press, 2020.

Fernando, Christine. "Collaboration with Police Divides Social Workers across US." AP News. April 20, 2021. https://apnews.com/article/us-news-race-and-ethnicity-police-chicago-racial-injustice-a4753d5ea6b545b40f1e1fe5793d2af4.

Fitzsimons, Tim, Alexander Kacala, and Minyvonne Burke. "Tennessee Teen Dies by Suicide after Being Outed Online." NBC News, September 30, 2019. www.nbcnews.com/feature/nbc-out/tennessee-teen-dies-suicide-after-being-outed-online-n1060436.

Foster, Kimberly N. "WAP and the Spectacle of Sexual Liberation." For Harriet. YouTube video. August 30, 2020. https://youtu.be/ILApR36KgQw.

Freire, Paulo. *Pedagogy of the Oppressed*. New York: Bloomsbury Academic, 1970.

Frey, William H. "The US Will Become 'Minority White' in 2045, Census Projects." Brookings. March 14, 2018. www.brookings.edu/articles/the-us-will-become-minority-white-in-2045-census-projects.

Funders for LGBTQ Issues. "2021 Resource Tracking Report: Lesbian, Gay, Bisexual, Transgender, and Queer Grantmaking by U.S. Foundations." 2023. https://lgbtfunders.org/research-types/tracking-report.

Gates, Gary J. "How Many People Are Lesbian, Gay, Bisexual, and Transgender?" Williams Institute, UCLA School of Law. April 2011. https://williamsinstitute.law.ucla.edu/publications/how-many-people-lgbt.

Gibson, Thais. "How Men Confuse Sexual Attraction with Emotional Connection." YouTube video. July 24, 2020. https://youtu.be/3i2rYgn5H5Q.

Gilmour, Paisley. "Why Many Bisexual People Don't 'Just Come Out.'" *Cosmopolitan,* May 21, 2018. www.cosmopolitan.com/uk/love-sex/relationships/a20769881 /coming-out-bisexual.

Gino, Francesca. "Another Reason Top Managers Are Disproportionally White Men." *Scientific American*, September 12, 2017. www.scientificamerican.com/article /another-reason-top-managers-are-disproportionally-white-men.

GLAAD. "In Focus: Reporting on the Bisexual Community." April 11, 2016. www .glaad.org/publications/focus-reporting-bisexual-community.

Glover, Cameron. "Not Formally 'Coming Out' Didn't Make Me Less Queer." *Glamour,* August 22, 2017. www.glamour.com/story/formally-coming-out.

Guess, Teresa J. "The Social Construction of Whiteness: Racism by Intent, Racism by Consequence." *Critical Sociology* 32:4 (2006), 649–73. www.cwu.edu/diversity /sites/cts.cwu.edu.diversity/files/documents/constructingwhiteness.pdf. https:// doi.org/10.1163/156916306779155199.

Gupta, Kristina. "Compulsory Sexuality: Evaluating an Emerging Concept." *Signs* 41:1 (Autumn 2015). https://doi.org/10.1086/681774.

Harney, Stefano, and Fred Moten. *The Undercommons: Fugitive Planning and Black Study.* New York: Autonomedia, 2013.

Harrison, Da'Shaun L. *Belly of the Beast: The Politics of Anti-Fatness as Anti-Blackness.* Berkeley, CA: North Atlantic Books, 2021.

Headlee, Celeste. "Racism vs. Discrimination: Why the Distinction Matters." n.d. https://celesteheadlee.com/racism-vs-discrimination-why-the-distinction-matters.

Hill, Marc Lamont. "Never Too Much." In Burke and Brown, *You Are Your Best Thing.*

Hizon, Nora. "Is Your Boyfriend Gay?" *Cosmopolitan,* October 26, 2010. www .cosmo.ph/relationships/is-your-boyfriend-gay.

hooks, bell. *All about Love: New Visions.* New York: HarperCollins, 2018.

Human Rights Campaign. "Health Disparities among Bisexual People." September 10, 2015. www.hrc.org/resources/health-disparities-among-bisexual-people.

Human Rights Campaign. "Sexual Assault and the LGBTQ Community." April 10, 2015. www.hrc.org/resources/sexual-assault-and-the-lgbt-community.

Humble Bee, The. "The Effects of TV on Your Brain." Steemit. 2017. https://steemit .com/tv/@thehumblebee/the-effects-of-tv-on-your-brain.

Ikpo, Nnanna. *Fimí Sílè Forever: Heaven Gave It to Me.* London: Team Angelica, 2017.

I Love Veterinary. "What Animals Have Sex for Pleasure?" July 16, 2021. https:// iloveveterinary.com/blog/what-animals-have-sex-for-pleasure.

Jackson, Zakiyyah Iman. *Becoming Human: Matter and Meaning in an Antiblack World.* New York: New York University Press, 2020.

Jenkins, Barry, dir. *Moonlight.* Los Angeles: Plan B Entertainment, 2016.

Kates, Jennifer, Usha Ranji, Adara Beamesderfer, Alina Salganicoff, and Lindsey Dawson. "Health and Access to Care and Coverage for Lesbian, Gay, Bisexual, and Transgender (LGBT) Individuals in the U.S." KFF Health News, May 3,

2018. www.kff.org/disparities-policy/issue-brief/health-and-access-to-care-and
-coverage-for-lesbian-gay-bisexual-and-transgender-individuals-in-the-u-s
/view/print.

Kerner, Ian. *She Comes First: The Thinking Man's Guide to Pleasuring a Woman*. New
York: HarperCollins, 2010.

Kinsey, Alfred C., Wardell R. Pomeroy, and Clyde E. Martin. "Sexual Behavior in
the Human Male, 1948." *American Journal of Public Health* 93:6 (June 2003),
894–99. https://doi.org/10.2105/ajph.93.6.894.

Kinsey Institute. "The Kinsey Scale." Indiana University. n.d. https://kinseyinstitute
.org/research/publications/kinsey-scale.php.

Konigsberg, Bill. *Openly Straight*. New York: Scholastic, 2015.

Kuadli, Jenifer. "32 Disheartening Sexual Assault Statistics for 2021." Legal Jobs.
Blog post. February 26, 2021. https://legaljobs.io/blog/sexual-assault-statistics.

Lambert, Sheela. *Best Bi Short Stories: Bisexual Fiction*. Cambridge, MA: Circlet
Press, 2015.

Lawson, Richard. "The Reagan Administration's Unearthed Response to the AIDS
Crisis Is Chilling." *Vanity Fair,* December 2015. www.vanityfair.com/news/2015
/11/reagan-administration-response-to-aids-crisis.

Levesque, Brody. "Bisexuality Not Covered by Federal Employment Law Lawsuit
Claims." *Los Angeles Blade,* September 27, 2022. www.losangelesblade.com
/2022/09/27/bisexuality-not-covered-by-federal-employment-law-lawsuit
-claims.

LexualMedia. "Boosie, Black Boys, and Rape Culture." YouTube video. June 10,
2020. www.youtube.com/watch?v=KHebIPQSJWk.

Ley, David J. "Where Are All the Bisexuals Hiding?" *Psychology Today,* April 30, 2018.
www.psychologytoday.com/us/blog/women-who-stray/201804/where-are
-all-the-bisexuals-hiding.

Lin, Jae. "What Is Toxic Monogamy?" Allgo. 2020. https://allgo.org/what-is-toxic
-monogamy.

Linstead, Stephen A., and Garance Maréchal. "How to Overcome Phallus-Obsessed,
Toxic Masculinity." The Conversation, November 3, 2017. https://theconversation
.com/how-to-overcome-phallus-obsessed-toxic-masculinity-84388.

Livingston, Jennie, dir. *Paris Is Burning*. 1990; Academy Entertainment.

Lodge, Guy. "Queer Fears: The Problem with *Black Mirror*'s 'No Homo' Episode."
Guardian, June 10, 2019. www.theguardian.com/tv-and-radio/2019/jun/10
/black-mirror-charlie-brooker-striking-vipers.

Longo, Chris. "*Black Mirror:* 'Striking Vipers' Star Breaks Down a Complex Relationship." Den of Geek, June 11, 2019. www.denofgeek.com/tv/black-mirror
-striking-vipers-star-relationship.

Mandriota, Morgan. "6 Signs You Might Have Sexual Shame—and How to Overcome It." Well+Good, November 11, 2020. www.wellandgood.com/sexual
-shame-signs.

Marcus, Nancy. "Immigration and Seventh Circuit Judges Reject Bisexual Man's Request for Protection; Here's Why They Were Wrong." Lambda Legal. August 19, 2016. www.lambdalegal.org/blog/20160819_ray-fuller-judges-reject-bisexual -mans-request-for-protection.

Martin, Alfred L. Jr. "Re-Watching Omar: Moesha, Black Gayness and Shifting Media Reception" *Flow,* February 1, 2021. www.flowjournal.org/2021/02 /rewatching-omar.

Maurice, Emma Powys. "Bisexual Student Battered in 'Unprovoked and Completely Random' Homophobic Attack." *PinkNews,* June 19, 2021. www.pinknews.co.uk /2021/06/19/bisexual-student-josh-ormond-homophobic-attack-liverpool.

Mguzmanvogele. "Queer Baiting." 21st-Century Interdisciplinary Dictionary. Blog post. March 29, 2016.

Miller, Stephen. "Black Workers Still Earn Less than Their White Counterparts." SHRM. June 11, 2020. www.shrm.org/ResourcesAndTools/hr-topics /compensation/Pages/racial-wage-gaps-persistence-poses-challenge.aspx.

Mingus, Mia. "Medical Industrial Complex Visual." *Leaving Evidence.* Blog post. February 6, 2015. https://leavingevidence.wordpress.com/2015/02/06 /medical-industrial-complex-visual.

Mitchell, Nissa. "On Being 'Uber-Gay,' Trans Women and Sexual Orientation." Medium. March 13, 2018. https://transsubstantiation.com/on-being-uber -gay-ad360448e170.

Mock, Janet. "Being Pretty Is a Privilege, But We Refuse to Acknowledge It." *Allure,* June 28, 2017. www.allure.com/story/pretty-privilege.

Moss, Emily, Kriston McIntosh, Wendy Edelberg, and Kristen E. Broady. "The Black-White Wealth Gap Left Black Households More Vulnerable." Brookings. December 8, 2020. www.brookings.edu/blog/up-front/2020/12/08/the-black -white-wealth-gap-left-black-households-more-vulnerable.

Movement Advancement Project. "Invisible Majority: The Disparities Facing Bisexual People and How to Remedy Them." 2016. www.lgbtmap.org/policy-and-issue -analysis/invisible-majority.

Movement Advancement Project, BiNet USA, and Bisexual Resource Center. *Understanding Issues Facing Bisexual Americans.* September 2014. www.lgbtmap.org /lgbt-movement-overviews/understanding-issues-facing-bisexual-americans.

Nagoski, Emily. *Come as You Are: The Surprising New Science That Will Transform Your Sex Life.* New York: Simon & Schuster, 2015.

National Coalition Against Domestic Violence. "Domestic Violence and the LGBTQ Community." Blog post. June 6, 2018. https://ncadv.org/blog/posts /domestic-violence-and-the-lgbtq-community.

National Institute of Public Health of Quebec (INSPQ). "Consequences." 2009. www .inspq.qc.ca/en/sexual-assault/understanding-sexual-assault/consequences.

Nellis, Ashley. "The Color of Justice: Racial and Ethnic Disparity in State Prisons." The Sentencing Project. October 13, 2021. www.sentencingproject.org /publications/color-of-justice-racial-and-ethnic-disparity-in-state-prisons.

Nichols, Margie. "The *DSM-5* and LGBT Rights: Still Crazy after All These Years?" Institute for Personal Growth. December 4, 2012. https://ipgcounseling.com /queer-mind/the-dsm-5-and-lgbt-rights-still-crazy-after-all-these-years.

Noel, Gabrielle Alexa. *How to Live with the Internet (and Not Let It Ruin Your Life)*. Melbourne: Smith Street, 2021.

Oakley, Lewis. "Researchers Need to Acknowledge Bi Men's Unique Needs." Bi.org, November 4, 2016. https://bi.org/en/articles/researchers-need-to -acknowledge-bi-mens-unique-needs.

Ochs, Robyn, and H. Sharif Williams. *Rec-Og-Nize: The Voices of Bisexual Men: An Anthology.* Boston: Bisexual Resource Center, 2014.

Okafor, Kelechi. "The Way to Discuss Racism in the Workplace Is to Listen." People Management, July 16, 2020. www.peoplemanagement.co.uk/article /1741923/way-discuss-racism-workplace-listen-kelechi-okafor.

Omi, Michael, and Howard Winant. *Racial Formation in the U.S.: 1969–1900.* New York: Routledge, 1994.

Open Society Foundations. "Ten Reasons to Oppose the Criminalization of HIV Exposure or Transmission." December 1, 2008. www.opensocietyfoundations .org/publications/ten-reasons-oppose-criminalization-hiv-exposure-or -transmission.

Oxford, Ed. "My Quest to Find the Word 'Homosexual' in the Bible." Baptist News Global. August 10, 2020. https://baptistnews.com/article/my-quest-to-find -the-word-homosexual-in-the-bible/#.Ya_1DS2ZPq0.

Pavco-Giaccia, Olivia, Martha Fitch Little, Jason Stanley, and Yarrow Dunham. "Rationality Is Gendered." *Collabra: Psychology* 5:1 (January 1, 2019), 54. https://doi.org/10.1525/collabra.274.

Peabody, Roger. "How Effective Is Post-Exposure Prophylaxis (PEP)?" Aidsmap.com, April 2019. www.aidsmap.com/about-hiv/how-effective-post-exposure -prophylaxis-pep.

Peralta, Marina. *Barriers To Love: Embracing A Bisexual Identity.* Los Angeles: Barriers, 2013.

Pilgrim, David. "The Brute Caricature." Jim Crow Museum, Ferris State University. 2023. www.ferris.edu/jimcrow/brute.

Plank, Liz. *For the Love of Men: From Toxic to a More Mindful Masculinity.* New York: St. Martin's Press, 2019.

Pontin, Jason. "The Importance of Feelings." *MIT Technology Review,* June 17, 2014. www.technologyreview.com/2014/06/17/172310/the-importance-of-feelings.

Pornhub. "Girls Who Like Boys Who Like Boys—Pornhub Insights." October 13, 2017. www.pornhub.com/insights/girls-like-boys-who-like-boys.

Pornhub. "More of What Women Want—Pornhub Insights." July 25, 2015. www .pornhub.com/insights/women-gender-demographics-searches.

Pornhub. "Pornhub's 2016 Year in Review—Pornhub Insights." January 4, 2017. www.pornhub.com/insights/2016-year-in-review.

Rabger, AVENite. "Primary vs. Secondary Sexual Attraction Model." Asexuality.org. July 19, 2022. https://wiki.asexuality.org/Primary_vs._secondary_sexual _attraction_model.

Randall, Clarie. "Coming Out (or Not): A Celebration of Autonomy." Feminist Campus, October 11, 2017. https://feministcampus.org/coming-out-or-not-a -celebration-of-autonomy.

Rape, Abuse & Incest National Network. "Sexual Assault of Men and Boys." 2000. www.rainn.org/articles/sexual-assault-men-and-boys.

Resnik, Ariana. "What Is Unicorn Polyamory?" VeryWell Mind. February 5, 2022. www.verywellmind.com/what-is-unicorn-polyamory-5215473#:~:text=A%20 unicorn%20is%20a%20person,nonsexual%2C%20companionship%20time%20 together%20too.

Rich, Adrienne. "Compulsory Heterosexuality and Lesbian Existence." *Signs* 5:4 (1980), 631–60. https://doi.org/10.1086/493756.

Richards, Bedelia Nicola. "Is Your University Racist?" *Inside Higher Ed,* May 25, 2018. www.insidehighered.com/advice/2018/05/25/questions-institutions -should-ask-themselves-determine-if-they-are-operating.

Rizzo, Rhonda. "5 Ways Playing the Piano Makes Us Healthier in Times of Stress." *Pianist.* Blog post. April 15, 2020. www.pianistmagazine.com/blogs/5-ways -playing-the-piano-makes-us-healthier-in-times-of-stress.

Romano, Aja. "Kevin Spacey Sexual Assault Allegations: Everything We Know So Far." *Vox,* December 24, 2018. www.vox.com/culture/2017/11/3/16602628 /kevin-spacey-sexual-assault-allegations-house-of-cards.

Rose, Charlie. "Toni Morrison." Video. May 7, 1993. https://charlierose.com /videos/18778.

Rouse, Lauren. "Suicide Rates Are on the Rise among Older White Men in Rural Areas." Vital Record, March 29, 2021. https://vitalrecord.tamhsc.edu/suicide -rates-are-on-the-rise-among-older-white-men-in-rural-areas.

Rubel, Barbara. "What Is Vicarious Trauma?" Grief Work Center. 2020. www .griefworkcenter.com/what-is-vicarious-trauma.

Ruthstrom, Ellyn. "Bisexual Health Awareness Month Draws Attention to Community's Urgent Health Needs." National LGBTQ Task Force. March 5, 2014. www.thetaskforce.org/news/bisexual-health-awareness-month-draws-attention -to-communitys-urgent-health-needs.

Ryan, Jules. "Why I Don't Use the Term 'Straight Passing Privilege.'" Medium. October 16, 2020. https://radiantbutch.medium.com/why-i-dont-use-the -term-straight-passing-privilege-f7f0b06a2c49.

Sánchez, Francisco, and Eric Vilain. "'Straight-Acting Gays': The Relationship between Masculine Consciousness, Anti-Effeminacy, and Negative Gay Identity." *Archives of Sexual Behavior* 41:1 (2012), 111–19. https://doi.org/10.1007 /s10508-012-9912-z.

Sandoiu, Ana. "Brushing Your Teeth May Keep Your Heart Healthy." Medical News Today, December 3, 2019. www.medicalnewstoday.com/articles/327208.

Savage, Dan. "Peg, Pegging, Pegged." Savage Love. August 9, 2007. https://savage
.love/savagelove/2007/08/09/peg-pegging-pegged.

Schmidt, Samantha. "1 in 6 Gen Z Adults Are LGBT. And This Number Could
Continue to Grow," *Washington Post*, February 24, 2021, www.washingtonpost.com
/dc-md-va/2021/02/24/gen-z-lgbt.

Schneider, Andrew. "How Conservative Activist Steven Hotze Became a Harris
County Power Broker." Houston Public Media, January 28, 2021. www
.houstonpublicmedia.org/articles/news/politics/2021/01/28/390247
/steve-hotze-gop-republican-activist-houston-harris-county-politics.

Scott, Katie. "Nickelodeon Announces SpongeBob Is Member of the LGBTQ2
Community." Global News, June 15, 2020. https://globalnews.ca/news/7066112
/spongebob-lgbtq-community.

Senzee, Thom. "Bisexual Seeking Asylum Resorts to Photos When Asked to Prove
It by UK Officials." Advocate.com, May 11, 2015. www.advocate.com/world
/2015/05/10/bisexual-asylum-seeker-humiliated-trying-prove-sexuality-uk
-officials-0.

Simien, Justin, dir. *Dear White People.* Netflix TV series. 2017.

Simonefiii (@simonefiii). "Do any of y'all use bisexual and pansexual interchangeably? Or do they mean different things to you and if so . . . can you explain the
difference?" Twitter. March 5, 2021, 2:22 p.m. https://twitter.com/simonefiii
/status/1367918370671063041.

Slowiczek, Lindsay. "Truvada." Medical News Today, October 26, 2018. www
.medicalnewstoday.com/articles/325820.

Smith, Laura. "How a Racist Hate-Monger Masterminded America's War on
Drugs." Medium Timeline. February 28, 2018. https://timeline.com/harry
-anslinger-racist-war-on-drugs-prison-industrial-complex-fb5cbc281189.

Spacey, Kevin. "Let Me Be Frank." YouTube video. December 24, 2018. www
.youtube.com/watch?v=JZveA-NAIDI.

Stiborova, Edita. "The Equality Wheel (The Duluth Method)." Social Workers Toolbox
.com. 2016. www.socialworkerstoolbox.com/the-equality-wheel-the-duluth
-model.

Strings, Sabrina. *Fearing the Black Body: The Racial Origins of Fat Phobia.* New York:
New York University Press, 2019.

StrongHearts Native Helpline. "Healthy Relationship Bill of Rights." December 10,
2022. https://strongheartshelpline.org/abuse/healthy-relationship-bill-of-rights.

Sunfrog. "Pansies Against Patriarchy: Gender Blur, Bisexual Men, and Queer Liberation." In Tucker, *Bi-Sexual Politics,* 319–24.

Tello, Monique. "Diet and Depression." *Harvard Health Blog,* February 22, 2018.
www.health.harvard.edu/blog/diet-and-depression-2018022213309.

Therapist Lauren L. "The Bigot Who Wrote 'The 5 Love Languages' Might Hate
You." Medium Blunt Therapy. November 13, 2021. https://medium.com
/blunt-therapy/the-bigot-who-wrote-the-5-love-languages-hates-you
-e2f65771a1c0.

Tracy, Natasha. "What Is Biphobia?" Healthyplace, January 10, 2022. www
.healthyplace.com/gender/bisexual/what-is-biphobia.

Trotta, Daniel. "U.S. Psychoanalysts Apologize for Labeling Homosexuality an Illness." Reuters. June 21, 2019. www.reuters.com/article/us-usa-lgbt-stonewall
-psychoanalysts/u-s-psychoanalysts-apologize-for-labeling-homosexuality-an
-illness-idUSKCN1TM169.

Tsantani, Maria S., Pascal Belin, Helena M. Paterson, and Phil McAleer. "Low Vocal
Pitch Preference Drives First Impressions Irrespective of Context in Male Voices
but Not in Female Voices." *Perception* 45:8 (April 13, 2016), 946–63. https://
doi.org/10.1177/0301006616643675.

Tucker, Naomi, ed. *Bi-Sexual Politics: Theories, Queries and Visions.* New York: Harrington Park, 1996.

TV Tropes. "Bury Your Gays." 2015. https://tvtropes.org/pmwiki/pmwiki.php
/Main/BuryYourGays.

U.S. Federal Bureau of Prisons. "Statistics: Inmate Race." July 8, 2023. www.bop.gov
/about/statistics/statistics_inmate_race.jsp.

U.S. Substance Abuse and Mental Health Services Administration. "Top Health Issues
for LGBT Populations Information & Resource Kit." March 2012. https://store
.samhsa.gov/product/top-health-issues-lgbt-populations/sma12-4684.

Underwood, Steven. "Black Boys and Bird-Chests, or the Racialized Legacy of Body
Dysmorphia in African-American Men." Medium. February 22, 2019. https://
blaqueword.medium.com/black-boys-and-body-dysmorphia-b85cf97dd32c.

Matteson, Dave. "Bisexual Feminist Man." in *Bi Any Other Name: Bisexual
People Speak Out,* 2nd ed. Edited by Lani Ka'ahumanu and Loraine Hutchins.
Riverdale, NY: Riverdale Avenue Books, 2015.

Von Malachowski, Joe. "Sleeping with Men Taught Me How to Be a Better Partner
to Women." *Cosmopolitan,* September 22, 2020. www.cosmopolitan.com/uk
/love-sex/sex/a34107580/bisexual-man-sex.

Walters, M. L., J. Chen, and M. J. Breiding. *National Intimate Partner and Sexual Violence Survey: 2010 Findings on Victimization by Sexual Orientation.* Atlanta: U.S.
National Center for Injury Prevention and Control, 2010. www.cdc.gov
/violenceprevention/pdf/nisvs_sofindings.pdf.

Ward, Jane. *Not Gay: Sex Between Straight White Men.* New York: New York University Press, 2015.

Wilkinson, Alissa. "Kevin Spacey Released a Bizarre Video Evoking Frank Underwood, Apparently to Defend Himself." *Vox,* December 24, 2018. www.vox
.com/culture/2018/12/24/18155150/kevin-spacey-sexual-assault-arraignment
-frank-underwood-youtube.

Wilson, Christina R. "What Is Self-Sabotage? How to Help Stop the Vicious
Cycle." Positive Psychology, April 22, 2021. https://positivepsychology.com
/self-sabotage.

Wolf, Cam. "NBA Tells J. R. Smith to Cover Up His Supreme Tattoo or Else." *GQ,*
October 1, 2018. www.gq.com/story/jr-smith-supreme-tattoo-nba.

Yussuf, J.R. "Bisexual Virgins & How to Know Which Gender(s) to Date." YouTube
    video. November 20, 2020. https://youtu.be/yTQIuuMO1fQ.

Yussuf, J.R. "4 Questions Every Bisexual Guy Should Ask a Potential Therapist."
    Men's Health, September 21, 2021. www.menshealth.com/health/a37612551
    /bisexual-friendly-therapist.

Yussuf, J.R. "A 7-Day Mental Health Workout Plan." The Good Men Project. June
    30, 2018. https://goodmenproject.com/health/7-day-mental-health-workout
    -plan-dg.

Yussuf, J.R., and Rachel Siden. "Bisexuality+ and Christianity." Bi Resource
    Center. 2021. https://biresource.org/bi-info/bisexuality-and-christianity.

Zambon, Veronica. "What Is 'Biphobia'?" Medical News Today, January 12, 2022.
    www.medicalnewstoday.com/articles/biphobia.

Zane, Zachary. "10 Things You Should Know before Dating a Bi Guy." Out.com,
    September 27, 2018. www.out.com/lifestyle/2018/9/27/10-things-you
    -should-know-dating-bi-guy.

Zane, Zachary. "Why Some Women Love Watching Gay Porn." *Men's Health,* July
    26, 2019. www.menshealth.com/sex-women/a28493364/why-women-watch
    -gay-porn.

Ziyad, Hari. *Black Boy Out of Time: A Memoir.* New York: Little A, 2021.

Zoppi, Lois. "What Is Trauma Bonding?" Medical News Today, November 27, 2020.
    www.medicalnewstoday.com/articles/trauma-bonding.

INDEX

ABOUT THE AUTHOR

 **J.R. Yussuf** is the award-winning author of *The Other F Word: Forgiveness* and creator of the hashtag #BisexualMenSpeak for bisexual+ men and masculine-identified folks to have the space to speak for themselves and talk about how being bisexual+ impacts the way they move through the world. Yussuf maintains a podcast called *Let's Heal Already,* revolving around mental wellness, self-improvement, and emotional literacy. Yussuf secured a peer support certification from the Black Emotional and Mental Health Collective (B.E.A.M.) and has used his training to support countless Black bisexual+/pansexual men. Yussuf's writing has appeared in *Men's Health Magazine, Thrive Global, Black Youth Project, Queerty, Queer Majority, Positively Positive, The Good Men Project, Escarp, Instigatorzine,* and *The CultureLP.*

ABOUT
NORTH ATLANTIC BOOKS

North Atlantic Books (NAB) is a 501(c)(3) nonprofit publisher committed to a bold exploration of the relationships between mind, body, spirit, culture, and nature. Founded in 1974, NAB aims to nurture a holistic view of the arts, sciences, humanities, and healing. To make a donation or to learn more about our books, authors, events, and newsletter, please visit www.northatlanticbooks.com.